# What Do I Do With My Pain?

# What Do I Do With My Pain?

## PROCLAIM LIBERTY TO THE CAPTIVES

### VOLUME 2

*Ann Gwen Mack*

publish your gift

### WHAT DO I DO WITH MY PAIN? VOLUME 2

Copyright © 2021 Ann Gwen Mack

All rights reserved.

Published by Publish Your Gift®
An imprint of Purposely Created Publishing Group, LLC

No part of this book may be reproduced, distributed or transmitted in any form by any means, graphic, electronic, or mechanical, including photocopy, recording, taping, or by any information storage or retrieval system, without permission in writing from the publisher, except in the case of reprints in the context of reviews, quotes, or references.

Printed in the United States of America

ISBN: 978-1-64484-357-4 (print)

ISBN: 978-1-64484-358-1 (ebook)

---

Special discounts are available on bulk quantity purchases by book clubs, associations and special interest groups. For details email: sales@publishyourgift.com or call (888) 949-6228.

*For information logon to:* www.PublishYourGift.com

# TABLE OF CONTENTS

Preface ................................................. 1

A Dedication to God & Letter of Gratitude .............. 11

Acknowledgments ................................... 15

**RECOGNITION: IN HONOR OF MY MOTHER, RUBY HINNANT MACK**

Born to Die! ......................................... 21

Creation and Purpose .............................. 27

**SALVATION IS A GIFT FROM GOD! IT IS FREE!**

**INTRODUCTION**

Go Show Them What He Told You – Part 2 .............. 35

The Pain We Cause Others! Even as Christians – Part 2 ... 41

Proclaim Liberty to the Captives ...................... 47

The Meaning of Faith ................................ 59

The Desires of the Heart ............................. 65

Stop Denying the Holy Spirit ......................... 71

Bearing Witness to the Pain and the Glory:
A Moment of Truth! ................................. 75

**PURPOSE: REALIZING YOUR GOD POTENTIAL**

Divine Purpose ....................................... 87

The Significance of Purpose .......................... 91

Challenges Come! .................................... 95

The Capacity to Love ................................. 97

Speaking Up and Speaking Out! ...................... 107

Doubting Thomas .................................... 109

Ministering in the Earth, the Church, the Marketplace,
and on the Job ...................................... 113

Those Who Are Sent ................................. 117

Why Do I Praise Him Like I Do? Because Praise
Is What I Do! ....................................... 123

Brokenness: Broken, Mended, and Second-Winded ...... 129

Brokenness, Part 2 ................................... 135

What Is the Nature of a Scribe? Part 2 ................ 139

## THE REALITY OF IT ALL: FROM REVELATION TO REALIZATION

These are Some Challenging Times! .................... 145

Witnessing ........................................... 149

Time ................................................. 155

This Present Darkness ................................ 159

Order: Divine Order .................................. 163

Time-Out for the Okey-Doke! .......................... 167

The Highest Honor .................................... 175

When You Know Who You Are! ........................... 181

What Is Perception? .................................. 187

Covering ............................................. 191

Church Hurt Is Real .................................. 195

Fight, Take Flight, or Freeze ........................ 201

From Revelation to Realization ....................... 205

## BIBLICAL TOPICS, TESTIMONIES, AND OTHER

What Is a Testimony? ................................. 213

Spiritual Maturity ................................... 217

A Call to Unity ...................................... 221

My Deliverance Is Continuous ........................ 227

Soul'd Out ............................................ 235

In the World, but Not of the World .................... 247

The Final Authority .................................. 257

A Microwave Society ................................. 261

The Key to Healing Is Forgiveness ..................... 265

In This Season, Trust and Belief in God Are Vital ........ 271

Supernatural Manifestation Defeating Flesh ............ 275

The Unparalleled State of Our Race .................... 281

The Souls of My Ancestors ........................... 287

No More Apologies! .................................. 293

Really? .............................................. 299

Frequency ........................................... 305

A Rebel 4 Christ! .................................... 309

You Can Move Past the Pain! ......................... 313

The Real World ...................................... 317

What Is Endurance? .................................. 321

Post-Traumatic Stress Disorder (PTSD) ................ 325

God Is My Source and My Strength ................... 333

Until Now ........................................... 337

Long-Suffering ...................................... 343

Passion ............................................. 345

Arrogance, Ignorance, and Fear! ...................... 351

Lead with Integrity, Not Discretion! .................. 357

What Is Truth? ...................................... 361

The Ugliness Inside .................................. 365

Poetic Justice ....................................... 373

Second to No One ................................... 381

The War in the Earth ................................ 385

Something Is Missing! ................................ 389

Things Are Unfolding! ................................ 395

The Storm Is Raging! ................................ 401

Integrity ............................................ 403

Culture ............................................. 411

Struggling to Understand ............................. 415

The Government Shutdown ........................... 419

Martial Law ......................................... 427

You Are More Than .................................. 431

Justice or Just Us! .................................... 435

There Is Evil in the World! ........................... 441

Chain of Command: New Level, New Devil ............ 445

What Is Your Definition of Essential? ................... 451

## BONUS

In the Line of Fire ................................... 457

Deborah the Bee: Judge, Prophet, Deliverer, Mother,
Wife, Warrior—and More ............................ 473

Amazing Grace ...................................... 483

God, All I Want for My Birthday Is More of You ......... 487

## APPENDIX

The Names of God ................................... 493

References .......................................... 497

Biblical References ................................... 519

About the Author .................................... 523

# PREFACE

*Meanwhile, live in such a way that you are a credit to the Message of Christ. Let nothing in your conduct hang on whether I come or not. Your conduct must be the same whether I show up to see things for myself or hear of it from a distance. Stand united, singular in vision, contending for people's trust in the Message, the good news, not flinching or dodging in the slightest before the opposition. Your courage and unity will show them what they're up against: defeat for them, victory for you—and both because of God. There's far more to this life than trusting in Christ. There's also suffering for him. And the suffering is as much a gift as the trusting. You're involved in the same kind of struggle you saw me go through, on which you are now getting an updated report in this letter.*

**~ Philippians 1:29-30 MSG**

September 20, 2020

This book (Volume 2) and the previous edition (Volume 1, released in 2010 and the revision in 2017), are to be a part of an ongoing series under the same title, *What Do I Do With My Pain?*, until God announces the end of this assignment. Early on in my life, I did not realize God had planted a **seed** of interest within me for writing and sharing my testimonies with so much *transparency* and passion. And, I most certainly could not have imagined being **called and chosen** to represent Him as an Ambassador of Christ while struggling with physical and emotional pain along **my journey of hope** in being *free* and thriving to reach my God-appointed destiny. Pain *so* great at the very beginning, that I couldn't imagine it growing to intensify any more deeply than it had already! It was, most certainly, unthinkable for it to serve any importance in my life to propel me from a position of unbelief into a greater understanding of my **spiritual growth**. I didn't even know that there was such a thing as a God-appointed destiny or purpose; and now, I believe!

When you find yourself deeply riddled with pain, physical and/or emotional, it is a struggle to want to push forward. Sometimes, *deep-rooted mental and emotional pain* overshadow the physical pain, thus proving to be devastating if you don't move beyond it! Emotional pain can be the definitive link between you, your health, and your physical pain, depending on how you are willing and able to manage it and possibly seek help. My physical pain was much more manageable than the emotional pain that was contributed to by the invasion of unwanted and unhealthy encounters with people. Fighting to endure, I attempted to ignore and deny my emotional pain as it grew with each and every life experience involving relationships with people, on top of unfortunate, growing disappointments. I even attempted to limit my association with others as much as possible! But how can you live and function in a world full of people without having to come in contact with them? People—no, not all—can be so mean, disheartening, and selfish; I desperately wanted to escape it all! Unless you are willing to climb under a rock and become a hermit, it is almost impossible not to interact with people!

*For those whom He foreknew [and loved and chose beforehand], He also predestined to be conformed to the image of His Son [and ultimately share in His complete sanctification], so that He would be the firstborn [the most beloved and honored] among many believers. 30 And those whom He predestined, He also called; and those whom He called, He also justified [declared free of the guilt of sin]; and those whom He justified, He also glorified [raising them to a heavenly dignity].*

~ Romans 8:29-30 AMP

God, the creator of us all, has a well-thought-out plan for using every encounter or experience in our life to prosper us. His adversary, our common enemy, *the thief* who *cometh not, but for to steal, and to kill, and to destroy* (John 10:10) will stop at nothing to derail God's plan for our life! Amazingly, God has provided a way of escape to any given situation! We simply have to get into a physical and spiritual position to receive God, to believe and follow the necessary strategies outlined throughout His word to stay on course in allowing the *process* to work in the earth as in Heaven to fulfill His Kingdom Mission.

*All Scripture is God-breathed [given by divine inspiration] and is profitable for instruction, for conviction [of sin], for correction [of error and restoration to obedience], for training in righteousness [learning to live in conformity to God's will, both publicly and privately—behaving honorably with personal integrity and moral courage]; so that the man of God may be complete and proficient, outfitted and thoroughly equipped for every good work.*

~ 2 Timothy 3:16-17 AMP

Nothing is too hard for God! *We can do all things through Christ*, the ultimate strategist, *who strengthens us* (Philippians 4:13)! *For His yoke is easy and His burden is light* (Matthew 11:30). Through the gifting of the *Holy Spirit*, God, our comforter, has downloaded all of what we need to be victorious. Challenges will come, obstacles and hurdles will be put before us, but we simply must not give up or give in to the wiles of our adversary, the devil (Ephesians 6:11)! His objective is to hit us with everything he has, to include using our greatest fear in an attempt to keep us ignorant to truth; our true identity and purpose. Our purposed design is a greater threat to Lucifer, the devil, than he is to us; and he wants to drive a wedge between us and our Heavenly Father to keep us bound by sin. *For the wages of sin [is] death; but the gift of God [is] eternal life through Jesus Christ our Lord* (Romans 6:23).

God loves us so deeply that He actually entrusted us to not only keep His commands, but He wanted us to appreciate that which He had freely given of Himself; His only begotten Son to show us the way to receive *salvation*! And He did not intend for us to replace Him with false idols—for He is a faithful and jealous God; although He loves us—unconditionally! *So, watch yourselves, that you do not forget the covenant of the Lord your God which He made with you, and make for yourselves a graven image in the form of anything against which the Lord your God has commanded you. For the Lord your God is a consuming fire, a jealous God* (Deuteronomy 4:23-24 NASB).

> **Salvation:** A word which is rendering of various Hebrew and Greek words, which carry the general idea of "safety, deliverance, state of security, saved, rescued, or forgiveness of sins."[1]
>
> **Strong's Concordance:**
>
> - Hebrew
>
>   > 3468[2] – **yesha** (pronounced yeh'-shah): deliverance, rescue, salvation, safety, welfare.
>
> - Greek
>
>   > 4982[3] – **sózó** (pronounced sode'-zo): I save, heal, preserve, rescue.
>
>   > 4991[4] – **sótéria** (pronounced so-tay-ree'-ah): welfare, prosperity, deliverance, preservation, salvation, safety.

---

1 *The New Combined Bible Dictionary and Concordance*, page 367.
2 http://biblehub.com/hebrew/3468.htm
3 http://biblehub.com/greek/4982.htm
4 http://biblehub.com/greek/4991.htm

In an attempt to disclose and reinforce my spiritual journey, much of what you will read on these pages may be reiterated in an effort to express my exact feelings of regression and/or progression on any given day as it was written in my journal. The dates denote my mindset on that specific day to include the *revelation* I gained in getting me over a particular hurdle! There were also times when I thought I had overcome a particular situation only to find out that there was still much more work needed to be done to move past my pain. **I never thought that I could embrace my pain on the road of *deliverance* in allowing God to use it to give me *revelation* about my God-purposed identity.** And He actually told me that my deliverance concerning many things in my life would be continuous! So I will not attempt to tell you that this "game called life and survival" is easy, but I will tell you that it encompasses a series of lessons, quizzes, and tests meant to *fortify* you and equip you to stay in the race and go the distance. Enduring with the right guidance is possible, if you are willing to allow God's revelation knowledge to flow from Him to you! As encouraged, I will not attempt to use His word, the Bible, to beat you over the head with it; however, I am willing to sit down with you to show you the difference between His word, religion, and tradition to explain His love for you. Happily, I will tell you how God's Spirit touched my heart, nurtured me, and saved me; and how He can and will do the same for you if you are willing to surrender to His Spirit and His ways!

> **Deliverance:**
>
> The root word in deliverance is "deliver," which means to free, redeem, or save. Deliverance is the act of being set free, redeemed, rescued, or *saved*.[5] Saved as in Salvation!

Revelation knowledge is a very vital part of my spiritual growth and yours. It's the ability and blessing to embrace God's wisdom, knowledge, and understanding for discerning truth. It cannot be obtained through a form of reasoning or a process of elimination. Nor can it be taught from textbooks in a classroom setting through an accredited educational system. For I neither received it of man, nor was I taught it, but through a revelation of Jesus Christ (Galatians 1:12). It comes from spending time and developing a relationship with the Lord. Revelation is the knowledge of truth, and when you receive revelation knowledge, it will be extremely hard for anyone to be able to convince you that what you know, you don't! Simply put, it is the divine revealing or uncovering of a hidden truth. As untruths or mistruths are discovered, it gives us the opportunity to reassess our programming (the mental computer called our mind) and delete the incorrect information to restore it with truth. *My people are destroyed for lack of knowledge [of My law, where I reveal My will]. Because you [the priestly nation] have rejected knowledge, I will also reject you from being My priest. Since you have forgotten the law of your God, I will also forget your children* (Hosea 4:6 AMP).

---

5  *The New Combined Bible Dictionary and Concordance,* page 128.

> **Strong's Concordance:**
>
> - Revelation[6] in Greek is *apokalupsis* (phonetically pronounced ap-ok-al'-oop-sis): an unveiling, uncovering, revealing, revelation.
>
> - Knowledge[7] in Greek is *epignósis* (phonetically pronounced ep-ig'-no-sis): knowledge of a particular point (directed toward a particular object); perception, discernment, recognition, intuition (a strong gut feeling).

I pray that after reading this book, each and every individual is blessed enormously by my testimonies to be delivered, healed, and set free as well as encouraged to develop a deeper walk with the Lord. I pray you are compelled to go above and beyond, to push past the boundaries or limitations placed on you by others to reach your destiny. I pray you never get bored or stop seeking God's face to experience *His love* for you to embrace your calling. I pray you never grow weary of doing good or become discouraged in the midst of your trials and tribulations to know **you can do all things through Christ who strengthens you (Philippians 4:13)**. Regardless of what it looks like, I pray you are able to keep your focus, hold on, and endure until the end to receive your reward in appreciation of your God inheritance. May you overcome your pain and all your fears to know you are victorious (more than a conqueror), and know in your heart, soul, and

---

6  https://biblehub.com/greek/602.htm
7  https://biblehub.com/greek/1922.htm

mind that the battle is already won by Him and through Him for you! You just have to believe and trust the Lord!

No matter what, continue to pray without ceasing and thank Him often! Praise Him in the morning! Praise Him in the noonday! Praise Him in the midnight hour! Praise Him when you are happy! Praise Him when you are sad! Use your weapon of praise to confuse the enemy! In fact, *I will praise thee; for I am fearfully [and] wonderfully made: marvellous [are] thy works; and [that] my soul knoweth right well* (Psalm 139:14).

> *For I am not ashamed of the gospel, for it is the power of God for salvation to everyone who believes, to the Jew first and also to the Greek.*
>
> ~ Romans 1:16 NASB

# A DEDICATION TO GOD & LETTER OF GRATITUDE

September 23, 2020

Dear God,

THANK YOU! Words cannot express just how grateful and committed I AM to Your mission and my journey to go the distance with You and for You! In spite of my reluctance, time and time again, to answer Your call, You were always there, though I lacked the knowledge of Your presence. So much pain, strife, and despair came upon me that I lost all hope of You ever rescuing me from myself to include those in the world who were being influenced by darkness and wanted so much to steal my joy and dim my light. Little did I know, You were standing near and never far away just waiting for me to catch hold of You all along the way!

Deceived by many in my life—especially those I assumed were supposed to do right by me and love me with no hesitation—I became discouraged, bitter, and even a little angry as

I held on to the hurting memories of my past and trusted no one. And, unfortunately, not even You! Instead of me running toward You and standing firm on Your every word, I let fear grip me and put a wedge between us. Mainly, because my focus was off! It seemed as if those who had chosen darkness over doing what was right were getting ahead while putting limitations on me! The more I gave of myself, the less I received in return and my pain grew deeper! As I looked around me, I saw others being hurt and taken for granted too! So I started to doubt Your existence and I assumed You had turned Your back on me!

Over the years, I have grown wiser by immersing myself deeper into Your word. Reading and studying, I gained greater insight concerning who You are to include the love within Your heart for me. Loving me as You do, unconditionally, I now know You felt my pain and You even hurt with me when I hurt, thus feeling every agonizing imprint. Determined to fortify me and prepare me by equipping me for the fight and my assignments, I understand the necessity of You allowing **the choices that I made** to play out! By doing so, You were ushering me through a process to get me to this point in my life where I AM today in You. How could I have ever doubted You and Your love for me?

When I once thought You heard me not, I knew nothing about the concept of spiritual warfare. I assumed You were ignoring my prayers, but now I believe each prayer was intercepted and did not make it to Your ears. Also, not knowing or understanding Your ways, I lacked the knowledge of doing things decently and in order (according to Your Will) to receive Your blessing. But lately, amazingly, You answer every thought in my heart and in my mind more quickly than imaginable. As I learn to forgive myself, I AM learning to let go of the memories of the hurt and pain stamped on my heart. In doing this, I will also evict the thoughts and images from my mind of those who have wounded my soul. And I will forgive their transgressions against me in the same manner You have forgiven me of my sins to give me this chance to prove myself—once more. You have given me more chances than I deserve and bestowed upon me much love, which is evident by the manner in which You revealed Yourself to me.

> *Let your conversation be without covetousness; and be content with such things as ye have: for he hath said, I will never leave thee, nor forsake thee.*
>
> ~ Hebrews 13:5

My baptism, for the second time, represented the rededication of my life to You as a symbol of my conscious awareness and acknowledgment of a needful relationship with You. I never knew I could reach a place of having such joy and inner peace. You restored me and made my life worth living! Thank You for this opportunity and Your confidence in my ability to carry out the assignment You entrusted to me. Thank You for helping me to understand that my assignment is my assignment until **You** tell me otherwise in giving me a new one. Because of the anointing of the Holy Spirit that You gifted to me (and many others like me), I know I can do all things through Christ who strengthens me. Today, I AM totally depending upon You to guide my life as you continue to **order my steps**!

In openly and boldly saying YES to Your will and YES to Your ways, I not only dedicate my life to You, but this book, which honors the presence of Your existence in my life forevermore. This book is also a representation of or my attempt to impress upon man his purpose here on Earth, a lifelong assignment we, unfortunately, seem to have overlooked or consistently taken for granted. I pray and hope that those who get the opportunity to read this book will allow You in their lives and see You much differently through my heart, as well as experience You to love You as I do. I will praise You continuously forevermore and look forward to developing and sustaining a lifelong relationship with You. Thank You for not giving up on me, for I long to be deeper in You!

> *For I am persuaded, that neither death,*
> *nor life, nor angels, nor principalities, nor powers,*
> *nor things present, nor things to come, nor height,*
> *nor depth, nor any other creature, shall be able to*
> *separate us from the love of God,*
> *which is in Christ Jesus our Lord.*
>
> ~ Romans 8:38-39

Committed to please YOU,

Your UNIQUE and COURAGEOUS one

# ACKNOWLEDGMENTS

### Dear Father God

Your **continued** persistence in my life to reveal who I was created to be is making me whole! For I now know that my healing through deliverance is continuous and You are blessing me with **new mercies** each day! I cannot begin to tell You just how grateful I AM for **Your unconditional love** and guidance to pioneer me in the direction of my purpose. No one but You truly knows how excited I AM to be growing spiritually toward gaining your knowledge, wisdom, and understanding in learning and appreciating Your ways! I want my ways to mirror Your ways! I want my flesh to take a back seat to Your Spirit in allowing Your Spirit to have a dominant presence over my life! Your confidence and belief in my ability to speak on Your behalf means more to me than I could have possibly imagined. Thank You for Your trust and for saving me from myself as well as rescuing me from the world. More importantly, THANK YOU for the opportunity to serve You!

### Dear Mom

Although you are not here in body, you are forever here with me in *spirit*! From the beginning, you taught me, in your own way, how to be strong in dealing with the pain of life to overcome while pushing forward. I would be remiss if I didn't thank you for your encouragement and enthusiasm in what God has called me to do.

### Dear Mary Bryant Lampley

Words cannot begin to express my gratitude for your patience, kindness, and friendship over the years! You have always been there to offer words of encouragement and redirect my focus back to the Word of God when I found myself feeling discouraged. And, although I know I could be challenging at times, you held your position in honor of God to continue to minister to me to penetrate the layers of my carnal mind to usher in the Lord to appeal to my spiritual mind. Thank you for putting in the time to extend to me, Grace and Mercy! Thank you for loving God so deeply that you were willing to believe in me to see beyond the surface in discerning and confirming my God-appointed purpose! Thank you for being accepting of my personality that's been so easily rejected by others but unconditionally loved by God to help me understand myself. From the very first time I spoke of my vision to write and dedicate the first of many books to God, you have continued to celebrate—with me—my growth and spiritual walk with God. I AM forever grateful!

## Dear Dr. Marcia Boyce Levi

Who knew when I came into your office in 2011 that we would still be connected today? God knew! On that very first day, I came to you physically broken and in desperate need of more than just chiropractic care; I was also emotionally broken. I didn't have any knowledge of chiropractic care to understand God's plan for putting you in my path! Nor did I understand the needed preparation for the GREATER that's coming, but you knew! From then to now, **through your spiritual gifting, healing hands, heart, and knowledge in nutrition**, you are attending to my wholeness (body, mind, and spirit) in bringing me back into RIGHT alignment. You are and have been aiding me to be more effective to serve the Lord in a greater capacity! A capacity I have yet to fully realize but one that resonates within my spirit. Thank you!

# RECOGNITION: IN HONOR OF MY MOTHER, RUBY HINNANT MACK

# BORN TO DIE!

*For to me, to live is Christ and to die is gain.*
~ **Philippians 1:21 NIV**

August 18, 2014

September 26, 2020 – with the inclusion of memorable emphasis

When considering the process and concept of life and death, we were not meant to occupy space in the physical realm while on Earth forever! Just as Christ, who is referenced as being the second Adam, was born to die *to save us from ourselves*. We who are born in this world are also born to die to self—both in the physical and the spiritual. (*Emphasis needed here*: But when we die to self, we are able to soar in spirit to live eternity on another *dimension* [as if in Heaven] above the surface!) We are three-part beings; first and foremost, born of **spirit**, which is housed in a **body** (made up of flesh, blood, and bone), possessing a **soul**. The spirit is that part of God living within us and which returns to Him when our bodies have served their usefulness. Our bodies that were created from dust return to the earth in the form of dust; meaning, *the body one day ceases to function and dies while the spirit transcends back to our Heavenly Father.*

> *All go to the same place; all come from
> dust, and to dust all return.*
>
> ~ Ecclesiastes 3:20

Early Sunday morning on August 17, 2014, at exactly 2:02 a.m., my mother—born Ruby Hinnant Mack on July 20, 1936—took her last breath after a three-year-long battle with cancer. She was a child of God who was born on this earth with a purpose. She wasn't perfect, but neither am I. Yes, we had our ups and downs, but what relationship does not take hits to evolve into an everlasting union? Throughout the years of my life, I had the pleasure of learning more and more about this person who was my mother and to appreciate what she had instilled in me. She was a very special and soft-spoken individual who had a very loving, caring, and *forgiving spirit.* **She unselfishly gave much of herself and made many sacrifices for those she loved.** At times, I felt she made too many sacrifices for those who weren't deserving and appreciative of her love. However, she showed no evidence of any regrets and never looked back, as she spoke to me often about the importance of forgiveness. Even in her diminished state, she still found time to put others before herself and wanted nothing but the best for those around her.

As stated above, I know we are not meant to live here on Earth forever. But you can never really be ready or prepared to see the person who has given birth to you depart from you. Determined to succeed and live life, she was truly a fighter who refused to give up since the day God introduced her to me as my mother. And I saw much more of that determination when she was diagnosed in November of 2010 with stage 4 lung cancer. She learned of her diagnosis the day before Thanksgiving and wanted as many of us as possible to pull together for a Thanksgiving dinner at a restaurant, at which time she shared the unpleasant news. It was her spirit in how she accepted and handled her illness that gave me the strength to endure. For her to have held on for as long as she did was truly a blessing! I AM just grateful to have had the opportunity to have been with her up until she took her very last breath of transitioning to be with the Lord. In the onset of her illness, she refused to let anyone take her to her chemotherapy or radiation treatments. And even after her road to recovery became long, discouraging, and a little difficult toward the end, she still always threatened me with talks of getting in her own car to drive herself wherever she needed to go.

> *I consider that our present sufferings*
> *are not worth comparing with the glory*
> *that will be revealed in us.*
>
> ~ Romans 8:18 NIV

Just hours after her death, I began to dial her number, and upon realizing she would not be there, I forced myself to fall asleep. I AM sure there will be plenty more days of me reaching out for the phone, only to remember that the Lord took her home to be with Him. Like any child, I AM sure I AM going to deeply miss spending time with my mother and pulling up a chair to watch a daily episode of the soaps or hear her tease me about my weight. We used to joke about who had gained more weight than the other, and she would playfully refer to me as "whale tail" in that soft child-like voice of hers. She had a beautiful smile and wonderful sense of humor! The cancer, unfortunately, had begun to spread to her lymph nodes and then to her bones. Just weeks before her passing, she asked me, "Why does God keep leaving me here?"

*Disappearing into the bathroom, I cried, prayed, and had a talk with the Lord. I told Him, "I remember when I first heard the news of her cancer and I pleaded with YOU not to take my mother." I told Him that I wasn't ready to be without her! But, on that day, I asked Him to forgive me for being so selfish and to please listen to her request. I didn't want her to suffer. I wanted her to be happy and at peace, even if it meant being without her in the physical but always in my heart! After getting myself together and coming out of that bathroom, I responded to my mother.* "Tell Him what you want and He will give you the desires of your heart. If you are ready to go, just let Him know." God finally answered her request; she went peacefully, and many family and friends gathered around her those last **three** days! She is no longer suffering and she is no longer in pain. If God grants me just half her strength, strong will, and tenacity, I will be A-OK.

## *A TIME FOR EVERYTHING!*

*There is a time for everything, and a season for every activity under the heavens: a time to be born and a time to die, a time to plant and a time to uproot, a time to kill and a time to heal, a time to tear down and a time to build, a time to weep and a time to laugh, a time to mourn and a time to dance, a time to scatter stones and a time to gather them, a time to embrace and a time to refrain from embracing, a time to search and a time to give up, a time to keep and a time to throw away, a time to tear and a time to mend, a time to be silent and a time to speak, a time to love and a time to hate, a time for war and a time for peace.*

~ Ecclesiastes 3:1-8

# CREATION AND PURPOSE

*For by him were all things created, that are in heaven, and that are in earth, visible and invisible, whether they be thrones, or dominions, or principalities, or powers: all things were created by him, and for him.*

**~ Colossians 1:16 KJV**

June 4, 2021

While writing a message to my supervisor, I inadvertently wrote the word *mother* in place of the word *doctor*. I literally had to stop and take a minute to give this some extensive thought! Subconsciously, my mother, who is with me always, has been on my mind a lot lately, and she has a birthday coming up soon in July. She was born on July 20, 1936. My mother was a very strong woman. She was diagnosed with lung cancer in November of

2010 (a day before Thanksgiving), and she fought that disease/illness with **grace** until August of 2014, a month after her 78th birthday.

- Together: 7+8 = 15 = 1 + 5 = 6
- 7 = completion
- 8 = new beginnings
- 1 = unity
- 5 = grace
- 6 = man (human race/human form) was created on the 6th day

On August 17, 2014, my mother completed (7) her assignment here on Earth to start or begin a new assignment (8) in Heaven. Her body was returned to the Earth and her Spirit returned to God to reunite with HIM in unity (1); as one! While here on Earth as an alien to this World, she loved deeply and attempted to live her life as gracefully (5) as possible in her human form (6) until she returned/transcended back to her Heavenly home.

- 08.17.2014
- 8 + 1 + 7 + 2 + 1 + 4 = 23 = 2+ 3 = **5**

Today is June 4, and in the Bible, June is the 4th month of the year; 4 symbolizes CREATION. **Today, I honor the CREATOR and the CREATION of the entire human race with the hope and prayer of us ALL completing an impactful assignment here on Earth with GRACE and LOVE.**

On July 20 of this year, my mother would be 85 years young. There's that 8 (new beginnings) and 5 (grace) again! 8 + 5 = 13 = 1 + 3 = **4** (creation)

- 1 = unity

- 3 = TRINITY (Father, Son, and the Holy Spirit) = complete, completion, completeness

There is meaning and symbolism in and through everything! In the Bible, July is actually the 5th month! God does everything with purpose!

## REFERENCES

- The number 5 symbolizes God's grace, goodness, and favor toward humans.

- God's grace = FAVOR

- The 4th month Bible references: Zechariah 8:19, Ezekiel 1:1-2, Jeremiah 39:2, Jeremiah 52:6-7.

- The 5th month Bible references: Numbers 33:38; 2 Kings 25:8; 1 Chronicles 27:8; Ezra 7:8-9; Nehemiah 6:15; Jeremiah 1:3, 28:1, 36:9, 52:12; Ezekiel 1:1-2, 8:1, 20:1, 33:21; Zechariah 7:3, 7:5, 8:19.

**SALVATION IS
A GIFT FROM GOD!**

**IT IS FREE!**

# INTRODUCTION

# GO SHOW THEM WHAT HE TOLD YOU!
## PART 2

*Hearing of thy love and faith, which thou hast toward the Lord Jesus, and toward all saints; That the communication of thy faith may become effectual by the acknowledging of every good thing which is in you in Christ Jesus.*

**~ Philemon 1:5-6**

## THE PROMISE, PURPOSE, AND PLAN

As far back as I can remember, to include every life-changing event I have experienced, this has been an incredible journey of spiritual growth for me! God has granted us the right to choose in making choices concerning our lives, but those choices also come with consequences. Making a right or positive choice may yield a positive outcome. Making a bad or negative choice may yield a negative outcome. In some instances, many of us may find ourselves having to deal with situations not of our own choosing; and, contrary to popular belief, we don't all necessarily possess the power or control to redirect certain events to work in our favor. But God has the ability to reshape, create, and recreate every scenario to work out for our good if we are willing to take Him at His word, put our lives in His hands and simply TRUST Him.

I have come to realize, many situations in my life were beneficial for propelling me toward my God-ordained purpose. It just took me quite a while to understand my calling to know I was CHOSEN by God for such a time as this long before I was conceived and birthed here on Earth! For many years, I attempted to compartmentalize various parts of my life from the most important to the least important in accordance to how I was able and willing to handle the pain associated with those areas. As I grew in age and maturity to redevelop and consider healthier coping strategies, the order from the most important to the least important changed often. Early in my life, school, education, and graduating with honors to assist with landing a good-paying job was very important. After that phase of my life was over and it was time to be an adult and move out of my parents' home, developing a career and excelling on the job became very important. I never considered or imagined needing a back-up plan for addressing any issues that would or could arise overtime to threaten my mental sanity.

Life creates challenges that may unfortunately induce pain. This pain is not similar to the hurt you could obtain from falling off a bike or a sliding board on a playground. This isn't the kind of hurt that may produce visible scars and bruises that you could soak away in a tub of warm or hot water and mineral salts. "You can accept or reject the way you are treated by other people, but until you heal the wounds of your past, you will continue to bleed. You can bandage the bleeding with food, with alcohol, with drugs, with work, with cigarettes, with sex, but eventually, it will all ooze through and stain your life. You must find the strength to open the wounds, stick your hands inside, pull out the core of the pain that is holding you in your past, the memories, and make peace with them."[8]

When the timing was right and I was ready to openly receive instruction from the Lord, He revealed His purpose and plan for my life to me. Then it was my turn to put things in order to move forward by allowing God full reign to transform me from the inside out. First, it was necessary for Him to renew my way of thinking and take me through an extensive process for my healing. He forced me to address every unresolved issue I had attempted to bury deep within the far corner of my mind. *But without thy mind would I do nothing; that thy benefit should not be as it were of necessity, but willingly* (Philemon 1:14). Through years and years of emotional abuse and attacks from the enemy (invisible spirits) through people (lost souls), my mind became clouded and I became damaged goods. I started carrying around baggage that prevented me from having confi-

---

[8] Iyanla Vanzant; https://www.oprah.com/oprahs-lifeclass/iyanla-vanzant-how-to-heal-the-wounds-of-your-past#ixzz6qMnx3Gg7

dence and trust in God, not to mention, confidence in myself. I honestly didn't know or think I had the authority and power to reject the way I was being treated by others until God showed me how! *Wisdom is the principal thing; therefore get wisdom: and with all thy getting get understanding* (Proverbs 4:7).

God is nothing like any person I have physically encountered on Earth. He allowed me to connect with Him in ways I did not think was possible to give me an in-depth understanding into who He is! He is a persistent and jealous but loving, kind, and gentle person who wants nothing other than the very best for me and you. He creates you out of a need (purpose) and gives you a set of instructions (a plan) for carrying out your assignment (according to His will or mandate). He tells you up front, with no hidden agenda, what He expects and how He plans to reward (or prosper) you. Unlike those in the world, God is the same today, yesterday, tomorrow, and always. He does not change in the middle of a covenant promise. He is no respecter of persons, meaning He does not discriminate but instead gives everyone the same opportunity to excel and be righteous.

God changed my outlook on life, healed my mind and my heart as He increased my *faith*. Allowing me to see myself through His eyes, He not only revealed Himself to me by making a believer out of me, but He restored my confidence and trust in Him. He took an ordinary person, absent of fame and fortune (as defined by society, not God), who was no different from anyone else in the world to reach others by giving me an assignment to show you what He told me! I AM commissioned to show you, through the sharing of my testimonies,[9] how I AM learning and have grown to depend on God—not man! He can and is willing to do the same for you, if you let Him! *Trust in the LORD with all thine heart; and lean not unto thine own understanding* (Proverbs 3:5).

> *But let all those that put their trust in thee rejoice:*
> *let them ever shout for joy, because thou*
> *defendest them: let them also that love*
> *thy name be joyful in thee*
>
> ~ Psalm 5:11

---

9  Testify, testimony, testimonies: To bear witness. For more information, see http://biblehub.com/topical/t/testify.htm

# THE PAIN WE CAUSE OTHERS!
## EVEN AS CHRISTIANS - PART 2

*And this is my prayer: that your love may more and more overflow in fullness of knowledge and depth of discernment, so that you will be able to determine what is best and thus be pure and without blame for the Day of the Messiah, filled with the fruit of righteousness that comes through Yeshua the Messiah - to the glory and praise of God.*

**~ Philippians 1:9-11 CJB**

December 31, 2020

Finalized March 13, 2021

Approaching the end of 2020, I couldn't help but inventory all of what has taken place to include the impact of COVID-19 and reflect backwards concerning my life. I spent a great deal of time and unnecessary energy giving too much thought to how people, the walking wounded just like me, accept me, and view me on the surface while trying to earn their approval. Here's the problem with that:

I assumed I could rely on people to teach me who and how to be! But, unfortunately, we're all struggling and trying to find our way in and through the maze of life. If you rely on people to approve of you and validate your worth, you will forever be lost, disconnected, roaming around in circles feeling hurt, angry and caught in the crossfire of their web of deception without any clear direction of your true God-ordained purpose!

Hurting people only hurt other people. Those who are confused about themselves only confuse others in creating a deeper kind of hurt. People seeking to control others lack self-control themselves. It is impossible to please everyone you come in contact with including members of your family! People who don't have a real connection to God and relationship with Him to know who He is or what is expected of us by Him as His children are possibly more influenced by darkness than they are the light.

God is love and the divine source of light in whom our energy (life force) flows from and He wants nothing other than the very best for us all! The greatest thing we can do is love and be loved in return without compromising our God-appointed position on Earth. We most definitely cannot be in position for God and by Him to please others above Him! It took me a while to understand that as well as to accept my God-appointed role on Earth and I am still learning and growing to master God's expectation of me while experiencing persecution from others!

My objective through it all is to resist being pulled backwards in allowing my emotions to derail me and strongholds to take root in undoing what God has already accomplished in my life this far! Staying connected and tapped into the deep-rooted power of

God's spirit within me which has revealed my purpose in giving me a greater joy than I could have ever imagined is my only saving grace. Before this realization, I was literally holding on by a single emotional thread, swinging back and forth like a pendulum. I was trying to stay steady and afloat while being controlled by the World to believe that the principles of the World were the only way. Then I discovered another way! Jesus the Messiah!

People, including some Christians, believe God is controlling and His ways are too strict to be fully committed to Him. But God is the only person I know who honors His unchanging word 100% and loves me unconditionally even when I backslide! His mercy, grace and compassion are unprecedented! This is enough for me to want to be as true to Him as He is to me; and, I will continue trying to fulfill His every command until I get it right – completely and without hesitation or apology to others! Yes, He is a jealous God who wants and expects our loyalty! But, He also extents loyalty in return unlike the World which teaches and encourages "do as I say and not as I do!"

I needed to realize the necessity of having to be alertly watchful and aware of my surroundings in an effort of unmasking spirits through discernment while working on myself to keep from being drawn into and influenced by the darkness! Over the years, I have encountered a great deal of pain centered around family, friends and throughout my career in corporate America in the government and private sectors trying to live up to the expectations of others. I started over so many times in an attempt to reinvent myself only to discover that I was encountering some of the same obstacles. Why was that?

I actually remember the day I began to acknowledge that there was an extreme void in my life which hindered my confidence in myself. It was partly due to me allowing the insecurities of others through influence and their false understanding of growth and humanity to attack me and beat me down! I even attempted to compartmentalize my pain as a fighting strategy to keep moving forward. Now, I couldn't very easily escape my family, entirely; but I could try to find a happy medium by going from church to church and from job to job in search of a peaceful co-existence. No, that didn't work either! Continuously running and closing myself off in isolation was not the answer.

Going inward to embrace my pain, I needed to explore the word expectation from God's point of view to see the connection for a greater understanding! There is purpose in everything that is allowed by God including the pain along with the order in which you experience it! To emerge, take root and heal emotionally to escape the prison of my mind and soar beyond the hurt and pain, I needed to figure out what was missing and what was most important to God for my life! Especially if I am to believe that nothing happens without God's permission! And, no matter what comes our way, God expects us to conduct ourselves in a manner worthy of the gospel of Christ.

Each person's path, abilities and tolerance level are different! Although, at times, our paths may cross, that which makes us tick or keeps us afloat is different! That which compels us forward, slows us down or threatens to hold us in captivity is different!

**Here's the ultimate question:** How do you navigate through the hurt and pain without being offended by the persecution to grow as expected by God?

In consideration of your answer, I would like to encourage you to read all of Philippians to think of Paul's position. In addition, keep in mind Exodus 20:5, 34:14, Deuteronomy 4:23-24, 5:9, and 6:15.

**Here's my answer:** From the inside out!

# PROCLAIM LIBERTY TO THE CAPTIVES

## THE UNFOLDING OF MY PURPOSE, MISSION, AND VISION

> *The Spirit of the Lord GOD is upon me;*
> *because the LORD hath anointed me to preach good*
> *tidings unto the meek; he hath sent me to bind up the*
> *brokenhearted,*
> *to proclaim liberty to the captives, and the opening*
> *of the prison to them that are bound.*
>
> ~ Isaiah 61:1

August 26, 2010

God has created each and every one of us *with a purpose for a purpose* and sent us to Earth to carry out our assignments. Jeremiah 1:5-7 AMP states, *Before I formed you in the womb I knew you [and approved of you as My chosen instrument], And before you were born I consecrated you [to Myself as My own]; I have appointed you as a prophet to the nations." Then I said, "Ah, Lord God! Behold, I do not know how to speak, For I am [only] a young man." But the Lord said to me, "Do not say, 'I am [only] a young man,' Because everywhere I send you, you shall go, And whatever I command you, you shall speak."*

When we were in our rightful form (spirit) and mind, we gladly accepted our assignments with honor and gratitude according to the *Will of God*. But something unexpected happened to us through a chain of events as dictated by this world. *Be not afraid of them [their faces], for I am with you to deliver you, says the Lord* (Jeremiah 1:8 AMPC). The greater the distance or separation from God (who is our light [John 12:35-36]), the greater the void in our *mission!* In allowing our flesh, through the temptations of this world, to rule our decisions, we lost our objectivity (our light) and became blinded by darkness. *To be blinded by darkness is like having a forgotten vision.* This darkness not only consumes our light, it clouds our judgment and threatens to destroy the very essence of who we are by stealing our mind! And should this darkness succeed, Heaven's wrath is against all who *suppress the truth* about God by living as they please (Romans 1:18-25) and falling prey to the enemy through the *captivity of our mind*. Lost identity! God, very adamantly, tells us to *be not conformed to this world: but be ye transformed by the renewing of your mind, that ye may prove what is that good, and acceptable, and perfect, will of God* (Romans 12:2).

*Don't become so well-adjusted to your culture that you fit into it without even thinking. Instead, fix your attention on God. You'll be changed from the inside out. Readily recognize what he wants from you, and quickly respond to it. Unlike the culture around you, always dragging you down to its level of immaturity, God brings the best out of you, develops well-formed maturity in you.*

~ Romans 12:2 MSG

Being in the right mind is very important! We should stay alert (be sober), keep our eyes open (be vigilant; watchful), and be ready for spiritual warfare because our adversary (also referred to as the enemy, Lucifer, Satan, devil, or the anti-Christ) is roaming around pacing like a hungry lion, desperate to find anyone he can destroy (1 Peter 5:8). He is an expert at manipulation and trickery! His main objective is to steal your joy, kill your spirit, lead you astray (away from God), hold your mind in bondage, and take your body hostage as leverage to have complete control over you. But God has given us something much greater to lead us, guide us, and sustain us. He has given us a set of written instructions to live by: the Bible. Then He took time and care in molding that word and giving it life.

*The living word*, Jesus Christ, through obedience and sacrifice, honorably carried out his assignment with passion and purpose to proclaim liberty to the captives. Never wavering or losing site of his objective, he spoke with clarity when spreading the gospel of truth and walked boldly as a living testimony in showing us how to escape and conquer captivity, withstand evil (*Be not overcome of evil, but overcome evil with good* [Romans

12:21]), and love our neighbors as if loving ourselves (Mark 12:31). Jesus came so we could have a real, eternal life—a better life than we could ever imagine or dream of; He came so we could have abundance (to the fullest, till it overflows) (John 10:10). *For God so loved the world, that he gave his only begotten Son, that whosoever believeth in him should not perish, but have everlasting life* (John 3:16). Jesus is the good shepherd who giveth his life for (us) the sheep (John 10:11).

It is time to wake up! Follow Christ and do that which He has done. Hear the voice of God and obey. In Psalm 27:1, David says, *The LORD is my light and my salvation; whom shall I fear? the LORD is the strength of my life; of whom shall I be afraid?* True followers deny their own will to obey the commands and teachings, which *they* hear Him, the Holy Spirit, speak to them from the word in their heart. *For God hath not given us the spirit of fear; but of power, and of love, and of a sound mind* (2 Timothy 1:7).

*My sheep hear my voice,
and I know them, and they follow me.*

~ John 10:27

## ACCEPTING THE CALL

While fellowshipping at 7:45 a.m. with Unity Life Christian Ministries on Sunday, August 15, my heart was overflowing with truth as the Word was being preached and came forth through Minister Sharon Capel. Hebrews 11:1 was the topic: *Now faith is the substance of things hoped for, the evidence of things not seen.*

Many times, I not only questioned my faith, but I also wanted to understand everything there was to understand about faith. More importantly, I knew I wanted nothing else other than to please God and do all of what was asked of me. Listening to Minister Capel, I understood my faith was greater than I had imagined, and I could feel the presence of God all around me. Such power and force emanated through my feet and traveled up my legs and out through my hands. It was like fire shut up in my bones. God was anointing me and preparing to use me in a mighty way.

> *It is the spirit that quickeneth;*
> *the flesh profiteth nothing: the words*
> *that I speak unto you, they are spirit, and they are life.*
>
> *~ John 6:63*

Joining hands to pray, I could feel an electrifying sensation in my hands and noted an intense increase of heat. I could not help but wonder if the people holding my hands could feel it too. As I let go and prepared to leave, I was given a Word from a visiting prophet, Karyn Collins, which spoke to my heart, and the tears began to flow down my face. If you know and understand how God works, you know He does not always give you complete sentences, but He speaks to you in parables: *All these things spake Jesus unto the multitude in parables; and without a parable spake he not unto them* (Matthew 13:34).

> *A **parable** is a short tale or story that illustrates universal truth; one of the simplest of narratives. It sketches a setting, describes an action, and shows the results. It often involves a*

*character facing a moral dilemma, or making a questionable decision and then suffering the consequences.*[10]

Upon being told my gift was healing and my purpose was in my testimony, I was also told to read Psalm 61 or Isaiah 61 to learn more. Exiting the church, my mind desperately tried to recall every word and event that took place. I wasn't ready to go home! My spirit was soaring, and my excitement was leading me to seek more praise and worship. So out the door I went in search of another church service to attend before heading home.

Upon sitting to join the fellowship service that was already in progress at Living Word Ministries, Pastor Carter directed the congregation to turn to Matthew 7:13-14. After reading this scripture, I felt God telling me I was on the right path and then I was drawn to Isaiah 61. As I began to read, my mind raced from **Isaiah 61:1** and back to Matthew 7:13. At that point, I knew in my heart that I could no longer run from God and deny the calling on my life. God confirmed what I was feeling by bringing to my remembrance a dream I had on December 31, 1999. It was a vision of my future, but this was unbeknownst to me at the time.

***VISION:** A dream-like experience that God uses to deliver a message to someone.*

*Who hath saved us, and called us with an holy calling, not according to our works, but according to his own purpose and grace, which was given us in*

---

10   www.liquisearch.com/parable/characteristics

> *Christ Jesus before the world began, But is now made manifest by the appearing of our Saviour Jesus Christ, who hath abolished death, and hath brought life and immortality to light through the gospel.*
>
> ~ 2 Timothy 1:9-10

## SHARING MY DREAM: GOD'S VISION FOR MY LIFE

Background: Prior to the year 2000, the beginning of the millennium, there was much talk about a problem for both digital (computer-related) and non-digital documentation to include data storage resulting from using a four-digit year and changing over to an abbreviated two-digit year. It was believed that computers instrumental in regulating the operation of energy (power), water, and sewer plants would cease to function and people would be without water and electricity.

> *One minute past midnight on January 1, 2000, there is no source of electrical power anywhere in the world. The world is completely void of light and is entirely consumed by darkness. The doors to the prisons, hospitals, and insane asylums are disarmed. People are panicking; there are hordes of people stampeding through the streets. There are rats and rodents everywhere. I, on the other hand, have been given the responsibility to go into each and every area to direct people to safety (higher ground) toward the light. Upon bringing one group to safety and passing the torch to a person to head the group, I go deeper and deeper into dangerous areas, coming*

*out unharmed only to hand off more people and go in again. The deeper I go, the more difficulty I face in finding my way out of the maze to bring others to safety. Just when I think I have made a wrong turn and meet a dead end, I see someone who escaped the insane asylum that I passed earlier in my rescue mission. Though he is not able to speak, we are able to communicate in spirit and I learn that he was sent to help guide me out to safety.*

Upon waking up from my dream, I felt empowered and spiritually alive! What I did not realize was the unfolding or revealing of my purpose through my dream. God spoke to me about my mission! He showed me how victorious I was to not only overcome and conquer the captivity of my mind, but I was to assist in reaching others for their breakthrough in this same area.

## LESSONS LEARNED

- Many are called and chosen in accordance to God's purpose and your assigned mission.
- Don't judge a book by its cover.
- God is Spirit. He is neither male nor female.
- God does think as the world thinks.
- *God is no respecter of persons* (Acts 10:34). God views us all as being equally important and of value.
- God sees our full potential and wants nothing but the best for us all.

▸ God can **send you** deeper in the valley in the mist of darkness to be the guiding light for others.

Each one, reach one, teach one! As we are freed, it is our responsibility and purpose to help free others for the uplifting and glorification of the Kingdom.

**What is your purpose, your mission, and your vision?**

*Are you walking in your destiny? Are you obeying God? Do you know who you are? You are the child of the* ***Most-High God****, and your deliverance is in your praise.*

## WHAT IS FEAR?

False Evidence Appearing Real! Fear is a liar! The devil tries to use fear and other forms of roadblocks to control us and keep us from learning who we are in Christ. If the devil is successful at deceiving us, he is able to keep us from our destiny.

*Proclaim:*[11]

1. to **declare** publicly, insistently [with passion], proudly [boldly], or defiantly [in truth and love] and in either speech or writing: **announce**

2. to give outward indication of: show

    › Personal emphasis by author: **show** or demonstrate by way of examples and testimony.

---

11  www.merriam-webster.com/dictionary/proclaim

*Liberty:*

1. Freedom! *Now the Lord is the Spirit, and where the Spirit of the Lord is, there is freedom.* ~ 2 Corinthians 3:17

*Captives:*[12]

1. taken and held as or as if a prisoner of war
2. kept within bounds: confined
3. limited[13] – confided within limits; restricted or circumscribed; held under control of another but having the appearance of independence
4. *mental incarceration* – owned or controlled by another concern, thing, or entity and not fully operating in the capacity in which you were created. (*Enslaved in your mind by your mind!*)

## REFERENCES

**Isaiah 61:1 MSG** – [*Announce Freedom to All Captives*] The Spirit of God, the Master, is on me because God anointed me. He sent me to preach good news to the poor, heal the heartbroken, announce freedom to all captives, pardon all prisoners. God sent me to announce the year of His grace—a celebration of God's destruction of our enemies—and to comfort all who mourn, To care for the needs of all who mourn in Zion,

---

12  www.merriam-webster.com/dictionary/captives
13  www.dictionary.com/browse/limited

give them bouquets of roses instead of ashes, Messages of joy instead of news of doom, a praising heart instead of a languid spirit. Rename them "Oaks of Righteousness" planted by God to display his glory. They'll rebuild the old ruins, raise a new city out of the wreckage. They'll start over on the ruined cities, take the rubble left behind and make it new. You'll hire outsiders to herd your flocks and foreigners to work your fields, but you'll have the title "Priests of God," honored as ministers of our God. You'll feast on the bounty of nations, you'll bask in their glory. Because you got a double dose of trouble and more than your share of contempt, your inheritance in the land will be doubled and your joy go on forever.

**Luke 4:18-19** – The Spirit of the Lord is upon me, because he hath anointed me to preach the gospel to the poor; he hath sent me to heal the brokenhearted, to preach deliverance to the captives, and recovering of sight to the blind (darkness), to set at liberty them that are bruised (oppressed), to preach the acceptable year of the Lord [the Lord's favor].

**Leviticus 25:17** – Ye shall not therefore oppress one another; but thou shalt fear thy God: for I am the LORD your God.

**Deuteronomy 24:14** – Thou shalt not oppress an hired servant that is poor and needy, whether he be of thy brethren, or of thy strangers that are in thy land within thy gates:

**Deuteronomy 26:7** – And when we cried unto the LORD God of our fathers, the LORD heard our voice, and looked on our affliction, and our labour, and our oppression:

**Jeremiah 34:17** – Disobedience: failing to proclaim liberty to the captives: Therefore thus saith the LORD; Ye have not hearkened unto me, in proclaiming liberty, every one to his brother, and every man to his neighbor: behold, I proclaim a liberty for you, saith the LORD, to the sword, to the pestilence, and to the famine; and I make you to be removed into all the kingdoms of the earth.

# THE MEANING OF FAITH

*Now faith is the substance of things hoped for,
the evidence of things not seen.*

**~ Hebrews 11:1**

September 2, 2010

Upon birth, we come into this world clinging to those we grow to depend on to protect us and nurture us. Through this connection or union, we not only take on their preconceived beliefs and thoughts; we incorporate the values, norms, and thought patterns dictated by the condition of our environment. As we further develop, we become more aware of our surroundings, including the actions of man, as we struggle to choose sides in acknowledging the difference between right and wrong. Noting how different you are from what you have been exposed to, your mind seeks to break free from captivity.

*You neglected the Rock who begot you,
And forgot the God who gave you birth.*

~ Deuteronomy 32:18 NASB

Confused by man's teaching through something called education, I once believed I needed to see, touch, feel, and taste a thing to know it to be real. If it was not tangible or concrete as dictated by the world, it didn't exist. After questioning and attempting to make sense of what I was seeing and feeling, it did not meet with my approval and only contributed great pain, grief, anger, and frustration to my effort toward understanding. In need of hope and refusing to believe I was placed on this Earth and left to perish, I told God I had many questions that needed answers, and I wanted so desperately for Him to materialize before me, pull up a chair, and sit with me face to face so we could talk. For I was starting to lose faith and trusted no one to do what was right!

*Wherefore, if God so clothe the grass of the field, which to day is, and to morrow is cast into the oven, shall he not much more clothe you, O ye of little faith?*

~ Matthew 6:30

Little did I know that my desire to seek God's face was the beginning of a relationship I never knew nor realized was possible! *But seek ye first the Kingdom of God, and his righteousness; and all these things shall be added unto you* (Matthew 6:33). I called on God, and a Spirit I could not see with the naked eye spoke to the measure of my faith, which was the size of a mustard seed. Jesus said to his disciples, "Because of your unbelief: for verily I say unto you, If ye have faith as a grain of mustard seed, ye shall say unto this mountain, Remove hence to yonder place; and it shall remove; and nothing shall be impossible unto you"

(Matthew 17:20). That experience and the quickening of the Holy Spirit canceled my disbelief and became the beginning of a walk of faith not based on sight (Corinthians 5:7) but one based on trust and the desire to please God.

> *And without faith it is impossible to please him,*
> *for whoever would draw near to God*
> *must believe that he exists*
> *and that he rewards those who seek him.*
>
> ~ Hebrews 11:6 ESV

Because I wanted to see and hear, God not only revealed Himself to me, but He allowed me to see myself through His eyes. Through my out-of-body experience, my spirit separated from my soul and hovered over me for protection as my soul pleaded to God for mercy and deliverance. I have learned and come to know within my heart the very essence of who I AM and the necessity of *faith*! To have faith is to have confidence, belief, and trust in something or someone, seen or unseen. But that someone is not just anyone; it is God, the Father, the Son, and the Holy Ghost. I now know—regardless of the world's view—that which you cannot see *is* more real than that which you can see. You have to be willing to open your heart and your mind to Him who is within you. He who has faith to see shall see. He who has faith to hear shall hear.

> *So then faith cometh by hearing,*
> *and hearing by the word of God.*
>
> ~ Romans 10:17

In short, faith is about your willingness and ability to shift your state of consciousness. It is about making an attempt or conscious effort to rewind or unwind your mind. Let go of everything you believed to be truth and reprogram your mind to replace that which is false truth with God's truth—the living word. My reward is my deliverance and peace beyond peace to know the Father, my creator, for myself. It is the faith of knowing and believing that God is the same yesterday, today, and always. Faith is the belief in the promise of God, the promise of things hoped for, and the *covenant* on the basis of God's unconditional love for us!

*Therefore being by the right hand of God exalted,*
*and having received of the Father*
*the promise of the Holy Ghost, he hath*
*shed forth this, which ye now see and hear.*

~ Acts 2:33

This world and everything in it are temporal and put in place to take your mind off of that which is really important. It is set up in a way to redirect your focus, your emotions, and your actions and bring about destruction to our being—the very essence of who we are or were meant to be—to keep our soul from waking up and realizing who we are! It is an attempt to keep us from realizing our God-created purpose, which is carrying out our mission (assignment) and connecting to the vision. Yet, we know that God will make everything that happens to us in this life come out to our eventual good, as long as we trust Him and remain true to the purpose for which He called us (Romans 8:28). In the world, not of the world!

> *For everyone who has been born of God overcomes the world. And this is the victory that has overcome the world—our faith.*
>
> ~ 1 John 5:4 ESV

God wants nothing but the best for us! He has given us everything we will ever need to succeed, live, and enjoy life. How? *God has predestined those who believe in Him to be like His Son, so He gives us the help we need. Therefore, whoever accepts His Son, He justifies; those whom He justifies, He intends to glorify* (Romans 8:30 CWB). We must hold onto our faith and the belief that God is forever with us to walk with us and carry us along the way, if necessary. So shout with joy and claim your victory! I can do all things (done decently and in order) through Christ who strengthens me. *And Jesus said unto him, Go thy way; thy faith hath made thee whole. And immediately he received his sight, and followed Jesus in the way* (Mark 10: 52).

> *And all things, whatsoever ye shall ask in prayer, believing, ye shall receive.*
>
> ~ Matthew 21:22

The Covenant[14] Promise: First, there is a very distinct difference between a contract and a covenant. Although both are and can be a written and verbal agreement, a contract may specify a particular period to include a beginning and an end date with con-

---

14  https://www.dictionary.com/browse/covenant; an agreement (promise or pledge), usually formal, between two or more persons to do or not do something specified.

ditions or agreed-upon guidelines; a covenant is a permanent unconditional arrangement between two or more people or groups of people involving promises on the part of each individual or group. **A biblically based or divine covenant is an agreement between God and His children as initiated by God, and it covers certain promises made by God to His children.** Jeremiah 32:40 states, *And I will make an everlasting covenant with them, that I will not turn away from them, to do them good; but I will put my fear in their hearts, that they shall not depart from me.* The "covenants of promise" as referenced by Ephesians 2:12 are God's guarantees that He will provide *salvation* in spite of people's inability to keep their side of the agreement because of sin—a true testament of God's unconditional love for us.[15]

---

15  For more information, please reference the Nelson's Compact Bible Dictionary, http//www.thomasnelson.com/compact-bible-dictionary, Thomas Nelson, Inc., 2004

# THE DESIRES OF THE HEART

*But without faith it is impossible to
[walk with God and] please Him,
for whoever comes [near] to God must
[necessarily] believe that God exists
and that He rewards those who
[earnestly and diligently] seek Him.*

~ **Hebrews 11:6 AMP**

March 7, 2018

Revised June 14, 2019

As little children, we, intently, watch the people, places, and things around us while yearning to be and imitate what we see! As we get older and to know right from wrong, some of us put plans in place to help us succeed at obtaining what we want while choosing various paths. Many of us never quite anticipate being greeted by obstacles or roadblocks along the way as some of us stray far from God and others draw nearer.

Each person's journey is different! Some are born with silver spoons to know no obstacles, and some are born to suffer with each step we take. However, according to the word of God, pain and suffering has its unique place and purpose. *For Christ also suffered once for sins, the righteous for the unrighteous, that he might bring us to God, being put to death in the flesh but made alive in the spirit,* in which he went and proclaimed to the spirits in prison (1 Peter 3:18-19). Therefore, *as we share abundantly in Christ's sufferings, so through Christ we share abundantly in comfort too* (2 Corinthians 1:5). The late Elisabeth Elliot through her sermons and teachings described it best and said, "God often teaches us the deepest lessons through our deepest suffering." *And the* **God of all grace***, who called you to His eternal glory in Christ, after you have suffered a little while, will Himself restore you and make you strong, firm and steadfast* (1 Peter 5:10 NIV; emphasis added) in Him.

When we slow down to yield or surrender to our calling in honor of Christ in allowing God to prune us, shape us, and mature us, a bond takes place. By developing a deeper walk and relationship with God, trust builds up on both sides. As we learn to trust God through our trials and tribulations, we come to a greater understanding of who God is to include a greater assurance of His love for us and His sovereignty as the Head and Creator of us all. *And we know [with great confidence] that God [who is deeply concerned about us] causes all things to work together [as a plan] for good for those who love God, to those who are called according to His plan and purpose* (Romans 8:28 AMP).

## SHARING A HEARTFELT TESTIMONY

The Bible is very clear, but not many of us review the word of God as truth to believe it and commit to it. *Jesus told this simple story, but they had no idea what he was talking about. So he tried again. "I'll be explicit, then. I am the Gate for the sheep. All those others are up to no good—sheep stealers, every one of them. But the sheep didn't listen to them. I am the Gate. Anyone who goes through me will be cared for—will freely go in and out, and find pasture. A thief is only there to steal and kill and destroy. I came so they can have real and eternal life, more and better life than they ever dreamed of* (John 10:6-10 MSG).

For the most part, a number of us have been taught to review the word of God as any other book or form of literary work in which we give no credence to until we are forced by a life-altering spiritual experience to change our mindset! *Jesus said to him, "Because you have seen Me, do you now believe? Blessed [happy, spiritually secure, and favored by God] are they who did not see [Me] and yet believed [in Me]"* (John 20:29 AMP).

Seeking the *American dream* like so many others, I was determined to put forth the effort to better myself at all costs. I kept applying for promotions through what I considered to be better positions only to be given excuses as to why I didn't qualify. And yet, I was expected to train others to perform in the same position I was told I didn't deserve because I didn't qualify to occupy it myself. So based on what I was told I was lacking, although I trained others, I would still attempt to obtain the experience, knowledge, specialized training, or education for an opportunity toward the next position for a promotion.

Upon experiencing this same scenario over and over again, I was beginning to lose hope, but I refused to give up no matter how great the pain.

Greatly disappointed but holding on, I would pray to God and ask Him to shield my heart by not allowing it to harden or grow bitter. I asked Him to give me the strength to endure and to be a much better person than those I was encountering. Attempting to move forward, I made a conscious decision to go back to school to get my bachelor's degree in business administration. But even after getting that degree, those in managerial leadership positions within my places of employment still refused to recognize my accomplishments while attempting to force me into roles they felt I was best suited to occupy—on the basis of who I was and what I represented (to them)! Unless you experience some of the same or similar for yourself, I'm sure it's hard for you to even imagine what I described as happening today. But, it does . . . more often than you think!

Overlooked time and time again and pushed into a corner while limitations mounted, I was now beginning to allow it to affect me and struggling to attempt to prove my value and worth to man to no avail! As my pain grew, I started to doubt God's existence, and I found it harder and harder to believe that a God who loved me unconditionally would allow people to bring so much strife against me—just because they could! Questioning God almost daily, I found myself challenging Him and growing closer to Him at the same time. Reading His word, I would give it back to Him! God, You said I have not because I ask not! You said to ask and it shall be given to me! Seek and I shall find! Knock and the door shall be opened! Well, I'm asking! I'm seeking and I'm knocking!

We were developing a relationship and my *faith* was growing stronger. God was opening my eyes as His word began to take root and come alive in me. I was learning to hold on to His every word and see it performing in my life. God and I were becoming inseparable! As I believed, I felt myself growing taller and becoming more confident, but not quite completely without fear, and God was talking to me about that as well. He reminded me of 2 Timothy 1:7: *For God hath not given us a Spirit of Fear; but of power, and of love, and of a sound mind.* He told me, *if I abide in Him, He would abide in me.* He even told me not to worry about being promoted by man. He was positioning me, but first I needed to trust Him. I needed to walk in my authority and take ownership! *For the word of the LORD is right and true; he is faithful in all he does. The LORD loves righteousness and justice; the earth is full of his unfailing love* (Psalm 33:4-5 NIV).

My love and commitment to and for God are real! He never ceases to amaze me, and He continues to make me aware of His sovereignty and presence in my life. First, there was a knock and I answered His call. Then there was training and a push to the front line. At times, I questioned my assignment; but still I forged ahead with reluctance and wanting nothing more than to remain in His perfect will. Many times, I even doubted my confidence to fulfill His every command, but He prevailed to reveal His confidence in me. On the third day of the first month of the year, March, as referenced by the sacred biblical calendar, which is also the birth and head position of our Lord and Savior Jesus Christ, God blessed me to receive an honorary doctorate in Divinity along with naming me as an Ambassador to the United Nations and gifting me with a Chaplaincy certification as His Kingdom representative. When God honors you and gives you the desires of your heart in accordance to His will, He does it big!

So on that glorious day, March 3, 2018, I attended my graduation, which was held on the grounds of Maryland University Chapel in College Park, Maryland, and received from Trinity International University of Ambassadors, not one, but three honorary acknowledgments in the name of Jesus Christ! When man pushes you in a corner and attempts to make you invisible (nonexistent), God pushes you out front to remind you that the *last will be first and the first will be last* as He makes you visible in letting you know just how relevant you are to Him. **When man condemns you, God redeems you! When man devalues you, God values you and makes your purpose known to you.** When man attempts to belittle you, God renames you by making your name great!

> *For promotion cometh neither from the east,*
> *nor from the west, nor from the south.*
> *But God is the judge:*
> *he putteth down one, and setteth up another.*
>
> ~ Psalm 75:6-7

# STOP DENYING THE HOLY SPIRIT

*I can do all things [which He has called me to do]
through Him who strengthens and empowers me
[to fulfill His purpose—I am self-sufficient
in Christ's sufficiency;
I am ready for anything and equal to anything through Him
who infuses me with inner strength and confident peace.]
Nevertheless, it was right of you to share
[with me] in my difficulties.*

**~ Hebrews 11:1**

September 9, 2018

Revised September 22, 2020

During the week, my time is normally very hectic, from the time I get up in the mornings until the time I sit at the end of my day and go to bed at night! I work before and after work; so some weekends, all I do is sleep like a newborn baby trying to rejuvenate unless God gives me an assignment and sends me out. In between the downtime and the waiting, I have conversations with God. I may even pray or cry myself to sleep in worship with my Bible or a book in my hand. There are also times in between when He gives me things to write or meditate on. Following through, I send out messages, check my Facebook page, and wake up two, three, or four hours later, still holding my cell phone or lying on top of it.

On the morning of September 9, 2018, at approximately 6 a.m., I woke up to something or someone banging as if they were furiously using a hammer. I jumped up and looked around to notice that every light in the house on the middle floor was on: the living room, bathroom, dining area, and kitchen. The television was on, and loud. Immediately, I called upstairs to my father to see if he was okay; perhaps it was him who had been using a hammer—for whatever reason. No, it wasn't him and he was okay! I knew it couldn't be my next-door neighbor because she was away for the weekend, so unless her home was being invaded, it wasn't her. All of a sudden, there was a sense of peace, quietness, and calm with the exception of the sump pump along with the sound of the rain outside—but it didn't sound like a hammer. Then I focused on the TV as I heard the voice of George Bloomer confirming a frustration that's plagued me for a long while. Because my DVR is set to record George Bloomer's Spiritual Authority series every Sunday and I had fallen asleep with the TV still on, I knew God wanted me to listen; so I did, intently!

George Bloomer was passionately talking about the Holy Spirit (or Holy Ghost, as referenced by some)! As I paid attention, I realized, like George Bloomer, my heart also aches concerning the lack of knowledge and interest that many people (believers and non-believers alike) have about who God is, to include their unwillingness to believe that God, the Father, the Son, and the Holy Spirit are one. Yes, even believers, those who call themselves Christians, deny the Holy Spirit like Judas did Jesus! I get so frustrated trying to explain the *supernatural* like a broken record—especially to those who should know or understand how God is able to communicate with me and others—if they are willing to listen and obey.

Interceding, I pray often that the eyes of people would be open and they would experience the day of Pentecost to know and believe in their hearts as I do! I pray they are not Christians in name only but believers with a *testimony* speaking in tongues, prophesying and moving step by step to the instructions of the Holy Spirit without shame or fear. I pray we stop attempting to hurt and deceive one another and start to embrace one another in love as sisters and brothers created by the same Father.

When God sends us out, we must get in *troop formation* like the Tribes of Israel and stay in position to fulfill our assignments while *trusting and leaning on the Lord without hesitation*! My challenge to reach others and spread the Gospel has not been as difficult as it has been to get people to believe in the existence of the Holy Spirit. We make the wrong compromises and sacrifices for career and false promises, which are never kept by people who lack the love of God in their hearts. We tie ourselves to sin while thinking there are no consequences. We attack one another while competing for recognition, power, and control with relentless passion. We stray away from the Lord while growing closer to the darkness and alienating ourselves from our one true comforter who was sent by God. And through it all, God still loves us unconditionally. Where is our passion and compassion for God?

# BEARING WITNESS TO THE PAIN AND THE GLORY:
## A MOMENT OF TRUTH!

*He told them, "You don't get to know the time. Timing is the Father's business. What you'll get is the Holy Spirit. And when the Holy Spirit comes on you, you will be able to be my witnesses in Jerusalem, all over Judea and Samaria, even to the ends of the world."*

**~ Acts 1:7-8**

May 6, 2019

Finalized June 5, 2019

People, unfortunately, have mastered how to compartmentalize! Prioritizing has evolved into a very systematic and delicate art form to include a disturbing order of importance which varies for everyone with an increasing lack of integrity! The Lord detests dishonesty, but accurate weights find favor with

Him. The integrity of the upright is guided by the light, but the unfaithful are destroyed by duplicity! (Proverbs 11:1, 3)

There are various situations and events in life that touch my heart. Some bring me joy, and some bring me pain. I AM deeply saddened by our lack of humanity and unwillingness to display love to one another and for one another. Pain is not enjoyable for me! And I'm sure no one but those who can be identified as masochistic like or receive pleasure from pain. However, I can't even imagine ever thinking or feeling pain to be pleasurable. I find it extremely difficult to understand how people can be so selfish, uncaring, cruel, and ruthless in how we regard and interact with one another! How are we so easily able to disregard the importance and value of another human being to feel nothing in the aftermath of it all? I understand not being able to shake a painful experience to the point of it being a nonexistent distant memory, especially when you are faced with having to relive some measure of a past experience each and every day, but **it is possible to move past the pain to embrace its deeper purpose!**

When God raises you up, puts you in position, and gives you an assignment to carry out, it is very important to make sure you activate your *divine filter* to be an effective and willing vessel! You must exercise unshakable faith! You must not allow people, fear, pain, or your *ego* (your emotions or personal feelings) to derail you! No matter how often you repeat the mission or the message to include being reminded of what people think or feel about you, you must also be mindful of who you are serving and whose you are! God or man? **You simply cannot follow** and please two *masters*! It is impossible to be and do what is expected of you in pleasing more than one person at the same time! So what is the *ultimate objective*?

You must not allow your intellect or that of others to block the flow of God! Much like Jeremiah, even if people object to what you have to say or share, you must not allow them to hinder or interrupt the deliverance of what must and should be shared as **a witness to truth**! Why? *This is the crisis we're in: God-light streamed into the world, but men and women everywhere ran for the darkness. They went for the darkness they were not really interested in pleasing God. Everyone who makes a practice of doing evil, addicted to denial and illusion, hates God-light and won't come near it, fearing a painful exposure. But anyone working and living in truth and reality welcomes God-light so the work can be seen for the God-work it is* (John 3:19-21 MSG).

The world is ruled by darkness (sin, corruption, and greed)! Iniquity (sin) is being demonstrated all around us and it is real! Classism and divisiveness are real! Racial inequality is real! Gender inequality is real! Social injustice is real! In fact, bigotry and chauvinism is as prevalent today as it was during the life and times of my great-great-grandparents! Corruption and criminal behavior from the least expected are real! Corruption and greed have taken a front seat to how people and justice are valued! *Double standards* along with the practice of black codes still exist! Retaliation, along with the need to silence truth, is real! There is also a widespread belief in something called a "code of silence"! **But God will always use what and who He pleases to unmask (reveal, uncover) truth when the time is right!**

## YOUR VALUE AND YOUR WORTH

People treat you based on how they value you! How they see you is how they value and measure your worth! Your perceived worth governs the respect or lack of respect (reverence) granted to you by others! But God is no respecter of persons! He is nothing like man; what He is willing to do for one, He is willing to do for all! He places the same amount of value, worth, and respect on each of His children—all of mankind! *For God shows no partiality [no arbitrary favoritism; with Him one person is not more important than another]* (Romans 2:11).

Many things are so obvious, but people tend to continue to deny the truth of what they see, and they are even more adamant about not engaging in objective conversations to discuss root causes. Refusing to discuss or reverence the truth doesn't solve a problem. Society, through cultural conditioning (influence), has dictated the level of importance and value we should place on people as a group or individually in accordance to our race, gender, and social status to include other possible idiosyncrasies![16] Let's take a deep look at *my* truth! I was born into this world a Black female, once a little girl and now an adult woman. When I lay my head down at the end of each and every day to go to sleep, I rise each and every morning a Black female. I have no magic wand that enables me to "change at will" from a female to a male or culturally change the color of my skin to live this life as anything other than a Black female. In fact, I have never even given any thought to pursuing a regimen or procedure for light-

---

16  www.dictionary.com/browse/idiosyncrasies; a characteristic, habit, mannerism, or the like, that is peculiar to an individual

ening my skin; although, I did desire to have a darker skin tone growing up! Now, I will admit that I have given some thought to the idea that the degree of my pain would be far less than what I have endured and witnessed in this life thus far if I were a Caucasian male (or female). And after losing my hair between the ages of thirteen and fifteen, many, without consulting me, assumed it was a desired lifestyle change to reflect a rebellious attitude against being born a female. No, not true! Although, I AM aware of the advancement of medical procedures to grant us the opportunities to change our sex and physical appearance to include the altering of our skin tone, that is not an option for me! I AM content and appreciative of who I have become, and it is my objective to be the person I was created to be in carrying out my God-ordained appointed assignment, **bearing witness to it all!**

God's adversary, who is the adversary to all mankind, is very strategic and will stop at nothing to keep you in the dark. It is his life's mission to kill, steal, and destroy you by any means necessary. If he can keep you ignorant to the truth, he has succeeded at keeping you from your destiny. There has been, in operation since the beginning of my existence, a plot and a plan to keep me from learning my true identity. Many obstacles have been put in my path in an attempt to distract and derail or delay me from moving forward in claiming my inheritance! Things were said to me and about me to instill fear and enslave my mind, designed to break my spirit and hold me in captivity! Pain was directed at me with the hope of stealing my joy and stopping me from prospering. But God, through the Holy Spirit, was determined to reign supreme in my life by not allowing me to be deceived by what it looked like! I needed to hold on to my faith and believe in the Word of God! Sitting quietly, I needed to trust God—no matter what—in allowing His plan to manifest in my life! There were times when I needed to bridle my tongue unless I was given strict orders from the Lord to speak. So I needed to learn to *put on the full armor of God [for His precepts are like the splendid armor of a heavily-armed soldier], so that you may be able to [successfully] stand up against the schemes* and *the strategies* and *the deceits of the devil. For our struggle is not against flesh and blood [contending only with physical opponents], but against the rulers, against the powers, against the world forces of this [present] darkness, against the spiritual* forces *of wickedness in the heavenly (supernatural)* places (Ephesians 6:11-12 AMP).

People, by design, have made many attempts to ignore me, silence me, and discredit me within the workplace or social settings when I have spoken my truth concerning negative and hurtful experiences or situations. Being shut down has become a normal practice to downplay, diminish, or suppress the truth about the presence of evil (and cruelty) within your immediate surroundings and in the world as a whole. Who you are or have become through conflict—the less entitled[17], the privileged,[18] the more tolerated[19]—speaks to how you process and handle information! Many have befriended me only to attempt to influence

---

17 Assuming or acting as though one has more right or claim to something than another
18 Belonging to a class or group that enjoys special privileges or favoritism over another
19 Belonging to a less than desirable group but more tolerated as a token and exploited

change in my life based on their misinterpreted truth. When interacting with others, how often do we act on our misconceptions and misguided teachings to exert some sort of control?

When I was in my first year of high school, I was excited to register for Driver's Education and Print Shop classes only to be removed from both classes because I was a female. That was my first experience and understanding of gender-specific, directed actions being influenced by a *spirit of chauvinism*. Yes, I'm sure that you would like to believe that that sort of thing only existed in the past prior to the 1960s or 1970s and is no longer an operating trait of gender discrimination, but I beg to differ! Much like today, some of us are still being forced into and considered for gender- and race-specific roles based on who we are in accordance to the mindset of others in position of power to impact our lives through limitations. I was extremely disappointed to be pulled out of those classes, which were substituted for Typing 101 and Beginning Shorthand—the more gender-appropriate courses for the female students, as deemed by the counselors at the high school where I graduated in 1978. Ironically, they had an outstanding female basketball team, and due to my height, I was encouraged to give that a shot! Unfortunately, I had no interest or skill for mastering the game.

## FAST FORWARD

**We are seeing (witnessing) mass destruction taking place at a very alarming, accelerated growth!** As outlined in a *Behold the Lamb* publication, **"Sin is the greatest destroyer in the universe. It destroys souls, families and nations!"** If you were to research "mass destruction," it is referenced as being a military term signifying death or injury on a large scale and specifically caused by nuclear or biological weapons. But who is holding the weapon, and what hands are pushing and directing the trigger?

There have been other references defining "mass destruction" as the "killing of large numbers of people." Ironically, an August 14, 2018, article featured on the Department of Homeland Security (DHS) website states, "The United States faces a rising danger from terrorist and rogue States seeking to use weapons of mass destruction."[20] I'm assuming the use of the word "States" was a typo or misprint and the writer meant to use the word country or countries in its place. Or, just maybe, it was an intentional Freudian slip and not an actual error! The greatest damage to the United States and the occupying people (human race) is being inflicted from within the United States as led by the controlling power base, and those on the outside are deliberate casualties of war being sacrificed to keep us from taking ownership or responsibility for our own demise. Many have tried to rewrite history to change or cover up the truth. We, the American people, have demonstrated atrocious acts of terrorism, one upon another, with the support of our judiciary system to tear down and destroy spirits! The wanton destruction of human life for selfish gain.

Government agencies are all outfitted with a nurse's station to include highly skilled staff to man and operate an "employee assistance program" for attending to the mental capacity of an employee dealing with stressful events (inside and outside of the

---

20  https://www.dhs.gov/topic/weapons-mass-destruction

workplace). But no one wants to consider or discuss the damage caused from inside the workplace! Can you imagine being passionate about wanting to help people and making career choices aligning you to accomplish that desire, but a shift in how business is being conducted has taken place to create obstacles directed at halting your goals? Civil rights and equal employment opportunity laws and policies are no longer being applied and enforced. People working within those offices who want to help preserve the rights, dignity, and integrity of others are being encouraged to turn the other way as employees are being violated!

Employees who were once valued and treated with importance have become less important and undervalued to be deemed disposable on the basis of their position (hierarchy status), class, and association! As an employee, you are being conditioned to fall in line without question like a robot. And be expected to adhere to the existing organizational culture of turning off your humanity switch for the sake of acceptance and career growth in being a part of a massive plot or plan to disregard the rights of people—depending upon who they are! Can you imagine transforming and being able to identify with the heart of God while being expected to deny all wrongdoing to please the heart of the people who have waged their souls to total darkness?

## THE BEAUTY AND THE GLORY

The beauty of my pain is in the knowing of its glory! Yes, the pain still stings and hurts through the enduring of it—but my pain is not without purpose! It is linked to the joy of my heart in refusing to conform to the ways of the world. My heart is the center and the brain of my spirit, which is connected to God. He sees and feels as I do! The pain that is etched in my heart is also etched in His! He has chosen me and positioned me, like many others, with a challenging assignment to bear witness to it all. Each of us has been outfitted with an assignment that may be considered to be challenging! My challenge is linked to my unwillingness to give in under pressure, no matter the threats or the humiliation inflicted or viewed by others. For it is not my desire to grieve the transgressions of this world but to learn and grow in observance of how not to be while striving to be the person I was created to be in well-doing! Why? Because the joy of the Lord is my strength, and Romans 8:28 gives me great confirmation!

# PURPOSE: REALIZING YOUR GOD POTENTIAL

# DIVINE PURPOSE

*And we know [with great confidence] that God
[who is deeply concerned about us]
causes all things to work together [as a plan]
for good for those who love God,
to those who are called according to His plan and purpose.*

~ **Romans 8:28 AMP**


June 25, 2018

Revised September 28, 2020

Life and growing old can prove to be very challenging! Certain events or trials and tribulations can cause you to question your sanity and your reason for being. When I was younger, I used to make references to God about not being in a position to cosign to being born on Earth to encounter the upsets and disappointments in my life. In other words, I didn't recall being given a choice! Initially, my greatest disappointment or issue was rejection and not being able to fit in! Then, I found myself struggling with hair loss due to a medical condition called alopecia.

This created an entirely different set of social problems for me to include being terminated from a job. Why? Imagine!

Coping with the pain of my existence while fighting to live or simply survive, I withdrew from socializing with others as much as possible to focus on self. To a certain extent, even that became a problem. Why? When you learn to block out the noise of unwanted influence and limit the amount of control or access that you are willing to give to people, you get labeled as being antisocial! But something else was happening! Through the isolation and quietness, I was developing a relationship with God and gaining spiritual growth to put things into perspective.

All things happen for a reason with divine purpose. Each and *every* human being is created by God. Before we were conceived in the womb of our mothers, we were simply a *thought* as perceived by God with a very specific and important role to perform here on Earth as in Heaven. Through our growth and development, from a thought to a seed or embryo that was planted by God, a *metamorphosis* took place. We were transformed from our spirit form into a fleshly form by human birth and born on Earth into sin as we became separated from our Heavenly Father.

If we were to study the birth, death, burial, resurrection, and life of Christ, we would learn a lot about being **purposed**! He was purposely created to fulfill a mission and position on Earth on behalf of the Kingdom. Each and every person is created with a purpose to fulfill a Kingdom role on Earth. Certain events concerning our lives set off a chain reaction for accomplishing desired outcomes—in accordance to the *Will of God*! That means every second, minute, and hour of your life has significance, although we may not understand the connection.

- **Purposed**: deliberate, intentional; to intend or resolve to perform or accomplish.

- **Purpose**: the object toward which one strives or for which something exists; goal; aim.

- **Metamorphosis**: a change in the form or nature of a thing or person into a completely different one or identity, by natural or supernatural means.

**There is divine purpose in all of it!** I remember the numerous conversations people were trying to have with me concerning the topic of immigration. They didn't understand why I refused to go along to get along on the subject. I needed to stay true to the expectation of my *mentor* to include all of His teachings! I needed to be mindful and very careful about my actions and my speech in not being disobedient to God!

> *"I don't think the way you think. The way you work isn't the way I work." God's Decree. For as the sky soars high above earth, so the way I work surpasses the way you work, and the way I think is beyond the way you think. Just as rain and snow descend from the skies and don't go back until they've watered the earth, Doing their work of making things grow and blossom, producing seed for farmers and food for the hungry, So will the words that come out of my mouth not come back empty-handed. They'll do the work I sent them to do, they'll complete the assignment I gave them.*
>
> ~ Isaiah 55:8-11 MSG

Many didn't like our current US commander and chief, but they still voted for him or cosigned on his immigration policy. Man tests the waters in using a smaller sample of his plan before he unleashes what's really coming that will eventually affect us all! Do you know what a test subject is? Do you know what a test sample is? Do you not understand the concept of "law of attraction" or "reaping and sowing"? Do you not know that everything is being recorded in Heaven? Your actions and your thoughts!

Jesus is my commander and chief! He is my mentor and divine example! He is the same, yesterday, tomorrow, and forever more! If you study the Word of God for yourself—not allowing outside influences to tip your understanding of who He was and is—you would note a very exceptional character who exhibits unquestionable *integrity*! He, God, and the Holy Spirit are one! God does not love on the basis of skin color, geographical location, gender, etc. He loves on the basis of being a creator who has given life to *all of His children*—unconditional love!

When you view individuals for whatever reason, you should try comparing them to the total content of their character as measured by the *ultimate example* we are supposed to be following. He, Yahweh, said follow me as I follow my Father—Abba Father! If man is not following the right path, why would you follow them and then complain about it later?

Nothing happens without God's permission. He is uncovering some things. He is pulling the wool and scales off eyes to reveal us to ourselves, the ugliness inside!

**Everything happens for a reason, and God always has a bigger plan called purpose!**

# THE SIGNIFICANCE OF PURPOSE

*"For I know the plans I have for you,"
declares the LORD, "plans to prosper
you and not to harm you,
plans to give you hope and a future."*

**~ Jeremiah 29:11 NIV**

January 9, 2019

Finalized January 15, 2019

God does everything with purpose, and He expects us to take His mandate seriously enough to get in position to honor our God-directed purpose, too! Each and every one of us is created by God with a purpose for a purpose! I cannot express just how gratifying it has been to know and walk out my purpose with *faith*! Developing a relationship with the Lord to know Him for myself has given me new meaning and direction. It has opened my eyes to His love, mercy, and grace. I AM so grateful for His persistence and willingness not to give up on me but to push me to strive for spiritual excellence.

I AM truly excited about how God communicates with me. Yes, He does and is willing to communicate with all of us, but right now I want to emphasize what it means to me to have a personal relationship with the Lord. Not many people understand the *true nature* of the importance of developing and having a relationship with God to appreciate Him knowing you better than you know yourself (flaws and all). I'm talking about the intimacy of getting to know Him and Him knowing you based on your personality, which speaks to who you really are and reveals who you were created to be! With that said, God knows what He put on the inside of me. In fact, He knows what He put on the inside of each and every one of us in getting the desired glory through relationship. In addition, not just our relationship with Him but our interaction and relationship with others!

Once a week, I have a regularly scheduled medical appointment with a natural healer who has been placed in my life and positioned by God in fulfilling her purpose on so many different levels on behalf of the Kingdom. She is a loving and caring individual with a heart for wanting to heal and treat people with open arms to restore their spirits! While in her office during my morning medical appointment on January 9, 2019, I had the pleasure of meeting two beautiful God-believing, God-fearing women (Katherine and Karen). We got lost in conversation about the goodness of the Lord. Although I have not had the opportunity to reconnect with them since that day, I know we will have many more conversations like that one in the near future. There is nothing like sharing and gleaning one from another as we show love and appreciation for the Lord. Matthew

18:20 states, *For where two or three are gathered in my name, there am I in the midst of them.*

God does nothing halfway, and He knows how to express His gratitude for our obedience and faithfulness. You just have to be willing to be flexible and available to hearing His heart to receive and give, learn, and grow, communicate, and glean! Nothing is by happenstance or coincidental. It is all by design: Divine Purpose! And guess what? God is watching!

> *But the plans of the LORD stand firm forever,*
> *the purposes of his heart through all generations.*
>
> ~ Psalm 33:11 NIV

\*

> *Many are the **plans in a person's heart,***
> ***but it is the LORD's purpose that prevails.***
>
> ~ Proverbs 19:21 NIV

# CHALLENGES COME!

March 24, 2019

*We are pressed on every side by troubles, but we are not crushed. We are perplexed but not driven to despair. We are hunted down but never abandoned by God. We get knocked down, but we are not destroyed. Through suffering, our bodies continue to share in the death of Jesus so that the life of Jesus may also be seen in our bodies. Yes, we live under constant danger of death because we serve Jesus, so that the life of Jesus will be evident in our dying bodies* (2 Corinthians 4:8-11 NLT). However, the Bible declares to count it all joy (James 1:2) when challenges and troubles (trials and tribulations) come! It took me a long while to understand the gravity of that concept and even longer to appreciate the reward of going through the process. Challenges, for some, do not come without pain and grieving, but there is a purpose for it all if you are willing to go the distance to uncover the secret treasure!

Pain creates, in some, a determination and drive to push forward to conquer our challenges. The process to include the challenge is not giving up or giving in at the start of an uncomfortable journey or situation. Once I stopped running to instead take a stand and face my opposition, in spite of the pain, much was revealed to me about my true identity and destiny. *I consider that our present sufferings are not worth comparing with the glory that will be revealed in us* (Romans 8:18 NIV).

Revelation gave me hope and increased my *faith*. The greater the challenges, the more God revealed Himself, His heart, and His expectations to me. The more I was willing to forsake my personal ambition to be the person God created me to be, my eyes were opened to the world and people around me! As children who proclaim to be Christians, we are to come to the aid of one another in spirit and in truth! Not many of us know how to defend others and are willing to *fight* for what we *believe* to defy the world in honor of the hurting or lost on behalf of the Lord! But I AM ready, willing, and able to get in position to hold my post to receive my treasure (my greatest reward) in Heaven!

> *Consider it pure joy, my brothers and sisters, whenever*
> *you face trials of many kinds, because you know*
> *that the testing of your faith produces perseverance.*
> *Let perseverance finish its work so that you may be*
> *mature and complete, not lacking anything.*
>
> ~ James 1:2-4 NIV

# THE CAPACITY TO LOVE

*If anyone boasts, "I love God," and goes right on hating his brother or sister, thinking nothing of it, he is a liar. If he won't love the person he can see, how can he love the God he can't see?*
*The command we have from Christ is blunt:*
*Loving God includes loving people.*
*You've got to love both.*

**~ 1 John 20-21 MSG**

November 23, 2018

Revised October 10, 2020

The world encompasses a conglomeration of people from various ethnic groups, backgrounds, and cultures within a culture with one thing in common: survival! Looking for new worlds to inhabit, many people from various geographical backgrounds outside of the United States come to America in search of the "American Dream" only to learn that it's not what they thought or hoped it would be! What exactly does the American Dream symbolize, and does it mean the same thing to and for everyone?

I've heard and have been led to believe that America is known to be the land of milk and honey, the land of opportunity and the good life! However, the same opportunities are not made available and granted to everyone for them to enjoy the good life equally. Yes—based on your perception, which is fueled by your experiences or *bias mental conditioning*, it's possible you may disagree and that's fine! But is equality valued and demonstrated as much as it should be to include *all* people? Especially since the central slogan or ideology in the wake of the current movement is to Make America Great Again! So what exactly does that really mean—and was it ever great? And for whom? Depending upon who you ask, the answer can display a very narrow-minded viewpoint laced with a selfish heart and loathing. *Then the Lord said, "I have seen how the children of Israel are still being treated in Egypt. I have heard their cries of pain and their pleas for help. I know they are finally ready to let me deliver them from the oppression they're under* (Exodus 3:7 TCW).

We, human beings, are creatures of habit who are easily influenced by our emotions. Without rationale, we have a tendency to operate in the moment, but whether we realize it or not, it all catches up to us in the end! And now, you are probably saying, at the end, when I cease to exist, it won't matter! So why should I care? Because you will reap what you sow—even at the end!

*Now [remember] this:*
*he who sows sparingly will also reap sparingly,*
*and he who sows generously*

> *[that blessings may come to others] will also reap generously [and be blessed].*
>
> ~ 2 Corinthians 9:6 AMP

We are products of our environment, and more often than not, we tend to mimic what we see rather than doing what we know to be true (or right) in spite of what we see! Everything and everyone we encounter, to include what we read, has the ability to create impactful life experiences. These experiences—good, bad, indifferent—can prove to be very challenging in opening and closing doors to our heart! Some experiences are processed without biases, and some are not so easily handled in a mature, forgiving manner. In fact, the outcome can be more devastating to one than it is to another in altering our way of thinking to distort our perception concerning how we respond and react (operate). That's why it is extremely important for me to conduct regular and daily self-checks of my heart. No matter the culture, environment, or situation, I must always be willing to carry the right spirit in my heart for creating the right attitude to display love for and toward others, even if it is not shown for or toward me! More often than not, I wonder "how?" in attempting to be positive and staying encouraged. Although, it has been known and proven to be true, hurt people hurt people. I must, in my brokenness, keep my heart open to love! So, although they slay me, I will trust the Lord—at all times!

On the night of October 27, 2018, my heart was very heavy. The intensity of what was going on around me—all the hate and iniquity—weighed so heavily on my heart! I got little to no sleep as I tossed and turned to get into a comfortable position in between the crying and agonizing thoughts of souls being tormented due to the growing lack of humanity and increasing dark cloud of evil moving amongst us and over us. The cruelty in the world is unbelievable! I AM truly baffled by it all and afraid at the same time. Afraid that one day my heart will break and become as seared as those around me! Afraid that with each offense brought against me, I may find it more and more difficult to forgive or to recover.

Sometimes, I get so lost in my pain and my compassion for others makes me angry, but I am passionate about making a difference not to conform! Often, I think about the children—the innocent, forgiving, and vulnerable children. Children who have been targeted for a while and set up to be abused. Children who have been separated from their parents as a result of the war on immigration and the growing acceptance for a culture that does more wrong than right. There are times when I want so desperately not to think or feel anything to be able to give my heart a rest! And then, I start to think about all of the things that I myself have experienced over the years in the name of cruelty to include people attempting to influence me to adapt to this horrid existing culture. Successfully, I have managed to remain resistant to this type of change! Not necessarily a good change—at least not for me! It is a change that would cause me to fit in, blend in, and be like countless others. A change with the possibility of opening up my chances for a promotion and a greater growth opportunity. But this kind of win—with the wrong motives and right incentives—would be a compromise to my values, beliefs, and faith! I cannot allow myself to rewrite wrongs in my mind as being right or rights as being wrong when my heart knows the truth as expected of me by God! The price would be too high!

As I lay awake that night, and as the days passed leading up to today, I sought God for answers. Why was it so easy for many to conduct themselves in such a corruptible manner without giving any thoughts to their actions and their impact on others? Not just the physical pain of wounding the heart and leaving scars but the possible long-term mental and emotional implications of invisible scars! How has it been so easy for me to resist temptation and bounce back from a wounded heart on numerous occasions? Determination? Why is it so easy for others to choose wrong over right? Discouragement? While pondering these questions, I heard in my spirit the condition of the heart and the capacity to love!

With each conversation or heart confrontation God has with me, He opens me up to an entirely different inspiring lesson and challenging writing assignment to convey His thoughts as it relates to me and everything going on around me. Listening intently to grasp every word or parable to document it correctly, revelation after revelation was being released to give me more hope and clarity about the importance of purpose and being positioned. Pain has its purpose—in accordance to the *Will of God*. Long-suffering has its purpose—in accordance to the *Will of God*. Being in position has its purpose—in accordance to the *Will of God*. Being purposed and positioned may not always be pleasant or easy, but it is necessary for the mission—in accordance to the *Will of God*. Everyone is not built (equipped) or created for the same mission, but our purpose is as equally important—in accordance to the *Will of God*. We are designed for different assignments, and there is a very distinct difference between God's mission and man's work of iniquity to deceive you.

According to God, I was purposed to handle pain and positioned to witness each experience on behalf of the Lord and His mission. In spite of the irony, as to how that sounds, I thanked God for His faithfulness in me to overcome and for setting me apart. I thanked Him for reminding me of who I was and who He had created me to be! Obedience is better than sacrifice, and each encounter with God draws me closer to Him in feeling good about fulfilling my purpose. When you are able to see (witness) and to experience things for yourself, no one can tell you anything differently; although, they will attempt to convince you otherwise!

Mark Twain wrote, "Of all the animals, man is the only one that is cruel. He is the only one that inflicts pain for the pleasure of doing it." Many of God's children are hurting and are falling into traps. Based on the number of different creatures on Earth, which were named by Adam, human beings are considered to be the most intelligent; but unfortunately, we struggle with not using common sense in how to treat one another with human kindness and decency. We have grown very comfortable in being led by our insecurities and dysfunctions while allowing our differences—race, color, religion, gender, pregnancy, national origin, age, disability, or genetics—to create barriers. Many civilian workplaces use a hierarchical[21] mana-

---

21  www.marketing91.com/hierarchical-organization/; A hierarchical organization is a structure where all the entities except the topmost are subordinate to another entity. It is considered one of the most traditional and popular structures in existence and is still dominant in governments, large organizations, religious groups, and corporations.

gerial leadership style, also referred to as a chain of command, similar to the military. In a hierarchical chain-of-command environment, specific employees have someone they report to at a higher graded level or rank and that individual is responsible for assigning and delegating tasks. There are times when the employee in the subordinate position is also subjected to a delegation of abuse of power. This type of behavior, lording over another, has a tendency to impact our mental state of mind to interfere with our mental health and challenging our innate desire to shower one another with love. Somewhere down the line, through our mental conditioning through trials and tribulations, we stop growing and maturing to reason, analyze, and understand the destruction and harm we cause to ourselves and others. As referenced by Proverbs 11:17 AMP, *The merciful and generous man benefits his soul [for his behavior returns to bless him], But the cruel and callous man does himself harm.*

The brain is a very delicate organ, and it has the ability to be programmed and reset to fit the desired stage! The manner in which our brains are wired speaks to how information and our experiences are filtered and processed through us to generate thoughts impacted by emotions such as pain, fear, joy, happiness, love, hate, and peace! Another name for these thoughts is perception, and each person's perception is different. In fact, while searching for answers, God said, as human beings, people unfortunately view everything in color or black and white! But it is not that simple! That's why we get so caught up on image. We've allowed ourselves to get distracted by debates concerning versions of Christian deity that were perverted by men who were jockeying for power and control along with creating division. In the process, they inflicted a great deal of deep-rooted pain and suffering on others who didn't measure up in comparison to fit their specific idealized image, and we are still doing it. If you were to create a chart using column headings to represent each race by name and an image, then expand each column to identify subcategories[22] with secondary subcategories underneath and so on, what would that look like? I would assume it would start out like this: tri-part being (spirit, body, soul), gender (mother, father, sister, brother), race, characteristics (personality or behavioral traits), issues or baggage, occupation, education, etc. It would be like peeling an onion with an overlap of similarities being exposed!

**Each and every human being is born and created in the image of God with the capacity to love ourselves and others!** Some of us may not be as resilient or mentally capable of rationalizing right from wrong to acknowledge the difference, but for the most part, we are equipped with the ability to choose. We, unfortunately, refuse to see the underlying issues of our actions as having consequences. We don't seem to understand or simply refuse to accept responsibility for how one is connected to the other as a significant part of our programming to consider every move we make before doing so. We have grown accustomed to ignoring our issues or hiding a problem as it develops and hoping the situation will cease to exist without addressing it appropriately, which creates another problem. Then the mountain gets bigger; a domino effect takes hold and creates

---

[22] www.thefreedictionary.com/subcategories; A subdivision that has common differentiating characteristics within a larger category.

layers of issues upon issues like tiny little compartments of computer code inside another code that was never deleted!

To get at the **truth** of a thing, you have to be willing to dig down deep below the surface to get to the root cause. Our unwillingness to demonstrate love, one to another, to see and appreciate individual equal worth is hurting us all. The mirror image or opposite of love is hate, and that hate has a very astounding impact on our position to receive love and live in the light! The central problem is, we never ever want to discuss the hate in the world to define it or to call it what it is to attempt to initiate mutually rewarding and cohesive change! *Anyone who claims to live in God's light and hates a brother or sister is still in the dark. It's the person who loves brother and sister who dwells in God's light and doesn't block the light from others. But whoever hates is still in the dark, stumbles around in the dark, doesn't know which end is up, blinded by the darkness* (1 John 2:9-11 MSG).

While listening to a track on William McDowell's artistic masterpiece, *Bending of Trees*, my spirit was able to identify with the following, as I listened to it, over and over again: *Our struggles or issues are not necessarily because we do not love ourselves (which is self-love from the inside out). In many cases, it is because of a lack of love from the outside in!* Love is an action! To love is a simple choice! Accountability is also a choice! To hate is to sin against God! God sees all and knows all, and He is the ultimate witness who has positioned His disciples in the earth. Justifications with the aid of manipulated laws as exceptions to the rules are being honored and substituted for accountability, but the truth will always prevail. *A nation without God's guidance is a nation without order. Happy are those who keep God's law* (Proverbs 29:18 GNT)! *Above all, have fervent and unfailing love for one another, because love covers a multitude of sins [it overlooks unkindness and unselfishly seeks the best for (and in) others]* (1 Peter 4:8 AMP, paraphrased).

# SPEAKING UP AND SPEAKING OUT!

*"Speak up for the people who have no voice,
for the rights of all the down-and-outers.
Speak out for justice! Stand up for the poor and destitute!"*

**~ Proverbs 31:9 MSG**

September 30, 2018

Like SARAI (Sarah), the faith of many women is being tested today! At the same time, like Abraham, the faith and actions of every man are also being tested! Will you continue to refuse to see what needs to be seen? Will you continue to put your faith and trust in the hands of people and not God? Will you keep turning your back on the God who created both men and women to give us an equal place (or footing) in this world? Regardless of the ruling in man's heart as well as a court of law, which has proven time and time again to lack justice and integrity, will you continue to believe that you don't matter or the lives of others—regardless of their geographical backgrounds—don't matter?

Will you continue to deny our ABBA Father who sits up high and looks down low in seeing all that has taken place (future and present)? He is the only One who will judge us all in due time for the condition of our hearts! No justification outside of *righteousness* will have a bearing on His ruling. No association of false allegiance will have any influence!

No matter what, I AM standing on the Word of the Lord! I have value! I AM worthy! I have a voice! I AM the apple of my Father's eye! I AM somebody! He who is within me is far greater than he who is in the world! **I can do all things through Christ who strengthens me!** *And we know that all things work together for good to those who love God, to those who are the called according to His purpose* (Romans 8:28 NKJV)! I AM called, and I have been chosen!

I have been tasked with a purpose to speak up and out as directed by God to expose injustices in the world. I have been given a platform to speak for those who cannot or are not willing to speak for themselves. I AM moving forward in accordance to God's plans for my life with purpose!

Experiencing a Holy Boldness!

What about you?

# DOUBTING THOMAS

*So the other disciples told him, "We have seen the Lord!" But he said to them, "Unless I see the nail marks in his hands and put my finger where the nails were, and put my hand into his side, I will not believe." A week later his disciples were in the house again, and Thomas was with them. Though the doors were locked, Jesus came and stood among them and said, "Peace be with you!" Then he said to Thomas, "Put your finger here; see my hands. Reach out your hand and put it into my side. Stop doubting and believe."*

~ John 20:25-27 NIV

April 29, 2018

God sits up high and looks down low. He is able to see all that goes on in the world. He knows us better than we know ourselves because He created us. He knows the number of hairs or lack thereof on the head of each and every one of us. He knows how we think to include when we will mess up before we actually do—and still, He loves us. He has divine insight into what will take place before it happens. He knows what to allow in our lives to redirect our paths or what will keep us on the straight and narrow! Ephesians 1:5 NIV states, *he predestined us for adoption to sonship through Jesus Christ, in accordance with his pleasure and will!* He does not have to ask for anyone's approval or permission as to who or what He chooses to use when or how!

God has taken into account every detail of my life: the good, the bad, and the ugly. But He did not let that stop Him from calling me into ministry and giving me a voice or a platform in which to reach others. And it is not my intent to sugarcoat or deny any part of my life in sharing my testimonies with others as directed by the Lord who is the *head of my life.* Through my experiences, He has used them to make a believer out of me! And Romans 8:28 NIV states, *And we know that in all things God works for the good of those who love him, who have been called according to his purpose.* So why would He not use an individual who was once a doubting Thomas and expose them to supernatural experiences to awaken them to the truth within and around them?

My initial supernatural experience, which took place during my volunteering assignment in the year 2001 as part of the World Trade Center cleanup, created a great deal of confusion and controversy for me! Mainly because, prior to that encounter, I had no real point of reference for what was taking place, and the best description or first thing that came to my mind was a movie I had seen or a book I had heard about called *Poltergeist.* For the first time in my life, I was being confronted by something that I had assumed was make-believe. Can you imagine having a life-altering, mind-blowing, supernatural experience that leaves you speechless, struggling to articulate it to others and process it for yourself?

The supernatural is real, and I, as a doubting Thomas who is also a runner, needed to be confronted with that truth to be able to move forward as planned by God! The existence of the natural (physical) world would not be possible on its own without the existence of the supernatural dimension. Hollywood, in how it presents the supernatural in accordance to how we receive it or process it, has desensitized the belief of its importance or realness for many. If you believe in Romans 8:28, then you must also understand that God knew just what to hit me with to get my attention—even if you don't agree with it!

There are things, fear or lack of confidence, that for one reason or another, we refuse to speak about; out of our silence, we give it power to continually hold us in bondage. When we are going through our trials and tribulations or conflict, the worst thing we can do is internalize it! We must be mindful of the spirits operating within our environment when we start to share our truth. On the basis of cultural differences and conditioning as dictated by this world system, truth is not encouraged; it is, unfortunately, freely denied while the *spirit of condemnation* takes center stage to arrest you!

When you are hurting, no one really wants to hear about your pain. But God cares, and He wants us to bring it all to Him in prayer! When you are being abused, battered, mistreated, and taken advantage of by others, people don't really want you to share your experiences. But God teaches us to value our experiences as testimonies to overcome our trials and tribulations with flying colors. For the most part, many are not necessarily interested in hearing our testimonies because it not only questions their level of spiritual maturity, but it may reveal their true nature as a doubting Thomas in disbelief of what God is capable of doing in our lives. There are many facets to God, and we must stop putting Him in a box. We must stop attempting to predict His potential like we do each other's! *Now to him who is able to do immeasurably more than all we ask or imagine, according to his power that is at work within us* (Ephesians 3:20 NIV). Unfortunately, not everyone is going to understand what God does in your life. But you must not get discouraged and you must not take the word of others above what God has already revealed to you! Yes, it is challenging! But, *for those God foreknew he also predestined to be conformed to the image of his Son, that he might be the firstborn among many brothers and sisters. And those he predestined, he also called; those he called, he also justified; those he justified, he also glorified* (Romans 8:29-30 NIV). Stay the course!

# MINISTERING IN THE EARTH, THE CHURCH, THE MARKETPLACE, AND ON THE JOB

*Saying, Father, if thou be willing, remove this cup from me: nevertheless not my will, but thine, be done.*

**~ Luke 22:42**

April 22, 2018

Revised September 29, 2020

This world and all in it was created by God, which means it all belongs to Him and nothing is off limits to Him! He is the *divine authority* over all of it; Heaven, Hell, and Earth! You do not have to take my word for it, but I would like to encourage you to read, research, learn, and experience God for yourself to obtain the same wisdom, knowledge, and understanding that has been made available to me through *revelation*. In fact, I AM still seeking, learning, and receiving new *revelations* every day! In the words and teaching of Pastor Randolph Davis, "**Revelation always produces a revolution to produce change!** You can never go back to the way you were once you get revelation. Revelation is God pulling back the veil of flesh and letting you see the spiritual reality of what is going on; and once God begins to show you that, it frees you up in so many ways!"

God is about *divine order*, and He has a *standard*! He sets the stage for what is and should be, regardless of man's deviation from God's structure. The Bible, which is the word of God, was inspired, spoken, and written for non-Christians (unbelievers) to awaken your faith and for Christians (believers) to encourage sustainability of your faith. For believers of the word of God, it is important to understand the position of the Son of God who is Jesus Christ, also known or referred to as The Living Word, who walked on Earth in the flesh amongst us! The Son of God is much more than just a physical image that many seek to deny in the same manner in which they attempt to deny the presence of the Holy Spirit. Salvation is obtained through Jesus Christ, the Son of God, and we must continue believing in Him in order to be saved in the end. We must not allow our situations or circumstances to shake us or redirect our beliefs. We must not allow outside influences to create doubt that alters our God-inspired mindset.

In the beginning was the Word, and the Word was with God because the Word is God! The Word took shape and became The Living Word to walk among us. Before the Word took form, He spoke into existence the order of the world to include all within it. The world was void of light and covered by darkness until God pulled out the light to separate it from the darkness. So, in the name of order, God created the day, which is represented by the light, and He created the night, which is represented by the darkness. Together, the combination of the day plus the night represents one full or complete day, which is equal to a twenty-four-hour period. The day, as defined during Biblical times, began at sundown (or sunset, whichever terminology you prefer), which is the going down of the sun or the fading away of the light to the rising of the moon well into the going down of the moon and to the rising of the sun just before the sun sets again. From evening to evening. The revelation gained through the ministering of this Word has granted me a greater understanding of God's order and authority as directed to me.

On more than one occasion, I have been asked, "Who gave you the authority to do this or that?" While sitting or standing quietly in disbelief about the tone or manner in which I was being reprimanded, I would hear in my spirit the answer to that question with clarity: "God!" There are times when I want so desperately to speak up and say exactly that! God gave me the authority! But cautiously, I am careful not to repeat what I'm hearing in my spirit to escape the possibility of being written up as being insubordinate or defiant; and I often feel as though I have let God down. However, even in my quietness, the awareness of that truth covers me to release an overwhelming **peace** that surpasses all understanding, as I AM reminded that the government sits on the shoulders of God; God doesn't sit on the shoulders of the government.

Remembering the order as orchestrated by God is very important! Why? Because we are created by God with a purpose for a purpose and positioned in the earth by Him to fulfill His mission in connection with our *destiny*. Knowing who you are in Him and Him in you to include your position in the earth on behalf of the Kingdom of God is important. My greatest objective is accepting my spiritual position in the earth—no matter the sacrifice—to minister God's Word in every arena as inspired by Him with the Apostolic Authority granted above and beyond man's perceived authority for my life! Not my will, but thy will be done in my life to follow through for the long haul to stay in position as commanded by the Lord even after He turns up heat for His glory to prosper me!

# THOSE WHO ARE SENT

*Are not all the angels ministering spirits sent out [by God] to serve (accompany, protect) those who will inherit salvation? [Of course they are!]*

**~ Hebrews 1:14 AMP**

January 7, 2013

Revised October 11, 2020

For the past month, I have been hearing over and over again in my spirit, "Those who are sent!" Why? Because God has been attempting to answer every question I have ever had about a particular matter, concerning not only my current working environment, but the world itself. Initially, I always said the world was a cruel, dark, and bad place to live or to raise children. But God, through the teaching of the Holy Spirit, is correcting my way of thinking by opening my eyes to view things much differently.

> *For we are not as many,*
> *which corrupt the Word of God:*
> *but as of sincerity, but as of God, in the sight of God*
> *speak we in Christ.*
>
> ~ 2 Corinthians 2:17

Each and everything created by God, which includes the world, is good! Just as He created the world, He created each inhabitant to include you and me. He has created each of us with good thoughts and good intentions with a purpose for a purpose. He has gifted each of us with a mind of our own to choose the path we seek. And the phrase, "A mind is a very terrible thing to waste" is a very true statement! Our mind can be as broad or as narrow as we would like for it to be, depending upon our desire for growth, should we be willing to put forth some effort, initiative, and determination. We can approach the empowering of our minds in the same manner in which we choose the appropriate path to take! The decisions are up to us! We get to choose how to utilize our mind and direct our thoughts. We get to decide who we will follow or avoid. We get to decide who we will allow to influence us with the best of intentions or the worst. We have the right to say yes or no to any given situation at any time, if we are intimidated by fear.

> *But if serving the LORD seems undesirable to you,*
> *then choose for yourselves this day whom you will serve,*
> *whether the gods your ancestors served beyond the Euphrates,*
> *or the gods of the Amorites, in whose land you are living.*

> *But as for me and my household,*
> *we will serve the LORD.*
>
> ~ Joshua 24:15 NIV

So on the basis of our actions, it is us (human beings) who impact the world in making it a good or bad place for ourselves as well as others. With that said, correcting my way of thinking, it is not the world that is cruel, dark, and bad; it is the people within the world who have allowed themselves to succumb to darkness in how they choose to live their lives in impacting others negatively. Influence! You can allow your mind to be consumed by faulty thinking and be condemned by a reprobate (degenerate, troublemaking) mind, or you can renew your mind and be transformed to think and act like Jesus! Again, the choice is yours!

> *Have this same attitude*
> *in yourselves which was in Christ Jesus*
> *[look to Him as your example in selfless humility].*
>
> ~ Philippians 2:5 AMP

I AM truly grateful to God for who He is! He is nothing like man! He gives us all the same opportunities. He starts us all out on the same path. The path of righteousness! God gives us free will, and He will never stand in our way to prevent us from choosing which way to go! He wants the same for all of us. We make the decision to deviate from the path or course He has set before us. He blesses us with the opportunity to meet those He has sent to encourage us and usher in the light. As we are sent out on our journey, it is complete with trials and tribulations to strengthen us and to increase our light in making our position stronger!

*He did not waver*
*at the promise of God through unbelief,*
*but was strengthened in faith,*
*giving glory to God, and being fully convinced*
*that what He had promised He was also able to perform.*

~ Romans 4:20-21 NKJV

God gives us assignments along the way to light the way for others. If we are not weary and do not faint, we can be effective and go onward to the next assignment or level. As we are sent out amongst the wolves into darkness, we must be mindful to stay strong. Some of us go the distance in understanding there will be challenges while being determined not to give up or give in. Some of us buckle under pressure while losing sight of the goal. Should you fall in the midst of trouble, that's okay as long as you get up and get back into the race. But should you fall and allow yourself to get lost in the shuffle, it's never too late to regain your focus; however, do not wait too long! Nonetheless, the key is obedience to God. Obedience is better than sacrifice, and the importance lies in pleasing God in all you do! It is not about seeking a shortcut or compromising the Kingdom mission or your destiny to go along to get along. It's about staying on track, pushing and forging ahead to the finish line (from your beginning to your end).

God does not subject you to more than what you can bear. Be confident in knowing the truth as you observe and take an accurate report of what you encounter along the way. So cherish being chosen and cherish being sent! Cherish your assignment and wait on the LORD to give you clear instructions to guide you while pushing forward toward your destiny in faith! Keep believing. Keep trusting. Speak and declare the works of the Lord. Decree and stand strong! You are more than a conqueror who has been sent to light the way!

*That is why I am so eager to preach*
*the gospel also to you who are in Rome.*

~ Romans 1:15 NIV

# WHY DO I PRAISE HIM LIKE I DO? BECAUSE PRAISE IS WHAT I DO!

*Among those nations you will find no peace (rest),
and there will be no resting place for the sole of your foot;
but there the LORD will give you
a trembling heart, failing eyes,
and a despairing soul.*

**~ Deuteronomy 28:65 AMP**

June 25, 2013

I truly cannot explain, relay, or tell you just how excited I AM about God and all of what He is doing, has done, and will do through His children. When we come into the world, we are birthed as spirits in a body of flesh with a soul, and we are entrusted to earthly parents to nurture, lead, and guide us. Those parents live in various conditions in various geographical areas and subject us (their children—God's children) to various situations (good and bad). Based on their spiritual maturity for enduring hardships (trials and tribulations) to be able to bounce back from whatever strongholds that bind them, they may or may not be equipped to be the loving parents we deserve, hope, or pray for to protect and see us through.

> *For the needy shall not always be forgotten,*
> *and the expectation and hope of the meek*
> *and the poor shall not perish forever.*
>
> ~ Psalm 9:18 AMPC

My father was not ready to be a parent, and he enjoyed his life as a single person although he was married with children. Raised in a certain era with archaic ideas about women, men in my father's day took very little responsibility in sharing the chores of the day-to-day home needs. The women were expected to do it all with no complaint of an absenteeism husband or father. The women were expected to care for the children, cook, make sure the bills were paid, and keep the house clean.

Women were told by other women who preceded them, in age, not to worry what a man did outside of the home as long as he went to work and came home with the money. So what if he stayed out all night or had a woman on the side? Men will be men, and the little women should let them do just that! But what about the respect of the household? What about the integrity and honesty of honoring the marriage vows? What about being the man needed by both wife and children as the head and male role model, the protector of the home?

At any rate, unfortunately, my father cared more about having fun and partying than he did about being a husband and father. He, in my opinion, was away from the home more often than he was physically present. His best friend, aside from his peers, was Jack Daniels, or some other form of grain alcohol.

My mother dealt with a great deal of pain from failed relationships and tried to keep up a good front in attempting to be a strong woman and mother. My mother was very unhappy. However, although she herself was hurting, she did the very best she could to instill certain values in her children.

*A healthy spirit*
*conquers adversity, but what can you do*
*when the spirit is crushed?*

~ Proverbs 18:14 MSG

As I consider the unfolding of the lives of my parents to include the impact of their situation upon me and my siblings, God only knows the reason and purpose for allowing the events to take place as they occurred. When I look back over my life and see how God is using me, I AM truly grateful for His confidence in my ability to serve Him in spite of the pain I endured growing up, from childhood to adolescence to adulthood. And I AM most certainly *grateful* for His opportunity and willingness to stay close to me as He made many attempts to reach for me and get my attention. He never gave up on me nor did He turn His back on me even when I failed to respond to His many attempts to call to ministry before I accepted. He kept throwing me a lifeline each time I messed up! Each time I made excuses for not getting back on track, still He loved me. And many times, I questioned the dysfunctionality of the family structure He placed me in, only to leave me there because I failed to see the bigger picture. Many times, I moaned and groaned in despair of the wrong choices I had made throughout my life, one disappointment after the next, until I realized God was developing me from the inside out. Unlike many parents, He didn't bail me out of my mess or make it easy for me to make the same mistakes over and over again—unless I was hardheaded and a glutton for punishment. He exercised tough love in allowing each choice I personally made to run its course. He was strengthening me and pruning me. He was hardening me, if you will, in preparation of being that spiritual warrior He could count on when the going got tough. He wanted to make sure I was not going to crumble under pressure at the first sign of trouble. He needed to know He could rely on me to do the right thing in the future and to take a stand when everybody else would run the opposite way. He needed to know my character would be fortified to exemplify a **Spirit of Excellence**.

*And endurance (fortitude) develops maturity of character (approved faith and tried integrity). And character [of this sort] produces [the habit of] joyful and confident hope of eternal salvation.*

~ Romans 5:4 AMPC

Today, I AM well on my way! No, not perfect! But striving and more determined than ever to be the person I was created to be as I chase after my Father into His loving arms. I cannot deny the love of a Father who knows me better than I know myself. A Father who is just as persistent as He is patient in setting the parameters in my life for a divine impact in propelling me from one position to another for His glory! For He knows exactly what He put in me to build my character to include the substances needed to carry out His will. I just never thought I would actually get to a place of acceptance in being transparent enough to use my story (testimonies) as shared with others in honor of a Father who has given me so much. Because to whom much is given, much is most definitely required. And I cannot deny this unspeakable, overflowing joy in my heart that was once broken. However, BROKEN TO SERVE and RENEWED!

*For godly grief and the pain God is permitted to direct,*
*produce a repentance that leads and contributes*
*to salvation and deliverance from evil, and it never brings regret;*
*but worldly grief (the hopeless sorrow that is characteristic*
*of the pagan world)*
*is deadly [breeding and ending in death].*

~ 2 Corinthians 7:10 AMPC

Do you really know what it is like to be loved so deeply and unconditionally to be put through a series of tests only to be refined? Do you know what it is like to have scars or wounds of life that serve only as a memory of how far you have come? Can you imagine those same scars or wounds no longer being a hindrance, but a joy and delight of your worth? Can you imagine being able to share your testimonies with complete strangers, not as an attempt to seek sympathy, but with complete confidence in the love of my Father to encourage others to seek His face in getting to know Him?

Can you imagine being condemned by man, but redeemed by the love of a Father who has healed you in making you whole? Can you imagine that love being so great that it covers a multitude of sins to cover up your scars to where they are no longer noticeable? Least of all not by me! Can you imagine receiving love so grand and penetrating that it extends beyond the surface of who you were to who you are to encourage you to love others in spite of their contributions to your past pain and hurt? But a love that encourages you to let go and forgive! Can you imagine still encountering hurt from those who wish to destroy you only because they don't know you, understand who you are, or understand why you have yet to or are no longer willing to give them the pleasure or the satisfaction of letting their iniquity take hold! Void of bitterness! Growing with forgiveness! That's why I praise Him like I do!

*He is your praise; He is your God,*
*Who has done for you those great and*
*terrible things which your eyes have seen.*

~ Deuteronomy 10:21 AMPC

# BROKENNESS: BROKEN, MENDED, AND SECOND-WINDED

*A cheerful heart is good medicine,
but a crushed spirit dries up the bones.*

~ **Proverbs 17:22 NIV**

November 11, 2013

Dear Lord,

As I look back over my life, I see that I was drawn to darkness and living in sin. Seduced by a world full of the walking wounded like me, I asked no questions and moved about like a puppet on a string. I was following instead of leading while hoping to be accepted by a world that only rejected me time and time again. Void of life with a dying soul, I struggled continuously to find my way. Identifying with no one and everyone, I quickly got lost in a sea of confusion, unaware of my actions and giving no thought to the consequences! I was gullible to the lies and seeking to fit in with no real knowledge of the truth until the day I realized something was missing. And then, I could no longer go through the motions while never being truly happy of who I was becoming.

> *If you do well, will you not be accepted?*
> *And if you do not do well, sin crouches at your door;*
> *its desire is for you, but you must master it.*
>
> ~ Genesis 4:7 AMPC

I was not living or growing, but sinking deeper and deeper into myself with such pain, grief, and despair! Tired of the rat race, I wanted much more than to be like the rest. Standing tall, I needed balance. Seeking truth became my ultimate mission. Getting free was the number one goal at hand. Escaping my pain to endure through the end is beneficial for my survival! And forgiving those who had hurt me was a matter of life or death to dodge the dis-ease that was inevitable. In choosing life, I could not do it alone. Choosing happiness, I needed an anchor—a steady rock that would not crumble under pressure. I finally realized I needed YOU. I needed to believe YOU existed. More importantly, I needed to develop a relationship with YOU to get to know YOU for myself! So I let YOU in when so many others in my life had let me down.

> *The strong spirit of a man sustains him in bodily pain*
> *or trouble, but a weak and broken spirit*
> *who can raise up or bear?*
>
> ~ Proverbs 18:14 AMPC

In spite of me and who I was, YOU loved me long before I loved YOU. YOU knew me better than I knew myself. YOU were always there just waiting for me to acknowledge YOU. All I had to do was reach for YOU. Lord, I AM forever grateful to YOU for YOUR persistence in my life. In creating me with a purpose for a purpose, YOU wanted nothing but the best for me. YOU never gave up on me. Even when I knew YOU "not" and turned my back on YOU while seeking to find my way through the darkness! YOU said YOU would never leave me nor forsake me (Hebrews 13:5)! YOU were always near, never far away. YOU were patiently waiting for me to come to my senses in realizing my one and only true love.

> *Before I formed thee in the belly I knew thee;*
> *and before thou camest forth out of the womb*
> *I sanctified thee, and I ordained thee*
> *a prophet unto the nations.*

~ Jeremiah 1:5

There I was being denied over and over again by the world, broken-hearted and in need of repair! My spirit was damaged beyond recognition, and I was looking for love in all the wrong places. Looking for man to validate me only made me more vulnerable. But You, Lord, are like no other person on the face of the earth, or within the entire universe for that matter! You believed in me when no one else did. You still believe in me! When people made attempts to tear me down, You lifted me and elevated me, and You keep on lifting me. When man speaks harsh of me, You redeem me and encourage me to go on. When

I AM too bruised and tattered to go any further, You carry me and give me the strength to endure—no matter what! You said I was the head and not tail, above and not beneath if only I would just take heed to your every command (*see Deuteronomy 28:12-14*). Because You are a man of Your word who honors every promise ever made to me, You have confirmed Your unconditional love for me, over and over again. Oh, God, how I love thee! You sacrificed Your only son for me. Then why should I not give my life to thee. Oh, how I want to tell the world about You. For my fire burns brightly!

> *By day the* LORD *went ahead of them*
> *in a column of smoke to lead them on their way.*
> *By night he went ahead of them in a column of fire*
> *to give them light so that they could travel*
> *by day or by night.*
>
> ~ Exodus 13:21 GW

You have touched my life in such a mighty way that there are not enough words in all the universe that I could use to express, explain, or describe my gratitude, joy, and yes, even the sorrow. Bittersweet is how I see thee, but awesome indeed are You! Your Grace and Mercy have shown me the way! You allowed me to go through situations needed to fortify me. Situations I would have never been able to accomplish in succeeding without You. For once in my life, I AM no longer afraid to say "no" to those who try to control me, use me, or abuse me. THANK YOU for being who You are and for allowing me to be who I AM in You! THANK YOU for choosing me. THANK YOU for being so relentless in Your pursuit of me, for I will continue to speak to the hills and all across the nations about YOUR goodness!

Broken to serve You,

Mended for Your glory,

Second-winded to fulfill my God-purposed destiny!

Dear Lord, I AM forever grateful!

# BROKENNESS
## PART 2

*He heals the brokenhearted and binds up their wounds
[healing their pain
and comforting their sorrow].*

~ Psalm 147:3 AMP

July 27, 2017

Revelation comes from God to offer insight (deep knowledge on the basis of wisdom) and encouragement. Sometime ago, He gave me the title Broken, Mended, Second-Winded. Months later, He gave me a more in-depth meaning to that title:

- **Broken** to serve
- **Mended** for His glory
- **Second-winded** to reach my destiny

By nature, when we experience that which brings us a great deal of discomfort and pain, we normally fall victim to self-condemnation. In this position of self-condemnation comes the pity party, along with shame, guilt, anger, and fear. Then many of us fall into a state of deep depression. I remember my conversation with God: "God, before I AM able to get over one test, trial, or tribulation, I seem to get hit with something else. Can you please intervene and wait until I get over one incident before you allow something else to come up against me?" I was beginning to feel numb. It was as if each part of my body was being affected. As shared with one individual, I have scars and bruises all over my body, from head to toe. There isn't one uncovered spot or place left on me. In fact, the bandages are starting to overlap and pile up! Can you imagine the expression on her face? Priceless! If you have not been there, you can't begin to understand the depth of one's despair!

Have you ever experienced pain and disappointment to the point of not wanting to leave the house, be around people, or simply function? Have you ever just wanted to give up or give in while knowing that deep down, that wasn't an option? We all experience pain in life, but not everyone will be willing to admit it. There are different types and levels of pain. No pain is alike, and each person processes pain differently. And it is up to us to figure out the best possible way to manage our pain without allowing it to arrest us and hold us in captivity forever. For me, I needed to know that my pain had purpose! So I pushed forward by staying in constant connection with the Father. I could actually visualize Him on that cross as I was going through it. With each painful situation, I would begin to wallow in my self-pity and then I would say out loud, "Who am I that I would think if He suffered that I myself would be spared?" Then I would apologize to God for my weakened state, but not once would He condemn me. He would console me to offer encouragement while teaching me to stand.

Attempting to view things differently, I remember:

- His ways are not my ways and my ways are not His, but it is my desire to grow in learning His ways above mine (Proverbs 3:5-10).

- Everything that takes place is in divine order in accordance to God's will and purpose. Nothing happens without permission from God. If it happens, it is allowed, and we must be still to see the salvation of the Lord.

- My suffering or pain is not in vain (1 Corinthians 15:58 and Psalm 127:1).

It is wrong of us to suggest or attempt to know how one individual should process their pain or **brokenness**. And we should never compare ourselves one to another in judging how a person should respond or react to that which brings them pain or grief. What you can do is pray for each and every individual in accordance to the *Will of God* for their peace and wholeness in any given situation!

# WHAT IS THE NATURE OF A SCRIBE?

## PART 2 - FOUNDATIONS OF THE SCRIBAL ANOINTING

*Now go, write it before them in a table,
and note it in a book,
that it may be for the time to come for ever and ever.*

~ Isaiah 30:8

October 25, 2020

Revised April 9, 2021

Too often, we are taught about God and religion through the lens of **tradition**. Tradition limits our growth and God by putting God in a box! God is so much more than religion[23] or tradition! He is a Divine Spirit and the source of our existence

---

23   www.dictionary.com/browse/religion

to include all creation (the entire universe as we know it); all inhabitants from bodies of water, galaxies, stars, planets, vegetation, animals, to the human race (all people). God knows us better than we know ourselves, to include our many gifts and talents in the natural and beyond.

When I started to exhibit signs of my spiritual gifts and talents, I had no point of reference for processing what was happening. My initial quickening of the Holy Spirit was an unexpected mystery to me! After my first encounter, it was hard to contain Him; and, although I actually never wanted to quench the Holy Spirit, I struggled with issues of fear and a lack of self-confidence around others concerning how they would view me. In fact, while in the presence of other believers in an assembly setting, some looked upon me as being strange, weird, or possibly crazy and losing my mind. Ironically, I was losing my mind as defined by man but gaining perspective about the existence of the Holy Spirit in my life. My mind was being rearranged, reprogrammed, or reordered. So, it is important for me to allow the Holy Spirit to have free reign as He pushes through with such intensity! I was coming into alignment with my true identity to fulfill a spiritual promise and purpose as designed and created by God.

Desperately seeking to understand and refusing to believe what others wanted me to believe, I reached out to God in agony. The Bible states *in all thy getting, get understanding* (Proverbs 4:7) and *God hears the cries of the righteous* (Psalm 34:17). So, I asked God to teach me what I needed to know and to guide me to all of what He wanted me to see, read, and learn. At that moment, things began to open up for me and to me, beyond what I could have ever imagined. As I began to grow in intervals and BE, God put people in my path like Apostle Dr. Theresa Harvard Johnson along my journey to aid me in grasping as much understanding as I could obtain and <u>contain</u> pertaining to the realness of who He is and the role I play in the Kingdom of God. Today, I am still growing and learning!

After reading *Graphic Design & the Prophetic: Foundations of the Scribal Annointing*, more was made clear to me. I used to joke about how I should have been a boy. The only bonding activity that I could remember between me and my father when I was younger was helping him put things together that needed to be assembled. Overwhelmingly, but in a good way, I could start to see why, early on in my life, there was such an interest in medieval movies with references to blacksmiths, the Knights Templar, and the heraldry behind the signet ring or crest worn by the king of a kingdom or empire. God began to teach me about gemstones in relation to the Twelve Tribes of Israel. The very first stone on the breastplate, as intended by God and representative of the blood of Jesus and His Kingship carnelian. Carnelian, also known as *Sard* and *Odem*, gets its name from the Latin word *carnis*, meaning flesh. For that reason, it was the stone of choice for the chiseled signet ring, which was also used to seal letters or notes prior to them being transported from one kingdom to another.

In addition, to my interest in medieval times, there was an early unexplainable interest in English, math, and science in grade school. Later, during junior high school, I developed an interest in sewing, crocheting, and knitting, which evolved to encompass a whole host of different arts and crafts like jewelry making. Throughout my school years, different teachers approached me with a recommended curriculum of study for college as a career choice from teaching to being a medical researcher and majoring in English, literature, and writing based on what they individually noticed as strengths. At the time, I had difficulty agreeing with any of them about the focus of a desirable career path for myself. Today, I can see how it's all connected! When I'm in a creative mode, I feel alive. When I'm writing about different subjects for the Lord, there's a certain spark of energy, like a relentless burning passion, that rises from within me. It's as if a channel opens up to give me a more direct and uninterrupted connection of dialogue with God as He fans the flame to encourage me to complete the writing assignment on His behalf. If you review biblical history, we were meant to get involved, use our hands, our mind, and our souls to recreate and BE what God intended us to BE as citizens of the Kingdom!

I urge you to take the opportunity to collect and read the teachings of Apostle Dr. Theresa Harvard Johnson to understand the concept and depth of a SCRIBE. Let the Holy Spirit minister to you through her and through you in gaining revelation to grow! Explore how it feels to verbally as well as in writing decree and declare a thing with authority and in agreement with God from a scribal position to see it manifest. There is so much to learn from prophecy, prophesying, the nature of a prophet, and taking your rightful position as God's mouthpiece, hands, arms, legs, feet, eyes, and ears.

# THE REALITY OF IT ALL

# FROM REVELATION TO REALIZATION

# THESE ARE SOME CHALLENGING TIMES!

*I can do all things
[which He has called me to do]
through Him who strengthens and empowers me
[to fulfill His purpose—I am self-sufficient in Christ's
sufficiency; I am ready for anything and equal to anything
through Him who infuses me with inner strength and
confident peace.] Nevertheless, it was right of you
to share [with me] in my difficulties.*

**~ Philippians 4:13-14**

August 26, 2020

**For a time such as this!** These are some challenging times indeed, but God didn't say that the storms wouldn't come. Challenges come and challenges go! I actually remember having a conversation with God and telling Him that I *believe* the hardest thing for me to have overcome in life was the acceptance of my hair loss to alopecia! It was difficult having to face the challenges of people staring at me and threatening to pull off my wig or my head wrap; and, on occasion, when I went out uncovered and completely bald, in all my glory, some asked, "What would you do if I smacked you across your head?" The nerve of them! Not very Christian-like. I don't want to tell you how I responded to one individual after driving approximately one hour and thirty minutes away from my home just to go to a mall where I thought I would be safe from such ignorance! On that day, I learned, God was challenging me to face my fears head on.

Depending upon the depth of my grief or disappointment on any given day at being faced with having to leave the house to interact with people, I would cry most mornings for hours attempting to get myself mentally prepared! The challenge of it all was very overwhelming! But through it all, I survived to recognize the victory of being challenged yet another day to move forward in God's strength. As I develop spiritual maturity and learn to exercise spiritual excellence through the Holy Spirit, my reactions or responses to the offenses of others against me have been addressed quite differently.

Verse **2 Timothy 1:17** assures us that *God has not given us a spirit of fear, but of power and of love and a sound mind.* **Romans 8:28** tells us that *all things work together for good to them that love God, to them who are called according to His purpose.* Each and every one of us has been created by a loving God with a purpose for a purpose to prosper and to be victorious! We just have to believe in Him, trust Him, and take Him at His word. Why? Because all of His promises are and should be, yes and amen (2 Corinthians 1:20)!

God has blessed us with *dominion and the authority to tread* (trample, stomp, tap dance) *on serpents and scorpions, and over all the power of the enemy* (Luke 10:19), which includes speaking to mountains and climbing hurdles to overcome them all. **Big storms or little ones, we are victorious, and the battle has already been won by He who was sent ahead of us!** When in despair, just think of the biggest challenge that you thought was too hard to bear and note how you made it through. No challenge is too big or too small for God! If He did it once, He can and will conquer it again. Are you familiar with the story about Jesus calming the storm? He decreed and declared, *Peace be still* with confidence! See Luke 8:22-25, Mark 4:35-41, and Matthew 8:23-27.

Let's review The Clear Word Bible version of Matthew 8:23-27, which offers an expanded **paraphrase** of the Bible to nurture faith and growth. It states:

> *Upon reaching the boats, Jesus boarded one of them with His disciples and began a trip across the lake. When they were about halfway across, an expected storm came up, and within minutes the waves were pounding against the boat, filling it with water. Jesus, totally exhausted, had fallen sound asleep. The storm was so violent, that finally His disciples shook Him awake and said, "Lord, do something to save us or we'll all be lost* [or in another version, drown]!" *Then Jesus said, "Why do you have so little faith in God? Our Heavenly Father is watching us and knows exactly what is happening. He'll protect us to make sure that our work for Him is not cut short." Then standing up, Jesus steadied Himself in the rocking*

*boat and rebuked the winds and the waves. Suddenly, everything was peaceful and still. The storm clouds lifted, the stars came out and the lake was quiet. The disciples, together with people in the other boats who saw this, ere speechless. Finally, they said to each other, "What kind of man is this who speaks to the winds and the water and they obey Him!"*

You just have to remain positive, stay focused, and stay in His word. No matter what it looks like, He said He would never leave you nor forsake you! So call those things that are not as though they were; keep standing firm (grounded and rooted in Him) and forge ahead. Challenging times, yes, but with them comes *divine opportunities for spiritual growth.*

# WITNESSING

*But you will receive power when the Holy Spirit has come upon you, and you will be my witnesses in Jerusalem and in all Judea and Samaria, and to the end of the earth.*

**~ Acts 1:8 ESV**

June 14, 2020

Revised July 15, 2020

Can you imagine the number of people in the world who *claim* to be divinely inspired by some form of faith-based religion but got it completely wrong? Each and every human being was birthed on the face of the earth and created by God with a purpose for a purpose! Nothing happens without God's permission (that He doesn't allow) for His glory. In other words, *there is nothing that cannot be used by God or turned around to fall into place to work in accordance to His mission-driven purpose!* Put another way, what the enemy orchestrates with the intention of using it for evil, God can take that same situation and transform it, remold it, and recreate something beautiful and positive to work in your favor, on behalf of your family members and countless others, to meet His ultimate agenda!

You just have to *hold on*, keep an open mind with your eyes fixed on Him, and place His word in your heart. In addition to that, you must keep your ears tuned to His Voice and exercise patience in seeing the *bigger picture*, along with His hand moving throughout the entire process, without becoming discouraged! Yes, at times, patiently waiting for something to open up or for change to finally emerge can be difficult or unnerving. But God encourages us through Psalm 46:10 to *Be still and know that I am God: I will be exalted among the heathen, I will be exalted in the earth.* The Message version expresses it this way: Step out of the traffic! Take a long, loving look at Him, our Most-High God, above the politics, above everything. Over the years, I have learned through trial and error (trials and tribulations) not to rush God through His process of pruning and perfection if *divine alignment* is to take place!

Growing up from adolescence to adulthood, I became discouraged and started to doubt the existence of God. My focus, unfortunately, was on people, to include the amount of cruelty that I was seeing in the world. As iniquity[24] began to impact me directly, I grew angry while struggling to protect my heart from darkness in an attempt to escape the adaptation of my surrounding environment. I ran from trouble and from job to job, starting over again and again, looking for a peaceful environment with no drama. Then I started seeking God for answers and reading my Bible for confirmation. More and more each day, I dove in

---

24  www.lexico.com/en/definition/iniquity; immoral or grossly unfair behavior, injustice, wickedness

deep to uncover its mysteries to shed some light on what I was seeing and experiencing to note how easy it was for others to claim to live without really living according to the Word of God. I had to understand that no situation (event or incident) is out of God's sight, reach, or reproach! And He was positioning me and strengthening me through every situation to be the person that He had created me to be in occupying a role He ordained!

## A WITNESS TO TRUTH

Let's assume that each and every individual has an important position and role to play out on Earth as a useful instrument similar to a pawn on a chessboard, representing this game called life. The Bible is explicit in describing how each of us is connected to God through His breath, which gives us life, and the Holy Spirit, which was made possible through the life, death, burial, and resurrection of Yashua. As time develops or evolves, each and every individual's path may cross directly or indirectly to yield a pass or failed result. Why? Because, **it's all a relational test of choice and will!** Not my will, God, but Your Will be done on Earth as it is in Heaven!

Do you see it? Can you feel the energy in the air? In this season, God is moving to uncover that which has been hidden and pushed aside or dismissed for a long while. No, He is not responsible for the negative way in which things have taken root, boiled over, and come to a head! He does not encourage nor does He condone[25] negativity; but He can use the aftermath

---

25  https://dictionary.cambridge.org/dictionary/english/condone; to accept and allow (behavior that is considered morally wrong or offensive) to continue

of negativity to *expose* (spotlight) the truth and direct change. And, if He wanted to—based on our unrighteous and wicked behavior—He could quite simply turn us all into a pillar of salt (Genesis 19:26), engulf us in fire (Genesis 18 and 19), or subject us to a flood (Genesis 6:9-9:17). God could choose to remove every inhabitant of Earth as quickly or as easily as He created it!

*Evangelism* takes place only when we share the message of Jesus' life, death, and resurrection and then encourage others to trust in Him above and beyond anything or anyone else. For me, witnessing is not just about evangelism, it's about witnessing and testifying to the truth and goodness of God's love for us to include how He has saved me and given me a reason to live. It's about being the eyes, mouth, hands, and feet of God on Earth as instructed. It's about pushing beyond the experiences of my personal pain, to include the actions of others who have so easily trespassed against me, to share my testimonies of spiritual growth. Simply put, witnessing for God through His only begotten Son and the Holy Spirit has opened my eyes to my purpose and position as part of His team in restoring my faith.

Witness

- Greek

    - Strong #3144, martys or martus: Phonetic spelling (mar'-toos). An eye- or ear-witness.[26]

    - Strong #3140. martyreō: Phonetic spelling (mar-too-reh'-o). To bear (be a) witness, testify; give evidence, give a good report.

---

26   https://biblehub.com/greek/3144.htm

- To be a witness, to bear witness, i.e., to affirm that one has seen or heard or experienced something, or that he knows it because taught by divine revelation or nspiration.[27]
- Hebrew
    - Strong #5707, ed: Phonetic spelling (ayd). A witness, evidence.
    - Strong #7717, sahed: Phonetic spelling (saw-hade'). A witness, advocate.

A witness in a courtroom tells what he or she knows about a given situation. Some have spoken the truth while others have fabricated a lie in place of the truth. A Christian experience describes and gives witness to the life of a believer's walk before and during the awakening of truth based on a developed relationship with the Lord. All believers are called to bear witness to the truth and relationship of God, the Father, the Son, the Holy Spirit, and self in addition to showing and expressing universal love!

To be used and sacrificed by God and be able to map out the transition fills me with unspeakable joy and peace. To be chosen to document my experiences in speaking out with such zeal, passion, and boldness concerning what I see, have seen, and know confirms my God-appointed role (assignment). A role I take seriously and no longer seek to be liked and approved by man! Gratefully, as a person who has been set apart and set

---

27  www.blueletterbible.org/lang/lexicon/lexicon.cfm?Strongs=G3140&t=KJV

aside for the Lord, I answer to Him and only Him who has given my pain as experienced on Earth a greater purpose, witnessing and put in position to tell about it! All of it—whether understood or misunderstood by others—as instructed freely without fear! I guess you could say that **I am a snitch for Jesus!**

# TIME

*Don't overlook the obvious here, friends. With God, one day is as good as a thousand years, a thousand years as a day. God isn't late with his promise as some measure lateness. He is restraining himself on account of you, holding back the End because he doesn't want anyone lost. He's giving everyone space and time to change.*

**~ 2 Peter 3:8-9 MSG**

December 30, 2019

**What is time?** Time is a unit of measurement that denotes distance, duration, and age in seconds, minutes, hours, days, weeks, months, and years. For one reason or another, many of us have difficulty shifting and shaking free to move forward in a timely fashion; we struggle to start, stop, and begin again. We have, unfortunately, allowed time to delay the breakthrough into our destiny with something called procrastination. For some, the fear of not knowing what to do or the fear of making a mistake stops us in our tracks and we neglect to move forward!

On the other end of that spectrum, there is such a thing as moving too quickly or too soon without devoting an effective amount of time to obtain a glorious victory. However, fortunately for us, although timing is everything, **time has no power over God!**

God has authority over time to slow it down, speed it up, or stop it altogether! A good friend once had this to say and has shared it with me many times as an encouraging reminder (paraphrased): "God can simply take your yesterday and put it into today. He can take your tomorrow and put it into your yesterday." To help bring that home for me, she was also kind enough to introduce me to a book by Renny McLean entitled *Eternity Invading Time*.

In a world of competitiveness, how often have you measured your success in accordance to someone else's? How often have you thought about your past to question your journey while condemning your growth and your progress? Imagine holding a yardstick in your hand while plotting your course of movement in noting where you are now in comparison to where you feel or think you should be! Many times, I have spoken about being so far behind in my walk with God with great disappointment. What value or purpose does self-condemnation have in your journey when God has the power to turn everything around for His glory?

I am constantly reminded of Romans 8:28 AMP: *And we know [with great confidence] that God [who is deeply concerned about us] causes all things to work together [as a plan] for good for those who love God, to those who are called according to His plan and purpose.* I've been stressing for far too long in the battle of my wilderness. I've been stressing for far too long in the battle of my storm. I've been listening to too many people who truly don't understand the mechanics of my heart to know what God is allowing to take place in my life and why. Yes, I know some mean well, but you cannot gauge God to know what He is willing and able to do behind or ahead of time.

It's okay to take a step back to reflect on your past to address your present in acknowledging and appreciating how far you have come; but it is not okay to wallow in self-pity while getting lost in your past to beat yourself up. Man browbeats you enough for every little thing without being willing to show some compassion for attempting to understand your plight to help you through it. But God, who can be relentless in His pursuit of you, can also be just as gentle in his approach to grant you the time needed! God does not view time in the same manner in which we have been taught by the world to express time! Time can be endless, or time can have an expiration. Just as faith is now, time is also now! Time is eternity! Simply keep on pushing forward in allowing the Holy Spirit to guide you in catching up and overcoming your obstacles! With the right attitude, altitude, and longitude, it's never too late to accomplish God's mission. In fact, God told me He was tired of me falling and rolling over; but if I was to fall, He was expecting me not to roll over any longer, not to stay down too long, but to get back up, jump to my feet, dust myself off, and move forward!

Nothing ventured, nothing gained! Nothing ventured, nothing won! Nothing ventured, nothing lost! Being behind is not a loss. It's a delay that can be overcome. It's not a denial or an unwillingness on my part to move. It could be a weakness, but God said, where we are weak, He is strong! It's all in how you look at it and where you direct your focus.

*So if you're serious about living this new resurrection life with Christ, act like it. Pursue the things over which Christ presides. Don't shuffle along, eyes to the ground, absorbed with the things right in front of you. Look up, and be alert to what is going on around Christ—that's where the action is. See things from his perspective.*

~ Colossians 3:2 MSG

# THIS PRESENT DARKNESS

*For our struggle is not against flesh and blood
[contending only with physical opponents],
but against the rulers,
against the powers, against the world forces
of this [present] darkness,
against the spiritual forces of wickedness in
the heavenly (supernatural) places.*

~ **Ephesians 6:12 AMP**

October 17, 2018

Revised October 2, 2020

Are you paying attention to what is going on *all* around you? You may not be able to see with your natural eyes, but you should be able to discern with your spiritual eyes. Are you not familiar with the tactics of WAR? We are in a battle, *spiritual warfare*!

Do you know the components of football and baseball? Do you know there is an ancient game plan at work to include defensive and offensive maneuvers? Why aren't you in position? There's an outfield, an infield, a middle, and a frontline! Just as the Army of Darkness is gearing up and getting in place, the Army of Light should be gearing up and getting in place. Don't wait until something happens to get ready; you should already be ready and in place. Why are you fighting amongst yourselves in allowing the Spirit of Offense and Competitiveness to take the lead? Why aren't you studying and rightfully dividing the word to understand what is taking place in this season as well as the seasons to come? Open your eyes! Get in position to work together and teach those who are to come behind you!

- Right flank!
- Left flank!
- Strategize and move out!
- You too should be seated in heavenly (supernatural) places to counterattack!
- You have been given *dominion* over the air, sea, and earth (Genesis 1:26-28)! Use it!

God is so awesome in how He communicates to us! When I heard right flank, left flank, I knew it was a military term, but I needed to look it up for a greater understanding of what He was conveying to me. Then one by one, God revealed other terms that He needed me to be aware of:

1. Formation!
2. Marching order!

3. Boots on the ground!
4. Visible!
5. About face!
6. Troops!

# ORDER: DIVINE ORDER

*But all things must be done appropriately
and in an orderly manner.*

~ 1 Corinthians 14:40 AMP

October 1, 2018

Revised October 4, 2018

There's order and there is **Divine Order**! Which would you prefer to have? I want to be in His perfect will and discipline myself to follow His Divine Order. I cannot follow a man—or any person for that matter—who doesn't follow God or pattern himself in accordance to the ways of the Lord. If he believes and follows the Lord step by step, he will live accordingly and treat me as a woman (a daughter of the Most-High God), a human being, with the utmost respect.

*This is what the Lord says: "Cursed is the one who trusts in man,
who draws strength from mere flesh
and whose heart turns away from the Lord."*

~ Jeremiah 17:5 NIV

## GOD'S GENERAL ORDER—AT A GLANCE

- The order is: God first, family second, then everything else including the job. In a family setting, it is husband, wife, children. There's even order among the children to include the grandchildren.

- In the family setting, the man is the head of his household in the right order and context of the will and Word of God. He, God, is also very specific about **all** things. Man (husband) should love his wife like Christ loves the church. They are to submit to each other; it should never be one-sided, but only one side is always addressed or referenced by society's standard—unfortunately! However, God has a standard too!

- Leading and believing as the Lord does: no cohabitation, no sex outside of marriage, living Holy. Yes, mistakes are made, but we don't have to keep making the same mistakes. When we know to do better, then we should move forward and do better to receive all of what God has for us!

Men are not the head of women because they are men. They become the head when they follow the right order in *divine context*. In a marriage, the husband is viewed as the head of the household or family structure to lead and protect with authority and Christ-like compassion! Have you ever taken the time to view a documentary about the characteristics of lions to see the dynamics of how they operate, from male, to female, down to the cub? Christ is the LION, and we are His cubs!

A man should never take the position of believing that he has every right to abuse and take advantage of his spouse. He should take the position of not allowing anyone to come in between him and his family, nor should he allow anyone else to abuse and take advantage of his spouse or children. He should be mindful to protect and abide by the sanctity of his Holy matrimony union!

No man should ever abuse the daughters of God or think that we were put here on Earth just to pleasure them! It's about accountability! When I was a child, I thought as a child; then I grew up and put away childish things. We *all* grow and mature at different levels and times, but hopefully we *all* will get there to allow our souls to prosper! You cannot follow the crowd or keep up with the Joneses! There is only one King of kings and one Lord of lords! Follow Him!

# TIME-OUT FOR THE OKEY-DOKE!

*For I, the Lord your God,
will hold your right hand, saying to you,
"Do not fear; I will help you."*

~Isaiah 41:13 NKJV

April 4, 2018

April 1, 2018, was Resurrection Sunday (a.k.a. Easter)! The day our Lord, Jesus Christ the Messiah (also known as Yashua/Yahshua and Yahweh), rose from the dead and sat at the right hand of our Abba Father. In Hebrew, He is called Yeshua HaMashiach, which means Jesus the Messiah[28]; also known as The Anointed One!

Easter is a season in which many stores' profit margins escalate in the areas of candy, clothing, and shoes. Target had eggs for sale, an eighteen-count carton for 99 cents, and by the

---

28  www.blueletterbible.org/search/dictionary/viewtopic.cfm?topic=BT0002907; anointed

time I got there on Saturday, they were already sold out! Easter Sunday is the only time of the year in which churches normally find themselves filled beyond capacity. For some, not necessarily in honor of the spiritual meaning of Easter, but for the opportunity to dress up and to be in attendance to walk the runway in the name of ritual. Why? Because many of us simply go through the motions; we put on airs by pretending to enter into discipleship with the Lord, but still have not learned the importance of developing a real relationship with God. A covenant relationship based on trust and commitment to allow God complete control over our hearts to change us from the inside out! This is why we are encouraged to transform through the renewing of our minds, not through conformance to the way of the world! *And do not be conformed to this world [any longer with its superficial values and customs], but be [a] transformed and progressively changed [as you mature spiritually] by the renewing of your mind [focusing on godly values and ethical attitudes], so that you may prove [for yourselves] what the will of God is, that which is good and acceptable and perfect [in His plan and purpose for you]* (Romans 12:2).

God the Father, the Son, and the Holy Spirit are ONE! God is a very loving and accepting Father. He knows us better than we know ourselves. We cannot pull the wool over His eyes about anything. Not one thing is He unaware of when it comes to His children, great or small, and yet we still make numerous excuses as to why we refuse to humbly surrender to Him and follow His commandments. However, we seem to have no problem surrendering to the misguided ruler or principles of this world system for the profit of material gain to get ahead by any means necessary! And when we die, we can take none of our material possessions with us.

Life, death, and simply living are choices! The ultimate desire should be living with purpose. Our soul is in jeopardy, and we are losing time. I refuse to say wasting time because God does not measure time as we do. All time is precious to Him, and everything—in the order in which it has taken place—has purpose. But it is up to us to value every minute or second that has been gifted to us—good or bad—to learn and embrace the lessons of life on our journey called spiritual growth as we awaken to truth while getting closer to God in fulfilling our destiny! First, we must start by unlearning to relearn and seek God with all our hearts, souls, and minds. Then we must worship Him in spirit and in truth to see beyond the natural into the supernatural. Lastly, we must humble ourselves to stay in step with Him as Jesus did and never cease to pray.

Just as Jesus accepted His God-appointed mission, it is our responsibility to follow Christ in getting to understand not only who He is, but who we are as well and should be in Him! Christ died for us to give us life! He is the sacrificial lamb whose blood was shed in place of ours to give us more time to get it right. Whether we choose to believe or not, we owe Him a great deal!

## THE POWER OF THE BLOOD: NATURAL AND SUPERNATURAL

Human blood is divided into four types: A, B, AB, and O. Blood types are inherited and consist of red and white blood cells, platelets, and plasma. Blood flows through the body from one cell to the next, traveling through our veins while carrying with it oxygen, nutrients, and antibodies. If blood flow is interrupted or cut off, our life support is hindered and any part of the body that ceases to receive blood will begin to die due to a lack of that which gives it life. The blood, with the aid of our kidney and liver, also carries away toxins and waste, flushing out pollutants from our cells.

Blood is transferrable through a process called transfusion. Those with compatible blood types can receive blood from others to help sustain life. The Blood of Jesus is universal; it is compatible with all blood types, and there is no limit to what it can do! If any part of our bodies is cut off from the flow of the Blood of Jesus, spiritual and natural death are imminent. Without the Blood of Jesus to remove the dirt of sin from our lives on a daily basis, our lives would be polluted and filled with filth just like the Pharisees in Matthew 23:27.

God created our bodies with a defense mechanism, which is fully charged and equipped to aid the body to heal and fight off sickness! But, through our actions, we compromise that process by allowing our spirit through the blood to be tainted. We open ourselves up to be invaded by what we engage, see, say, and do outside of the *Will of God*! We fail to protect ourselves by not appreciating the cost paid by the sacrificial lamb!

When you are in position and on the right frequency in alignment with the Lord, your natural blood is healthy and you are forever protected from dis-ease. When you are in position and on the right frequency in alignment with the Lord, you are spiritually healthy enough to defend yourself from the wiles of the devil and there isn't anything he can bring against you that the Blood of Jesus isn't able to overcome. Why? Because the victory is already His! Leviticus 17:11 states, *For the life of the flesh is in the blood: and I have given it to you upon the altar to make an atonement for your souls: for it is the blood that maketh an atonement for the soul,* which is true for both the spiritual and physical realms. There is life and liberty in and through the Blood of Jesus! The Blood of Jesus will never lose its strength or power, but it will only make a difference or impact in your life if you apply it to your everyday walk in how you live!

**Here's my personal story and testimony:** I was born a Negro (a member of a dark-skinned group of people originally native to Africa, just south of the Sahara) female to James and Ruby Mack. Most of my life, I have been fighting to figure out who I am and why I think the way I do, struggling to find my place in this world of chaos! Those within a position of leadership have been attempting to break me by chipping away at my humanity and threatening to strip away my purpose, dignity, and self-respect. I have been undervalued, mistreated, abused, cheated, lied to, talked about, and controlled. I have been held back or limited by others in my career while being denied promotions and growth. They have even attacked the God within me in an attempt to figure out how to exercise full control over me! There has always been some type of angle, hoop, or hurdle I have been expected to jump before being granted a little decency or hope of moving forward. I have never truly been allowed to be who I was created by God to be until I realized it wasn't up to others!

He who is within me is far greater and more powerful than the he (false god) within the world influencing those who have committed trespasses against me! The blood which flows through my veins has memory, and it has reconnected me to the truth! It has refused to allow darkness to have complete control over my mind in allowing captivity to dominate! The Blood of Jesus has been the soul source of my will to fight in search of liberty, which has been granted to me from the beginning by my Savior! That which **the Son sets free** is truly free indeed!

Through the Blood of Jesus, there is (to name a few):

1. Protection: *When I see the blood, I will pass over you* (Exodus 12:13).

2. Reconciliation to God: *Through him to reconcile to himself all things, whether things on earth or things in heaven* (Colossians 1:19-20 BSB).

3. Redemption and Forgiveness. *In Him we have redemption through His blood* (Ephesians 1:7 NKJV).

4. Fellowship with God: *Having boldness to enter the Holiest by the blood of Jesus* (Hebrews 10:19).

5. Healing: *By His stripes we are healed* (Isaiah 53:5 NKJV).

6. Authority Over the Devil: *And they overcame him by the blood of the Lamb, and by the word of their testimony* (Revelation 12:11).

Through the Blood of Jesus, I have received revelation about my *identity* and purpose, which has truly freed me to embrace who God has created me to be! Today, I am moving forward with boldness without fear!

# THE HIGHEST HONOR

*Beloved,
I pray that in every way you may succeed and prosper and be in good health [physically], just as [I know] your soul prospers [spiritually].*

~ 3 John 1:2 AMP

March 23, 2018

Revised October 14, 2020

Someone told me, approximately a month ago, that change is not easy or quick; it takes time! But he also forgot to take into consideration that I am a Black female born into a society that does not favor who I am—not even a little bit! And society, or the majority which represents those in position of power and control to influence or tip the scales in the name of *equality* and all fairness, refuse to change to include seeing me as being a very viable part of this world. As a woman, God has purposed His daughters and His sons. He has permitted us—His daughters—to partake of our inheritance in the absence of any sons born to our earthly parents (see Numbers 26 and 36)! Incidentally, the status quo wants us—and others who look like me—to believe that we have no place in this world, which was created by our Abba Father as having a right to legal citizenship with all the bells and whistles! Instead, we are viewed as legal aliens who should not feel entitled to a piece of the pie in peace!

Each and every person (everyone to include all colors of the rainbow) was created by God, the *divine true source*, with a purpose for a purpose in accordance to His will and not ours! Somewhere and somehow throughout the history of humankind, the created has put himself in the place of the Creator in being the head to decide who should belong and who shouldn't. Man has attempted to categorize and relabel in accordance to a level of importance or value, the hierarchy since the beginning of time. Some folks have even put their pets on a higher pedestal than people, depending upon who is doing the analyzing or grading.

God has a *divine order* in how He recognizes or views everything! And His value system is very unique! He sees all His children as being equal, but their roles as being unique to His order are significant to our position and purpose. Let's look at Noah and Abraham, for instance. Noah was given the role of bringing his family and others to safety out of the way of the flood, but a number of them who were intent on following their own will refused to honor Noah's God-appointed assignment, and they were destroyed by water. In obedience, Noah honored God by taking heed to His command and restarting civilization.

Abram was renamed Abraham (see Genesis 17:4-5), which means the father of many nations. He and his wife Sarah were the parents to Jacob, who was renamed Israel. Jacob, the patriarch from which the initial blood of the Twelve Tribes of Israel flows, in whom we are all descendants, although reluctant at first, accepted his calling on his life in honor of God. For this reason, I cannot and will not agree with deportation immigration laws. If the truth be told, as descendants of the Twelve Tribes of Israel, we are all immigrants who have migrated from our ancestors' native lands to take up occupancy in our current places of residency. Leviticus 25:10-13 (AMP) states, *And you shall consecrate the fiftieth year and proclaim freedom [for the slaves] throughout the land to all its inhabitants. It shall be a Jubilee (year of remission) for you, and each of you shall return to his own [ancestral] property [that was sold to another because of poverty], and each of you shall return to his family [from whom he was separated by bondage]. That fiftieth year shall be a Jubilee for you; you shall not sow [seed], nor reap what reseeds itself, nor gather the grapes of the uncultivated vines. For it is the Jubilee; it shall be holy to you; you shall eat its crops out of the field. 'In this Year of Jubilee each of you shall return to his own [ancestral] property.*

Ironically, it has taken me most of my life up until now to realize and embrace my God-given purpose to understand the true meaning of my greatest or highest honor—like Jacob after many wrestling matches with God! If only I had come to know much sooner what I know now, I would have saved myself a great deal of heartache, pain, and health issues. But then I would have no platform or testimonies in which to share with you concerning my journey or quest in honor of the highest honor!

**By yielding to God, it has no longer become important for me to prove myself to man in wanting to be a part of the rat race to climb to the top in pursuit of more.** *Thus says the Lord, "Cursed is the man who trusts in and relies on mankind, Making [weak, fault human] flesh his strength, And whose mind and heart turn away from the Lord. For he will be like a shrub in the [parched] desert; And shall not see prosperity when it comes, But shall live in the rocky places of the wilderness, In an uninhibited salt land* (Jeremiah 17:5-6 AMP).

Sure, we always want more and should be granted the same opportunities across the board to obtain more; but does having *more in accordance to man's definition or concept as dictated by the world system of success* fit in God's plans for our life? Would we be good stewards over more? Would we allow more to hinder us from fulfilling our God-appointed purpose? I want to fulfill God's perfect will for my life **without compromise!**

For years, I allowed double standards, worriation, the fear of the unknown, and bullying from others to create unnecessary stress in my life and impact my health in the name of wanting more. I was going around in circles while growing tired and frustrated from attempting to please man. I was grasping at air! The expectation to excel in our jobs or careers is different for each individual; not all of us are expected to work as hard to receive the same compensation. God's criteria for blessing us with goodness doesn't change, and the expectation for achievement is the same for everyone. Man, on the other hand, keeps moving the finished line with no intention of making good on his promises. *And my God will meet all your needs according to the riches of his glory in Christ Jesus* (Philippians 4:19 NIV).

Much of what we experience does not happen by coincidence! Nothing simply happens without permission from God. Everything is allowed by Him, not with the intent to harm us but with the intent of moving us into position for His Glory. The positioning can be a smooth transition or a struggle and quite challenging if we fail to honor God's will by leaning toward our own understanding.

## DIVINE LIBERTY

**What is honor?** What does true honor look like? How can we honor God, ourselves, and others? John 4:24 says, *God is a Spirit: and they that worship him must worship him in spirit and in truth.*

When I think back to my former self, I was wounded, messed up, and confused about God and the people in the world. Values weren't being respected, morals weren't being displayed, and every man, woman, or child was doing whatever whenever and however. Much of that still hasn't changed, but my perspective is different now. My entire focus has been readjusted! My desire to be who God created me to be in seeing myself through His eyes has intensified, and I AM no longer looking to man to validate me or approve of me as a person or a Child of God!

**Honoring man's idea of success in accordance to this world system is no longer a priority!** Honoring God for His persistence, faithfulness, and willingness to hold me close while my mind was twisting is my sole priority. Carrying out my divine purpose in connection with God's mission is my way of honoring Him for His unconditional love and confidence in me. He protected my heart and mind during my spiritual process in obtaining divine liberty through revelation. Man can do what he will, but my life and spirit belong to God forever! I AM internally free and eternally grateful!

The solution is life on God's terms as referenced by Romans 8:1-2 MSG: *With the arrival of Jesus, the Messiah, that fateful dilemma is resolved. Those who enter into Christ's being-here-for-us no longer have to live under a continuous, low-lying black cloud. A new power is in operation. The Spirit of life in Christ, like a strong wind, has magnificently cleared the air, freeing you from a fated lifetime of brutal tyranny at the hands of sin and death.*

I want to reverence God and *all* His glory!

# WHEN YOU KNOW WHO YOU ARE!

*I'll never forget the trouble,
the utter lostness, the taste of ashes,
the poison I've swallowed. I remember it all—oh, how well
I remember—the feeling of hitting the bottom. But there's
one other thing I remember, and remembering, I keep a
grip on hope: God's loyal love couldn't have run out, his
merciful love couldn't have dried up. They're created new
every morning. How great your faithfulness! I'm sticking
with God (I say it over and over). He's all I got left.*

~ **Lamentations 3:21-24 MSG**

July 9, 2017

It is *very important* to know who you are. In doing so, you must be willing to be extremely honest with yourself and God about the total you—meaning being totally objective in recognizing and acknowledging all of you to embrace the good and the bad, taking complete note of your shortcomings to include the changes you have made and need to make in your life. Willing to hold yourself accountable and taking full responsibility for your actions is a sign of integrity. That does not mean you should feel the need to take responsibility or ownership of what others attempt to saddle you with while they exercise their false sense of power and control over you or the situation in question to feed their egotistical desire for thinking of themselves more highly than they ought to (see Romans 12:3).

Let me share some history! My parents, based on their upbringing, were passive—to a point—which was a learned behavior as dictated through cultural conditioning and intimidation to always know their place. If you know anything about culture, then you also know it incorporates biases and double standards on the basis of unfairness and inequality, in many cases. And people normally don't question culture; they simply, out of habit and conditioning, fall in line to conform to the controlling and unwritten inherited doctrines as laid out before them to follow. Being passive is generally about going along to get along, even if it means allowing yourself to knowingly be taken advantage of by others simply because it is culturally expected and accepted. Adhering to a norm or doing the same thing over and over again as a ritual doesn't necessarily mean it's right!

My parents taught their passive behavioral traits of cultural conditioning to me. And for years, I allowed people and situations to dictate my decisions, my life as a whole. One day, really not that long ago, a coworker pulled me to the side and asked why I always, and so easily, accept blame when I am not the responsible party. At the time, I had no answer other than it had become the norm for me as taught and dictated by a way of life for coping. So I thought! But this way of coping was detrimental and unhealthy to my self-esteem and confidence as a human being. What I was actually doing was turning over my rights without a fight!

As the saying goes, "When you stand for nothing, you fall for everything." I'm truly starting to learn, understand, and appreciate that statement. While attending a meeting, a human resources director prepared me for a lie, to take the blame for a decision she made. I wasn't expected to disagree or say "no" to being used as a scapegoat if I wanted to keep my job. So she made a call to our Kansas City office to conference in the director for the second part of the meeting. Then, she proceeded to apologize for a very substantial financial error by telling the director that I was also present as a participant on the call. Then she nudged me to confirm my presence by saying hello and identifying myself. Like a puppet, I was not allowed to say anything else while the meeting continued as I became the sacrificial lamb; the entire blame was laid at my feet. I felt humiliated, angry, and sick to my stomach for not speaking up. I let the HR director use me to redirect her intentional management decision not to honor a contractual agreement to extend payment as a financial screw-up or error due to my oversight. After finding myself in yet another scapegoat, sacrificial-lamb situation, something within me said, "No, not this time or ever again!" I wasn't being defiant or disrespectful. I was being true to myself, and I was letting my yes be yes and my no be no, as instructed by James 5:12 and Matthew 5:37.

Can you imagine how easy it is for there to be so many innocent folks locked up behind bars? Mainly because they were easily sacrificed! They refused to speak up or didn't have any more fight left to remain true to themselves. While being interrogated, they gave up out of fear and gave in to a system or strategy that was carried out by the desires of others who used manipulation and intimidation tactics. Many of the underprivileged or disadvantaged lost hope and sight of the principle. They let the person ruling over them—who was wheeling the power—decide their fate. They falsely confessed to an act they did not commit! No, this isn't true for everyone, but this scenario most certainly isn't far-reaching either. That's why I'm so glad to know that God is nothing like man, that He should lie or feel the need to stoop to utilizing deceitful tactics to make Himself feel important. He does not use any type of coercion. He is no respecter of persons! And for that, I am truly grateful!

When you know who you are, doing not-so-easy things in life becomes the easiest, because it is right! I was accused of being a negative influence in the office and the main reason why those they had hired to serve as receptionists were all leaving. Unfortunately, the turnover rate for that position, because the management/leadership didn't know how to treat people, was very high! So, to my credit, what they really wanted to say is, we cannot have you going around preaching the gospel and giving folks hope when we have worked so hard to tear down their defenses to give us more leverage and control at getting them to conform. On that day, I suffered through that meeting of false accusations because I know who I AM! And, I would rather be like Shadrach, Meshach, and Abednego as outlined in Daniel 3.

If I am going to be accused of something, then let it be in line with me standing up for principles and my belief in Christ to be true to Him first and then to myself! For the last will be first and the first will be last in accordance to the *Will of God*!

Walk with confidence in knowing the Lord and live with purpose in the call of your destiny! Pray for our government! Pray for those in leadership! Pray for those in position of power! Pray for the *land* and the *nations* without ceasing!

# WHAT IS PERCEPTION?

*Their moral understanding is darkened and their reasoning is beclouded. [They are] alienated (estranged, self-banished) from the life of God [with no share in it; this is] because of the ignorance (the want of knowledge and perception, the willful blindness) that is deep-seated in them, due to their hardness of heart [to the insensitiveness of their moral nature].*

**~ Ephesians 4:18 AMPC**

November 10, 2016

Perception is a thought process—the way in which a person thinks or understands someone or something. A perception is normally void of truth, a false belief involving the senses or a feeling. And, unfortunately, feelings can change from one minute to the next—like the drop of a hat or the changing of the wind. Meaning no disrespect, but consider a schizophrenic[29] or

---

29  www.nimh.nih.gov/health/topics/schizophrenia/index.shtml; Schizophrenia is a serious mental illness that affects how a person thinks, feels, and behaves. People with schizophrenia may seem like they have lost touch with reality, which causes significant distress for the individual, their family members, and friends.

manic-depressive[30] personality, like being hot one minute and cold the next. Today, they like you and tomorrow, or two hours later, they don't, for something as simple as wearing the wrong color of clothing or refusing not to jump high enough.

I was actually called into an office by a former supervisor and told my clothes were too colorful for an office setting. What they really wanted to say is they would like for me to refrain from wearing clothing that speaks to an ethnic connotation. A couple of days later, I was approached and told that my appearance relating to my baldness was offensive, intimidating, and believed to be a militant statement that was not going to be tolerated.

Perception is similar to stereotyping and profiling on the basis of race, gender, age, etc. A preconceived notion[31] or idea about a person or group which is mostly fueled by a prejudiced attitude or uncritical judgment and fear.

Let's examine some other descriptions:

- Mental mapping or stereotyping.

- Representation; void of that which is real. Lacking truth!

---

30  www.nimh.nih.gov/health/topics/bipolar-disorder/index.shtml; Bipolar disorder (formerly called manic-depressive illness or manic depression) is a mental disorder that causes unusual shifts in mood, energy, activity levels, concentration, and the ability to carry out day-to-day tasks.

31  www.thefreedictionary.com/preconceived+notion; an opinion formed beforehand without adequate evidence

- An unrealistic or oversimplified opinion or viewpoint.

- A fixed or standardized and general mental picture (image) categorizing a person as a member of a group or thing.

The problem with attempting to please people is that you will forever be trying to win favor with them with no satisfaction in sight. Think of a revolving door on an endless roller coaster! But by pleasing God, not only can you obtain favor with Him, but He can grant you favor among men. Irrevocable favor!

When people with the wrong heart make a conscious effort to view you how they want to see you—which has nothing to do with who you really are in the eyes of God—it is going to take an earth-shaking event like a move of God to change their minds.

# COVERING

*Woe to the rebellious children,
saith the Lord, that take counsel, but not of me;
and that cover with a covering, but not of my spirit,
that they may add sin to sin.*

~ Isaiah 30:1

September 6, 2015

Everyone within the body of Christ does not believe the same thing to the same degree or extent of the word. Why? Mainly because each and every person is wired differently in our thinking and comprehension of the Word! We are at different levels in our thinking when it comes to our belief in Him and the Word. We are at different levels of spiritual maturity, but we are all called and encouraged to study to show ourselves approved, rightly dividing the word and being not ashamed of our covering. Our covenant is with God, not man. However, I will attempt to honor and be respectful of the person who is in position of leadership to rule as governed by the covering of us all. God commands us to assemble regularly to worship Him in spirit and in truth (Hebrews 10:25-27).

> *But [the time is coming when] the earth*
> *shall be filled with the knowledge of the glory of the Lord*
> *as the waters cover the sea.*
>
> ~ Habakkuk 2:14 AMPC

Many have been taught to believe the shepherd of the church was and is God's delegated authority and ambassador who communicates God's messages to the masses. Authority is granted (and allowed) to all men from God. However, more responsibility may be given to some than others; it is important for us to be mindful of our roles and perspective positions as ordained by God. We were *all* created by Him for a purpose with a purpose. We *all* have a part to play as part of a whole. Disobeying the shepherd is like disobeying God, but our divine objective should be to please God and not man—if man is operating outside of the *Will of God*.

> *And be not conformed to this world:*
> *but be ye transformed by the renewing of your mind,*
> *that ye may prove what is that good, and acceptable,*
> *and perfect, will of God.*
>
> ~ Romans 12:2

There have been times when I readily believed and followed all of what was told to me without questioning a single word. I simply went with the flow until I found out differently and became greatly disappointed and frustrated that what I had received and followed was wrong! Unfortunately, much of what we are told, believe, and follow, as it relates to the church, is taught as a result of tradition and religiosity, which stems from characteristics of the world that are introduced to the church in the name of control. We must be mindful to evaluate every teaching to ensure it lines up with the Word of God! *God's Word is very clear!* He provides us with explicit instructions and principles (the law of the Lord) in which to follow, should we take the time to read and to study them faithfully! God's Word is liberating; it encourages freedom from bondage and legalism. When what we learn threatens to hold us in captivity, it is not of God and proves to be false teaching.

> *But there were also false prophets among the people, just as there will be false teachers among you. They will secretly introduce destructive heresies, even denying the sovereign Lord who bought them—bringing swift destruction on themselves. Many will follow their depraved conduct and will bring the way of truth into disrepute.*
>
> ~ 2 Peter 2:1-2 NIV

Although it is equally important for us to withstand the wiles of the devil, it is also believed that finding the right church to attend is about finding the right covering and protection. We must not give in to the temptation that is wisely disguised to deceive us! Each and every time I hear someone tell me I need a covering, I shrink as if the Holy Spirit is warning me not to store that information in my thoughts or my heart. While giving me *revelation*, God reminded me that He is my covering and directs me to various scriptures of reference. *Now you [collectively] are Christ's body, and individually [you are] members of it [each with his own special purpose and function]* (1 Corinthians 12:27 AMP). *For just as we have many members in one body and all the members do not have the same function, so we, who are many, are one body in Christ, and individually members one of another* (Romans 12:4-5 NASB). Put in the proper context, *God has put all things under the power of Christ, and for the good of the church HE has made Him the head of everything* (Ephesians 1:22 CEV). When considering and choosing the right church, the prospective church environment should believe in the Bible and teach the Holy Ghost (Spirit) while trusting and leaning on the Lord to deliver, to heal, and to set the captives free, baptizing in the name of the Father, the Son, and the Holy Spirit!

*He is also head of the body, the church;*
*and He is the beginning, the firstborn from the dead,*
*so that He Himself will come to have first place in everything.*

~ Colossians 1:18 NASB

# CHURCH HURT IS REAL

*If God gives such attention to the appearance of wildflowers—most of which are never even seen—don't you think he'll attend to you, take pride in you, do his best for you? What I'm trying to do here is to get you to relax, to not be so preoccupied with getting, so you can respond to God's giving. People who don't know God and the way he works fuss over these things, but you know both God and how he works. Steep your life in God-reality, God-initiative, God-provisions. Don't worry about missing out. You'll find all your everyday human concerns will be met.*

~ **Matthew 6:30-33 MSG**

August 28, 2015

Revised October 14, 2020

Do you know "church hurt" can be the most devastating and deadly of any and all forms of hurt for some people? Why? Because there are people, including myself, who have come to church in search of refuge from the outside world. Therefore, it is not unheard of for the behavior of the world to be infused in the church. When we come to church, many of us do not expect to encounter the same spirit of division, *spirit of competitiveness*, or Jezebel greeting us at the altar! But, we have, unfortunately, succumbed to the ways of the world and have taken that outside behavior into the church with us. However, as leaders who have taken on the role of "pastoring" the church, we should be putting forth an effort to withstand the wiles of the devil in how we conduct ourselves as messengers of God.

> "The collateral damage (from church hurt) negatively affects the ministry and outreach of the church, too, and some churches never recover. Recognize that the behavior that brought such devastation to your heart is not much different than the hurt any of us can encounter in the workplace, marketplace, or home. The difference is we don't expect God's people to behave like those without Christ in their lives. The church is the one place almost everyone agrees should be safe, accepting, forgiving, and free from conflict and pain. Yet in most churches, at least some elements of strife, conflict, and hatred creep in and tarnish that ideal."[32]

We should be working toward growing in spiritual maturity. We should possess a knowledge and lifestyle unlike those who are coming to the church for refuge. We should be living examples, mindful of God's agenda and His word in working toward accomplishing our divine, assigned missions on behalf

---

[32] www.gotquestions.org/hurt-by-church.html

of the Lord as opposed to building a reputation for ourselves. What about our character? Does it resemble the character of Christ? What are we teaching others by way of our character and behavior?

We question terrorism! But we have not given any thought to the true meaning of that word to note our unrighteous, terrorist behavior with no regard for the hurt we cause others. People are hurting and seeking hope, while others have lost complete faith in humanity and the church. But their hope and faith should never be put in man. Man will disappoint you every time! Our faith should be put in God; *He is love.* He said He would never leave us nor forsake us. It is man who makes empty promises. It is man who seeks to belong and will do any and everything necessary to fulfill a need of self-realization at the expense of others. But as followers of Christ, we should not think as the world thinks. *Don't deceive yourselves. If any of you think you are wise in the ways of this world, you should give up that wisdom in order to become really wise* (1 Corinthians 3:18 GW).

By setting your sights on the world, you have become confused in your thinking. You see the wicked getting ahead as they trample you to climb to the top. The more wrong they do, the more they are rewarded and promoted. They go through life not being held accountable for their actions, causing them to think there are no consequences. When you lose your footing or moral compass, your actions start to mirror the actions of the world. Putting ourselves on that same pedestal, we start to see ourselves as giants. We forget about saving souls and conduct our services with the need to excite the senses to hold the interest of people. We plan programs to entertain and compete with other churches just to pull in a larger crowd. No one is paying attention to God's Word falling on good soil. No one is paying attention to the blessing of the offering for a plentiful harvest.

Where's the deliverance? Where's the power and the presence of the Lord? What about the miracles, signs, and wonders? People are hurting! Many are called, but few are chosen, and those of us who have chosen to serve the Lord on the basis of free will must make sure that we are following His example (1 Peter 2:21). Otherwise, you are out of order! None of us are without sin or blemish and must make sure that we, ourselves, have been delivered, healed, and set free from the challenges of that which threatens to hold us within captivity. Meaning, if we are finding it difficult to manage or deal with unresolved issues, we should know when it is time to step down or move back—temporarily or otherwise—in an attempt to keep from hurting others or to keep from scattering the sheep (Jeremiah 23:1 and Ezekiel 34).

## Matthew 22:34-40 MSG

## The Most Important Command

*When the Pharisees heard how he had bested the Sadducees, they gathered their forces for an assault. One of their religion scholars spoke for them, posing a question they hoped would show him up: "Teacher, which command in God's Law is the most important?" Jesus said, "'Love the Lord your God with all your passion and prayer and intelligence.'*

*This is the most important, the first on any list. But there is a second to set alongside it: 'Love others as well as you love yourself.' These two commands are pegs; everything in God's Law and the Prophets hangs from them."*

## THE CHURCH AND BAPTISM OF THE HOLY SPIRIT

1. The church, which is the body of Christ, is the temple of God. *And He is the head of the body, the church: who is the beginning, the firstborn from the dead; that in all things he might have the preeminence* (Colossians 1:18).

2. The baptism by the Holy Spirit is the means by which believers in Christ are incorporated into his body. For by one Spirit are we all baptized into one body, whether *we be* Jews or Gentiles, whether *we be* bond or free; and have been all made to drink into one Spirit (1 Corinthians 12:13).

3. The baptism by the Holy Spirit began on the day of Pentecost after Christ's resurrection. *For John truly baptized with water; but ye shall be baptized with the Holy Ghost not many days hence* (Acts 1:5; see also, Acts 2:1-4; 11:15-17). Therefore, the church began on the day of Pentecost after Christ's resurrection.

# FIGHT, TAKE FLIGHT, OR FREEZE

*Fight the good fight of faith,
lay hold on eternal life, whereunto thou art also called, and
hast professed a good profession
before many witnesses.*

~ 1 Timothy 6:12

October 21, 2014

When I first started to hear "fight, take flight, or freeze," I was very puzzled. I didn't know if it was a message directly relating to me or a subject matter (title) was referencing for me to speak on later—until God made His expectation very clear. He told me He was giving me one option while taking away two: (1) my option to take flight (run from trouble) and (2) my option to freeze (stand still and do nothing). So that leaves me with only the option to fight. Many want us to believe Christ was meek and passive, according to their interpretation. But according to God's interpretation, being meek is exuding *power under control*. And Christ knew when to speak, what to say, what to do, how to do it, and how to be still (freeze) when absolutely necessary! Unfortunately, we have allowed the enemy to push us in a corner and to deceive us about many things.

*The meek will he guide in judgment:*
*And the meek will he teach his way.*

~ Psalm 25:9

Growing up, I always took the low road. I never wanted to rock the boat or hurt anyone's feelings. I always neglected myself and opted to forfeit what I wanted or needed just to make others happy in getting their way. How many times have you heard "'Vengeance is mine,' said the LORD" being redirected at you by others as a result of you attempting to resist their control over you? Many who do not know the word and have not made a conscious commitment to following the Lord's example do not waste any time quoting the scripture to work in their favor against you. That's why it is very important to develop a relationship with the lord for yourself, study the word, and allow the Holy Spirit to give you revelation.

In fighting the good fight of faith, it is about believing in yourself and trusting in the Lord to see you through. But you have to be willing to listen to Him intently as He guides you and instructs you on what to do. Then you have to be willing to follow His instructions to the letter to carry out the assignment(s) He entrusts to you. He may push you outside of your comfort zone by telling you to take a stand, when in your past, you often took the approach to run, hide, or just cry in letting others walk all over you. He may tell you to speak up and speak out—to no longer keep silent. He may tell you to put something in writing and send it out to share it with others on a particular issue you have never considered taking on. He may even tell you to comfort the enemy at every turn, thus putting yourself in the line of fire to receive more attacks.

> *Jesus went straight to the Temple and threw out everyone who had set up shop, buying and selling. He kicked over the tables of loan sharks and the stalls of dove merchants. He quoted this text:*
>
> *My house was designated a house of prayer;*
>
> *You have made it a hangout for thieves.*
>
> *Now there was room for the blind and crippled to get in. They came to Jesus and He healed them.*
>
> ~ Matthew 21:12-14 MSG

As a child of God who is anointed and appointed with a special mission, you can no longer sit quietly on the sidelines doing nothing. In due season (the right timing), God raises up an individual or individuals by equipping them for battle (spiritual warfare) and sending them out for a specific task (or to a particular post) to uproot, tear down, or pull down (see Jeremiah 1:10). Indeed, the weapons we fight with are not the weapons of the world. On the contrary, they have divine power through the Holy Spirit to demolish strongholds (2 Corinthians 10:4). We must claim our rightful positions! Decree and declare with humbleness, says the Lord! We must take up our cross and walk with **boldness** to scope out the land as prophets of the Most-High God. It's time to move out as in the days of the old when John the Baptist was present (see Matthew 11:12-13)!

## WHAT IS A STRONGHOLD?

A stronghold is a faulty thinking pattern based on lies and deception, which could also result in others placing limitations upon you to keep you in a box. Deception is one of the primary weapons of the devil on the basis of perception and interpretation; it is the major building block for developing strongholds and limitations. What strongholds can do is cause us to think in ways (outside of the *Will of God*) that block us from receiving God's best. For example, James 5:16 AMPC states, *Confess to one another therefore your faults (your slips, your false steps, your offenses, your sins) and pray [also] for one another, that you may be healed and restored [to a spiritual tone of mind and heart]. The earnest (heartfelt, continued) prayer of a righteous man makes tremendous power available [dynamic in its working].* However, if you think you have to confess all your sins to *everybody* you have ever wronged in your life, this could possibly take you forever to accomplish and could send you on a downward, self-condemning spiral (to feel awful and extremely guilty), thus bringing about doubt and unforgiveness. You should, however, take every offense to God in prayer in seeking His wisdom, His knowledge, and His understanding for moving forward. Why? Because not everyone is at a level of spiritual maturity to handle your confession or transparency. Let God guide you all the way!

> *And take the helmet of salvation and the sword that the Spirit wields, which is the Word of God [and fight back].*
>
> ~ Ephesians 6:17 AMPC

SELAH!

# FROM REVELATION TO REALIZATION

*Teach me your way, LORD,*
*that I may rely on your faithfulness;*
*give me an undivided heart, that I may fear your name.*

**~ Proverbs 86:11 NIV**

Revised October 12, 2020

Good Morning God,

How are You today? I AM feeling great and on top of the world. After all, it was You who said I was the head and not the tail. I AM above and not below. I AM more than a conqueror. Father God, I thank You for not giving up on me and for being so patient with me. As I sit writing to You this morning, I must admit, I did not believe I would ever get to this point in my life. And I owe it all to You! You have increased my faith, renewed my mind, and filled me with the Holy Spirit that keeps me connected to You.

It is an awesome thing to finally know You for myself. As I look back over my life, I did not have this same awareness or deep-rooted connection to You upon my first baptism on June 30, 1995. That is why it was so *important* for me to rededicate my life to You on November 20, 2007. I have a better understanding of Your love for me *to include who You created me to be*!

I thank You for *Your persistence* in how You *revealed* Yourself to me like never before. I AM sure, without a doubt, that there is more You will reveal to me over time and I AM ready. The supernatural presence of You and Your holy power is real. I have made so many attempts to explain to others what it means to have a *revelation* that gives true meaning or confirmation to a *realization*. Wow! If only I had my tape recorder. The item that You keep prompting me to have with me at all times to be able to capture and play back over and over again my encounters with You. The incident that still blows me away even to this day was the erupting of the Holy Spirit within me during a Salvation Army World Service Office (SAWSO) corps meeting that was held on the same day as a National Commissioners' Conference. To think that they actually thought I was experiencing a nervous breakdown still boggles my mind, but I get it!

I was extremely overjoyed to be associated with them as an employee to the point of thinking or believing they would have a measurable amount of influence on my spiritual growth! I guess if it had not happened to me, I could possibly doubt such a charismatic move took place as well. But it did happen to me and I will be forever grateful to You for that experience. In fact, I AM looking forward to many more encounters with You like

Smith Wigglesworth! This has been an amazing journey, and I can't wait to see what else You have planned for me.

As You are aware, my mother made sure my sister and I were introduced to the church before we could walk or talk. As I listened to the sermons, I took to heart every word that was being presented. As I became older and adapted to my flesh that was influenced by the world, I was introduced to lust, want, need, and lack. These elements fueled my emotions and dictated my choices. Choices I did not feel or think were overly wrong in accordance to choices made by others. I didn't steal, cheat, or lie, nor did I take pleasure in mistreating or deceiving others in any way. The choices I made, I felt to some extent, did not harm anyone but me. However, knowing what I do now, I not only hurt me, I hurt You—yet You loved me still, unconditionally. You continued to love me as You made several attempts to reach me through my pain in extending to me a life raft.

As I studied Your word in familiarizing myself with Your expectations, I had many questions about the concept of forgiveness to include it being a reality for me. Feeling guilty about my less-than-Christ-like choices in life, I would not allow myself to get close to You for fear of You not loving me or forgiving me for not being perfect. In June of 1995, I had an extensive conversation with an Elder of the Holy Christian Missionary Baptist Church for All People who explained, I did not have to be perfect to turn my life over to You and be baptized. It was this misconception that kept me from taking the first step, although I knew within my heart that You were calling me. We are born sinners into a sin-infested world. We are not perfect, but we are given the opportunity to be ye therefore perfect, even as You, our Father which is in heaven is perfect (see Matthew 5:48). But You accept us as we are and work within us, through us, and around us to perfect us, which is why I greatly appreciate Your ways not being like our ways. I AM longing for You to teach me Your ways as You can teach me. I desire to denounce all the ways of man to think more like You to forever do the right thing!

As I have struggled often, forgetting has not been as easy for me as forgiveness, and You have discussed that with me too! So thank You for the confirmation; it is possible to forgive without forgetting. I find that many people tend to believe that discussing a situation or issue means I AM holding on to anger that prevents me from forgiving. On the other hand, I have come to learn through You that many people refuse to accept responsibility for their actions and would, therefore, have me to believe that their issues or problems have more to do with me than it has to do with them not willing to change. As Christians, we should be able to talk openly and directly in truth and in love about the things that need to be confronted.

Father, thank You for giving me the ability to see beyond my faults and blessing me with a heart to admit when I'm wrong. Thank You for teaching me about forgiveness and how to let go of guilt in seeking to change and improve my way of thinking. Because my past, present, and future experiences help to shape who I AM. You have taught me that forgetting is not necessary; however, for my growth, forgiveness is a part of a process. Thank You for allowing me to see myself through Your eyes in appreciation of knowing who I AM today in You!

*He suffered no man to do them wrong:*
*yea, he reproved kings for their sakes;*
*Saying, Touch not mine anointed,*
*and do my prophets no harm.*

~ Psalm 105:14-15

\*

*And David said to Abishai, Destroy him not:*
*for who can stretch forth his hand*
*against the LORD's anointed, and be guiltless?*

~ 1 Samuel 26:9

# BIBLICAL TOPICS, TESTIMONIES, AND OTHER

# WHAT IS A TESTIMONY?

*And they overcame him by the blood of the Lamb,
and by the word of their testimony;
and they loved not their lives unto the death.*

~ **Revelation 12:11**

August 4, 2019

Revised October 13, 2020

When I share my testimonies, they may speak to me as being the main character, as in specific to me, but it is not primarily all about me! When I share my testimonies, it is an opportunity for me to praise the Lord and to give Him honor for how far He has brought me through *endurance*! My testimony is a reflection of my trials and tribulations! It normally signifies an unpleasant or sad event with a happy ending concerning my growth. My growth speaks to moving from a place of unbelief to a position of belief and *trust in God* with my life! Therefore, my testimonies are a testament to my love for God, faith, and belief in Him as I stand on His word. Through my testimonies, I AM displaying a willingness to be an Ambassador for Christ and an act of evangelism!

When I share my testimonies, it is not about me reliving a disappointment or an upsetting time in my life; it marks a victory for not allowing that event to destroy me. Sometimes, keeping quiet only gives the enemy a false assumption to believe he has succeeded in tearing me down to keep me held in captivity (bondage and enslaved in my mind). If anything, with God, I AM able to emerge with strength from the ashes like a phoenix to tell my truth! God's phoenix is ready to mount up on wings like an *eagle* to soar and tackle another battle with greater confidence knowing *I can do all things through Christ who strengthens me*!

Souls are being challenged each and every day! People are being attacked by darkness in every area of their lives. People, unfortunately, are experiencing situations and encounters they never imagined seeing or taking place as it relates to them! Even in places they least expected because they thought they would be safe: on the job (in the workplace), in the church and outside the church, in schools, in the courts where justice should be obtainable, by law enforcement and US military soldiers sworn to protect and serve, in the sanctity of the home of a loved one (relative), etc.

Just to reiterate, people, unfortunately, are experiencing unbelievable, unexplainable, tormenting things, large and small. Things they wish not to share or don't know how to share, mainly because they fear no one will believe them or others will refuse to fight alongside them for moral support. If sharing a testimony gives closure or a sense of peace, pray for the strength of others to be able to do it in seeking *freedom* to move forward. Pray for their connection to the Father to overcome by the sharing of their testimony. Pray that they be surrounded by Saints who truly have a relationship with the Lord to help usher them through and toward the light! Pray they are encouraged to live with passion and not die with determination! Pray that there are no long-term devastating and debilitating physical and mental wounds keeping them from being whole!

Show some compassion!

# SPIRITUAL MATURITY

*And I, brethren, could not speak unto you as unto spiritual, but as unto carnal, even as unto babes in Christ.*

~1 Corinthians 3:1

February 27, 2013

One of the many things God cautions me about is not getting into a debate with anyone concerning religion. Each and every individual is different and unique in their own way. Just as we are different on the outside, we are most certainly different on the inside to include how we receive and process information. Therefore, it would be pointless to attempt to get someone to see your point of view if they are not willing and able to be open to at least embracing that which God has revealed to you. If what you have received to know is truth on the basis of revelation through the guidance of the Holy Spirit, don't sweat it! If that which you attempt to share with others is not your personal view, but is instead God's wisdom, knowledge, and understanding being poured through you as a willing vessel and it is not readily received by others, don't sweat it! Just do it! Spread the Gospel as instructed and move on!

There are a number of studies conducted by various individuals depicting detailed information about a particular subject matter. For instance, there are countless studies for first-time parents to tell them how to measure the expectant growth of their child from infancy to adulthood. It even spells out at what age you should expect your child to walk after their crawling stage. As they progress in age, you are also told when to expect them to form syllables, go from babbling to talking, or at what age you should expect them to have an interest in reading and writing. But if no two people are alike, then how is it possible for us to measure the stage of a person's growth in comparing one human being to another. And yet, we do it all the time while being encouraged by society to be competitive.

As we mature, we start to identify and categorize what is most important to us as we struggle to find our way. Our references increase or decrease to include a level of materialism as some things become more important and others become less important. Some of us become more driven by our flesh, while others become more driven by our need for spiritual growth. Along with our staying power comes an increase or decrease in our tolerance level. Our tolerance level is what normally dictates what and who we are willing to follow. If you are concerned with keeping up with others, what are you willing to do to be accepted by them? What reference will you value as being important to use as a measurement of your character? Will you choose them or God? In choosing God, He gave us a real life (flesh and blood in a physical body) example to combat our excuses before our excuses became an issue. He is Jesus Christ, our Lord, Master, and Savior! And He was willing to do whatever it takes to reconnect us back to the Father, including being a sacrificial lamb! Are you willing to live and die for Him?

What is the difference between a carnal mind and a spiritual mind?

# A CALL TO UNITY

*Behold, how good and how pleasant
it is for brethren to dwell together in unity!*

**~ Psalm 133:1 KJV**

November 13, 2013

Revised October 8, 2020

Why is it so customary for pastors to encourage members of their flock (or congregation) not to attend other church assemblies or gatherings? If God, the Father, the Son, and the Holy Spirit, are one, then what would be the common denominator or thread linking us to Him? The Holy Spirit! If there is one Spirit, one Body, and many members, what is the glue that connects us all together? Yahweh, Jesus Christ, who is the Son of God! Just as a body, though one, has many parts, but all its many parts form one body, so it is with Christ (1 Corinthians 12:12). If God is the creator and head (covering) of us all, shouldn't we be about our Father's business just as Jesus states He is about His Father's business? Then we should also be mindful to be on one accord, thus having the same agenda! Not my agenda or your agenda but a Kingdom-minded agenda in accordance to God's governmental order and expectation for His Church in Christ!

How else can we accomplish God's mission if we are divided and at war with competing priorities, thus attempting to prove we are more highly than we ought to be or think (Romans 12:3)? Then I would implore you all to put aside the things of the world and to *work toward unity, and live in harmony with one another. Make a conscious effort to avoid thinking you are better than others or wiser than the rest; instead, embrace common people and ordinary tasks* (Romans 12:16 VOICE) to accomplish the objectives of God's agenda.

*And he said unto them,
How is it that ye sought me? wist ye not that
I must be about my Father's business?*

~ Luke 2:49

Approximately less than two weeks ago, on November 1, 2013, to be exact, my spiritual sister Mary Bryant and I packed a bag and headed down the road for Martinsburg, West Virginia. We were extremely excited to attend a City-Wide Call to Unity conference, which was led by Jim and Carla Barbarossa (otherwise known as The Shofar Man and Company). When I think of the word "unity," I envision a number of people, diverse in nature but embracing each other's differences (one another) to include spiritual gifts and coming together with one common goal in mind. That goal or mission would be to acknowledge our Father, praise Him, and worship Him! Having the opportunity to come together with other like-minded willing vessels earnestly eager to obtain a Word and please our Heavenly Father through song and testimonies while sharing the goodness of His love was a joyous healing experience! We were, simply, overwhelmingly ready to be in His presence, experience His glory, receive His instruction and carry out His command in reaching others!

*Father, may they all be one as You are in Me and I am in You; may they be in Us, for by this unity the world will believe that You sent Me.*

~ John 17:21 VOICE

Upon receipt of the invite, I could not contain my emotion! I just love receiving confirmations from my Father, thus enforcing His plan for me and/or others pertaining to His directive guidance for the Kingdom. I like to refer to moments like this as being a sign of undeniable divine intervention! I don't know about you, but I just love it when a plan comes together and I can actually see it, taste it, feel it, and realize it with an undoubtable knowing deep down within my soul. I can imagine how God must feel when one of His children gets a revelation, acknowledges it, moves out, and follows through with it on His behalf to share it with others. You could see the excitement on Jim's face (to include those with him) when he talked about and demonstrated God's expected order to those of us who were in attendance. As I looked around the room, my spirit was soaring and overjoyed to be in the presence of so many like-minded Kingdom citizens holding on to every word from the Father through Jim Barbarossa. We sat attentively just waiting to absorb more of the vision and the message to carry that word back to any and everyone who would listen!

> *For who were the people who turned a deaf ear? Weren't they the very ones Moses led out of Egypt? And who was God provoked with for forty years? Wasn't it those who turned a deaf ear and ended up corpses in the wilderness? And when he swore that they'd never get where they were going, wasn't he talking to the ones who turned a deaf ear? They never got there because they never listened, never believed.*
>
> ~ Hebrews 3:15-19 MSG

*Jim Barbarossa is calling God's Leaders, from all over the world, across all denominational lines to join hands, in Unity and take the Gospel message beyond the walls of our buildings, out into our cities to reach and disciple the lost.*[33] What do you have to lose? We go to church at the appropriate time, but fail to take heed of God's call for us to unite. We simply go through the motions, insistently doing our own thing. We view the size of the congregation, even the square footage of the building, as a symbol of successful preaching, reputation, and popularity against other church communities. Too often, with a spirit of competitiveness, the focus, to be held in high esteem as one of the leading megachurches, hinders the presence and flow of the Holy Spirt! Sure, people are being reached; however, there is no evidence of the manifestation of miracles, signs, and wonders; and no one is getting healed or delivered from the ties that bind them. Many times, they come in wounded and are left broken because many

---

33 http://www.step-by-step.org/whatgat.htm

churches are not following God's order in allowing the gifts of the five-fold ministry to shine and work in unison.

> *See to it that no one carries you off as spoil or makes you yourselves captive by his so-called philosophy and intellectualism and vain deceit (idle fancies and plain nonsense), following human tradition (men's ideas of the material rather than the spiritual world), just crude notions following the rudimentary and elemental teachings of the universe and disregarding [the teachings of] Christ (the Messiah).*
>
> ~ Colossians 2:8 AMP

## QUESTIONS

1. What if I as a church have a vision and am able to articulate it, but lack the skills to implement the vision?

2. What if I am able to finance the vision, but lack the tools to construct it?

3. What if I possess one part of the plan, but need others who have the talent to produce part two, three, etc., to ensure the vision evolves and expands to fruition?

4. Will I let my pride hinder me from following through with God's plan in failing to reach out to other churches as a joint (team) effort?

5. Why limit the potential growth of a sheep from obtaining more training needed elsewhere to contribute to God's Kingdom?

6. Why limit the usefulness of a vessel who has been anointed by God to perform in a capacity of God's choosing?

*Also I heard the voice of the Lord, saying,*
*Whom shall I send, and who will go for us?*
*Then said I, Here am I; send me.*

~ Isaiah 6:8

# MY DELIVERANCE IS CONTINUOUS

*The Spirit of the Lord is upon me, because he hath anointed me to preach the gospel to the poor; he hath sent me to heal the brokenhearted, to preach deliverance to the captives, and recovering of sight to the blind, to set at liberty them that are bruised, To preach the acceptable year of the Lord.*

~ **Luke 4:18-19**

December 19, 2013

Revised October 9, 2020

**God is my ultimate teacher and guide!** He loves me enough to be relentless in His pursuit of me. Why? Because I AM His and He is mine. I AM fearfully and wonderfully made in His image. And He wants to make sure that I AM fully equipped to "not only" carry His torch in lighting the way through the darkness, but to be in a position to pass that torch along to others. So He takes such delicate care of His investment, His chosen vessel, as He leads me along the path of righteousness in leaving nothing to chance. He orchestrates or develops His plan for my life to include the importance of allowing the most intricate tests for my meticulous pruning. He knows my innermost thoughts, desires, and fears; He leaves nothing uncovered when it comes to my continuous deliverance.

*And it shall come to pass, that whosoever shall call on the name of the LORD shall be delivered: for in mount Zion and in Jerusalem shall be deliverance, as the LORD hath said, and in the remnant whom the LORD shall call.*

~ Joel 2:32

## DELIVERANCE

My conversations with God used to involve me asking Him, "Why have You allowed the trials and tribulations in my life to take place?" After recognizing the importance of those trials and tribulations for my good and His Glory, I moved on to asking Him to please put ample distance between me and each lesson before hitting me with another one so soon. But, I, who have never been a fan of controversy or confrontation of any kind, would often run to escape the inevitable, or I would quite simply keep turning the other cheek in doing and reluctantly agreeing with my adversary against my will. Especially, when you find yourself so often going above and beyond the call of duty to please others, only to be expected to give more of the same, unfairly as you drift further and further away from your goal or destiny! When you allow yourself to be pushed to the limit by others in giving them what they want, would you not expect them to do right by you? Not if no good thing exists within them to do the right thing in accordance to the condition of their heart! And yet, you keep putting your trust in man and giving him the benefit of the doubt, thus expecting him to bestow an honor of reward upon you. *For the LORD God is a sun and shield: the LORD will give grace and glory: no good thing will he withhold from them that walk uprightly* (Psalm 84:11). You just have to be willing to stay the course—no matter what! Therefore, running from your problems only intensifies the journey and prolongs you in receiving your "breakthrough." And, if your actions do not line up with your purpose *as ordained by God*, which is your reason for being, turning the other cheek and being amiable may not be an option for you! Not my will, but His will be done on Earth as it is in heaven.

> *For I know that in me (that is, in my flesh,)*
> *dwelleth no good thing: for to will is present with me;*
> *but [how] to perform that which is good I find not.*
>
> ~ Romans 7:18

Being a product of your upbringing speaks to you being conditioned by that which you have been exposed to within your environment: people, places, and things helped to dictate to your way of thinking. Be it right or wrong thinking, you have no reference of what that may be until your eyes and heart are open to hearing God. The more I thirst for God, the more is revealed to me about who I AM in comparison to who others think I should be. When you become more and more aware of truth in replacing what you thought you knew with what is, you become resistant to the false influences of others in the name of unmerited control as God starts to push you beyond your comfort zone. This process brings about controversy, which marks the beginning of your deliverance. However, you must be certain to consult with the *divine counselor (the Holy Spirit)* for confirmation of His direction even if it is unpleasant.

> *For men verily swear by the greater:*
> *and an oath for confirmation is to them an end of all strife.*
> *Wherein God, willing more abundantly to shew unto the*
> *heirs of promise the immutability of his counsel, confirmed*
> *it by an oath: That by two immutable things, in which it was*
> *impossible for God to lie, we might have a strong consolation,*
> *who have fled for refuge to lay hold upon the hope set before*
> *us: Which hope we have as an anchor of the soul, both sure*
> *and stedfast, and which entereth into that within the veil;*
> *whither the forerunner is for us entered, even Jesus, made*
> *an high priest for ever after the order of Melchisedec.*
>
> ~ Hebrews 6:16-20

## AUTHORITY

For quite some time now, I have had a constant struggle with the word "authority." Mainly because too often I have seen people in positions of leadership abuse their authority. I have even agonized about what to do when a person or persons in leadership roles deliberately give(s) me a command that falls outside of my character or the Will of God for my life. Not necessarily an order that takes me outside of my comfort zone, but falls outside of what I know to be right. In being told many times how important it is to honor authority, do I follow the lead of an immorally or politically incorrect delegated request? Will I be forgiven by God if that request falls outside of what I know is the opposite of what He expects of me, for the sake of "respecting authority"? How can I, then, honestly, serve two opposing masters or adhere to specific commands when one is truly contradictory of the other? As stated by Barbara Wentroble in her book *Praying with Authority*, "Authority has always been a subject of controversy in the universe!"

> *And without controversy great is the mystery of godliness:*
> *God was manifest in the flesh, justified in the Spirit,*
> *seen of angels, preached unto the Gentiles,*
> *believed on in the world, received up into glory.*
>
> ~ 1 Timothy 3:16

Amazingly, man will quickly appoint himself and others to positions of power that he is not worthy to uphold for the sake of prestige on the basis of favoritism, class, or an unrealized order of destructive structure and selfish gain. Until recently, I have learned to understand a position a person holds does not necessarily mean he or she is qualified to occupy the post to which he or she has been appointed. There is truly a difference between being appointed and anointed for a position. It took me a while to understand that although an individual may be elected and appointed to a particular position by man, they are not necessarily chosen and anointed by God to perform the task with ease! Contrary to popular belief, Christ was not a pushover. He knew His position and His rights and He governed Himself accordingly on seeking to fulfill His Father's business. My career or place in man's army is not as important as my purpose and position in God's Army. And through Him, I have been given dominion and authority to lead, do, and be. For it is He who has deemed me worthy and places the highest value on my life as He continues to deliver me and separate me from the unimportant things of the world (see 1 John 2:15-16 and 4:3-4) as I soar and thrive at obtaining spiritual maturity!

*Thou hast proved mine heart;*
*thou hast visited me in the night;*
*thou hast tried me, and shalt find nothing;*
*I am purposed that my mouth shall not transgress.*

~ Psalm 17:3

## A PROPHETIC MESSAGE

For some, our deliverance is instantaneous (immediate and all at once). And for others, our deliverance takes place over time in ensuring we reach our full destiny or potential to forever remember the journey of how far we have come. Each person's life plan (purpose and destiny) is different! We may not start from the same place and we may not end at the same time to reach the finish line together. It is even possible we may not head in the same direction. Our paths may intertwine or we may not meet at all! To some it may be easy and to others it may be hard, depending upon your will or determination to include your tolerance and endurance should you faint not or become weary. Nothing is done without rhyme or reason as purposed or allowed by God. To whom much is given, much is required!

> *But as for you, be strong and courageous,*
> *for your work will be rewarded.*
>
> ~ 2 Chronicles 15:7 NLT

# SOUL'D OUT

> *If any man serve me, let him follow me;
> and where I am, there shall also my servant be:
> if any man serve me, him will my Father honour.*
>
> ~ John 12:26

February 8, 2015

Revised February 28, 2015

Joyce Myers said it best when she stated, "We literally live in a war zone!" The world is truly engulfed in war, and there are battles happening all around us, everywhere we go. Matthew 24:6-8 (KJV) states, *And ye shall hear of wars and rumours of wars: see that ye be not troubled: for all these things must come to pass, but the end is not yet. For nation shall rise against nation, and kingdom against kingdom: and there shall be famines, and pestilences, and earthquakes, in divers places. All these are the beginning of sorrows.* Today, there are wars on the earth, wars in government, wars in developing countries, wars in the home, and wars on the job! There are attacks against your person (physical being) and your mind (mental psyche) affecting your way of life (socially, economically, financially, etc.); and, there are people attempting to control your idea of right and wrong just so they can feel in control and in charge. **Spiritual warfare is more real than you know, and it is definitely more serious than people are willing to admit!** That is why it is very important for you to make a conscious effort to choose who you will serve. And in doing so, your decision should not be made on the basis of following a fad or a person of human interest out of fear pertaining to their status, position, power, or level of authority! Unless you are entirely sure of the person's identity (character) to include where they are going! Even Paul recognized the importance and power of influence when he stated as referenced in 1 Corinthians 11:1 (paraphrased), follow me as I follow Christ or imitate me as I imitate Christ! Christ, the Messiah, is the operative objective and not just any man without a divine purpose and integrity! Matthew 6:24 (NIV) states, *No one can serve two masters. Either you will hate the one and love the other, or you will be devoted to the one and despise the other. You cannot serve both God and money.*

*My sheep hear my voice,*
*and I know them, and they follow me:*

~ John 10:27

Can you imagine being told by a supervisor that he or she did not think that "there was any room for God within a business or government office and people should not bring Him to work?" That we should leave Him at home? Nevertheless, is it not God who formed the light and created darkness, making peace [national well-being] and creating [physical] evil (calamity)? Is He not the Lord, who does all these things as referenced in Isaiah 45:7 AMPC (paraphrased) to include being the creator of government, heaven, and Earth?

Within my cubical at work, I have taken the liberty of surrounding myself with scriptures that speak directly to my heart. The entire Bible speaks to my heart, but I needed to post scriptures directed at projecting immediate reminders to stay focused and fixated on the Lord—no matter what! Scriptures packing an immediate blow to my conscious and subconscious mental layers to stay on track. Why? Because unfortunately, many people do not take God, the Father, and the Creator of the entire universe, seriously enough to view Him as being a real person. He is a tri-part being, fulfilling three different roles or functions all leading toward the same common objective. And man is a tri-part being, meaning we are (1) spirit first and foremost possessing a (2) soul inhabiting a (3) physical body! But God Himself is Omnipotent (all-ruling and almighty), Omnipresent (everywhere), and Omniscient (all knowing)! He is everywhere and nowhere all at the same time! He sits up high and looks down low upon all that is going on within the world, whether we choose to believe it or not. Amazingly, if He who is in me is greater than he who is in the world, then God is everywhere I am and it is important for me to stay connected to Him!

## LORD, I NEED MORE

God knew I needed to have my hope and faith restored. He knew I was near the end of my rope. He orchestrated a move on my life by blessing me with what I thought I wanted and needed the most: to return to employment with the federal government to make good on my plan to boost my career, with potential for growth, learning, and training opportunities! I mapped out a plan during a twenty-three-year hiatus (1985–2008) from the federal government while working various private-industry positions and returning to school to pursue an education in business management with an interest in human resources and employment/business law to meet my target objective. But, sometimes, there comes a point and time in our lives whereby we can do all we can to follow a plan we think would be instrumental in leading us toward our goal, only to be met by many obstacles and limitations intended to cripple us. You can either give in to it or you can make an attempt to rise above it!

We, unfortunately, live in a world fueled by chaos and human cruelty. People are running around like addicts chasing a feeling known as "more." But, ironically, more is never enough, and yet, more is pursued vigorously at the cost of selling our souls to the highest bidder. The more we attain, the more we want, and the more we attempt to appeal to the wants of our flesh as controlled by the thing (or entity) with the greatest influence. We are never satisfied but forever reaching, scratching, and clawing at that imaginary mark or measure of success we think will provide us with the greatest happiness. Some of us have actually reached that goal or plateau of wanton lust we have set for ourselves, only to find it still isn't enough to satisfy what we crave, or thought we wanted and needed to fulfill that blissful desire! So we keep looking around and searching unrealistically to feed our growing addiction while becoming more and more competitive in our approach to life as we trample and stampede over others to get it. Making comparisons of our life to others', we see an illusion of success and happiness on the outside in the name of false identity and material possessions unaware of the truth. On the surface, it looks good and inviting, thus leaving most of us reaching for things (idols of the world we put on a pedestal) while attempting to prove ourselves over and over again to impress others. At what cost? There is nothing wrong with being successful and happy with the right mindset and level of integrity in accordance to the Will of God! *Not that I have already obtained all this, or have already been made perfect, but I press on to take hold of that which Christ Jesus took hold of me* (Philippians 3:12 BSB).

Roadblocks can, unfortunately, impede our progress and threaten to open up our hearts to darkness, which grows with deep-rooted anger and resentment. Circumstances beyond our control as guided by others within our surroundings can impact our potential to move forward and get ahead. Starting to feel abandoned by God, I could not believe I was seeing and experiencing so much darkness. Darkness many people were expecting me to accept and to embrace because they themselves had done so. What I thought was not and could not be a real possibility for so many like-minded individuals to conform to became a reality. And they were trying to convince me of a majority rule. In fact, I once heard a coworker say, "if there are more people on the opposite side of your thinking and belief, then the side of those with the greater numbers is right and you must be wrong or the absolute problem." On the contrary, their way of thinking is faulty at best—a world view that's contributed by a world system operating outside of the Will of God to plant doubt and control! Therefore, you must be able and willing to think outside of the box in not allowing yourself to be influenced by darkness to encourage you to be led away from God or what He expects of you.

Finally, I was growing tired of going around in circles and making the same mistakes over and over again while being disappointed by man to let me move up or forward. For promotion and power come from nowhere on earth, but only from God. He promotes one and deposes another (Psalm 75:5-7 TLB). I needed more than surface enjoyment and happiness. I needed to understand what God was trying to get through to me. I needed to know the depth of my reason for being in this particular time zone at this particular time and precise season in my life. And He changes the times and the seasons; He removes kings and sets up kings. He gives wisdom to the wise and knowledge to those who have understanding (Daniel 2:21 AFV). I needed to fully grasp the understanding of God's knowledge to know where He was taking me and why. God, who is capable of putting an end to the nonsense, whose ways are not my ways, is able to use every obstacle, limitation, and roadblock for His glory and my good! *And we know that all things work together for good to them that love God, to them who are the called according to his purpose* (Romans 8:28). I needed to accept His truth for my life once and for all, thus allowing no compromise to intervene! *And this is life eternal, that they might know thee the only true God, and Jesus Christ, whom thou hast sent* (John 17:3).

## THE OVERALL BEAUTY OF IT ALL

For most of my childhood life, all I could think about was doing the right thing, getting a good education, graduating, choosing a career, and getting ahead in life. When one door closed in my face, I would spazz out a little, but I never gave up hope. I would simply retreat and devise another plan of action to achieve what I thought I wanted. I just never counted on having to encounter so much human cruelty along the way or feeling the need to be ruthless, cutthroat, and unkind to others to fit in as a testament to staying on the path I had chosen for myself. Nor did I feel the need to allow myself to be put in a box by those who did not understand me. But how bad did I want my idea of happiness, and why was it so difficult for me to reach what seemed to be so obtainable and close to the point of being taboo? It was more about will than anything else, a testament to my faith and belief in God!

God had a bigger plan and reason for directing me to the lion's den—a place He referred to as being the "Headquarters for Demonic Activity," where I would receive extensive training on the "battlefield" to force me to face all my fears for an expected end while gaining spiritual growth! I was being chosen and set apart by Him for Him! He was determined to separate the wheat from the tares (see Matthew 13:24-30) to show me who I am and what I was made of! He already knew because He created me; He just needed to convince me! So what better training ground to use as a lesson in spiritual warfare than such an overwhelming environment whereby God was forcing me to develop a backbone and stand up for myself and Him?

Imagine having to endure and conquer every situation that you had encountered in your life! Situations you despised, feared, possibly ran away from and avoided to include the bullies, the overbearing dictators, the oppressors, the naysayers, the chauvinistic sadistically racist and discriminative (prejudicial) behavioral patterns all on one playing field! And, having to reengage with those who take pleasure in standing on your neck to hold you at bay for no apparent reason other than because they can! The walking wounded believers and non-believers attempting to coexist while fighting to obtain more of the same!

Suddenly, I woke up to realize my perspective was all wrong! This world and all it has to offer is temporary. For our light affliction, which is but for a moment, worketh for us a far more exceeding and eternal weight of glory; While we look not at the things which are seen, but at the things which are not seen: for the things which are seen are temporal; but the things which are not seen are eternal (2 Corinthians 4:17-18). Can you see yourself shedding layer after layer like an onion, recognizing your true self and developing an entirely different outlook concerning (1) a want, (2) a need, and (3) just enough to being overly satisfied in Him with just enough? Putting God first above anything and everybody in reaching that sense of joy, peace, gratification, and happiness that no man can give or take from you feels good! *And fear not them which kill the body, but are not able to kill the soul: but rather fear him which is able to destroy both soul and body in hell* (Matthew 10:28).

*Answer this question: Does the God who lavishly provides you with his own presence, his Holy Spirit, working things in your lives you could never do for yourselves, does he do these things because of your strenuous moral striving or because you trust him to do them in you? Don't these things happen among you just as they happened with Abraham? He believed God, and that act of belief was turned into a life that was right with God.*

~ Galatians 3:5-6 MSG

## MIRACLES, SIGNS, AND WONDERS

Hollywood has tainted our view of the supernatural! Whenever something out of the ordinary that's unexplainable happens, we automatically start to link it or equate it to the workings of the devil or anything demonic. Yes, Satan is powerful; however, God is more powerful! *Thus says the Lord, In this you shall know, recognize,* and *understand that I am the Lord: behold, I will smite with the rod in my hand the waters in the [Nile] River, and they shall be turned to blood* (Exodus 7:17 AMPC). No one hardly ever discusses or testifies to experiencing "miracles, signs, or wonders." If more people were excited to get a visitation from the Lord and felt good about sharing those experiences with others, many people would believe in His existence. In addition to that, they would not think it was impossible to have a conversation with Him; actually, hear Him and talk to Him as in experiencing Him for themselves. In fact, I believe more people would praise Him and be overjoyed about worshiping Him. Did you know that many miracles have taken place during praise and worship? *And the Lord said to Moses, How long will this people provoke (spurn, despise) Me? And how long will it be before they believe Me [trusting in, relying on, clinging to Me], for all the signs which I have performed among them* (Numbers 14:11 AMPC)?

Prior to breaking my right leg on February 20, 2010, I had no idea as to the depth of the supernatural to come into the full understanding of God being real. On that cold morning approximately five years ago, I slipped on black ice in the alley behind my mother's house under her carport while attempting to shovel her snow and broke my leg in four places—not one, but four. It was as if I were a cartoon character and the ground was moving under me. My right leg snapped, and I was no longer able to support my weight as my left leg grew weak and gave out too. I went up in the air, and while coming down, I started to tense up and brace myself for the impact I knew I was going to feel from hitting the hard cement! But something else happened that day. While falling backward in a horizontal position, I felt myself being caught in midair. So there I was, levitating aboveground in shock while trying to make sense of what was happening. I felt as if I were a feather being gently handled and delicately placed on the ground on my right side. I did not feel the impact of the ground. I did not hit my head or my back. There was no excruciating, sharp-shooting pain. In fact, I lay there and started shouting and praising the Lord for loving me so much that He would send "angels" to catch me and to sustain me from my fall.

Yes, I can imagine what you are saying! She's making that up! That could not have possibly happened the way she makes it sound! Oh, but it did! And get this—had I hit that concrete, God told me I would have had to be fitted for a full body cast. So He spared me and showed me just how much I was worth to Him! Months before my fall, I was diagnosed with osteoporosis to the extent of having bones so brittle they were consistent with that of an eighty-year-old woman and not one who was forty-nine years old at the time of her fall. Many doubted I would ever be able to walk after that ordeal and rendered me useless. Those on my job even made a determination to attempt and suggest I be demoted or terminated on the basis of my injury. When a workhorse becomes lame, oftentimes, it is rendered useless and put to death!

As time went on and I began to improve, I wondered if I would be able to walk without a cane. My recovery has been a very long one, and although there is not a day that goes by that I am not experiencing some type of pain to my bones or joints, I am forever grateful to a God who would allow me to truly experience His existence in more ways than one. And He continues to enlighten me by allowing me to see myself through His eyes. I was shown these things so I would know that the Lord is God and that there is no other (see Deuteronomy 4:35). No matter what the task or the assignment, I owe Him everything that I am. My life is not my own; it belongs to Him! And I am overjoyed to be of service to Him!

I can honestly say, I never knew it was possible to love the Lord as much as I do. I never knew it was possible to be this *SOUL'D OUT for Him*! I am grateful to God for who He is and how He has touched my life. I never imagined getting to this point in my life whereby I would be consumed by everything

He is to be delivered from people! *For Him I live and for Him I die!* He is the only person in my life I can count on to tell me the truth and lead me through the darkness on a tightrope to bring me *safely* to the other side of light. I needed to see the Lord and to experience Him for myself to move to the next level. I needed to connect with other born-again believers (Christians) and be in the company of those who loved God with an intensity of true belief. I needed to know it was not impossible to have a mountaintop experience like Moses. I just did not know quite what to expect when I knocked on the doors of Heaven. But God, answering my request, has graciously obliged me, and He keeps on ministering His presence in confirming and declaring His miracles, signs, and wonders like never before.

How can I not be *SOUL'D OUT for Him*? That which I thought was real is not and that which I thought was not is indeed real!

# IN THE WORLD, BUT NOT OF THE WORLD!

*They are not of the world,*
*even as I am not of the world.*

~ **JOHN 17:16**

October 6, 2015

Revised October 7, 2015

There is a very good reason why we are instructed not to look to the left or to the right! In fact, Proverbs 4:23-27 from the Message Bible states, *Keep vigilant watch over your heart; that's where life starts. Don't talk out of both sides of your mouth; avoid careless banter, white lies, and gossip. Keep your eyes straight ahead; ignore all sideshow distractions. Watch your step, and the road will stretch out smooth before you. Look neither right nor left; leave evil in the dust.* In the world, we are surrounded by a number of possible distractions that are intended to derail us from our purpose. And, if you have taken the time to read and study the Bible, it gives you great insight into the war that began in heaven. Lucifer—whose name means "morning star," shining one, light bearer, and son of the dawn—was God's right hand. He, like all the angels, was created by God to include all living things in and outside of the universe. Lucifer and his minions challenged God's position, authority, and His love for mankind, so they were tossed out of heaven, exiled, and fell to Earth where they wreak the most havoc! Have you not heard it said many times before: "Earth is the devil's playground"? Meaning people here on Earth are influenced primarily by God's adversary more than they are by God Himself—unfortunately.

On another note, do you recall learning about something called Maslow's hierarchy of needs?[34] Have you ever considered how it applies to your life or to someone else's? For instance, what motivates you? I mean, really motivates you enough to compel you to go the distance to achieve your desires, good or bad? Is it the need to feel successful, important, and accomplished? What does success or being accomplished mean to you? And what are you willing to do to obtain that success? Are you willing to sell your soul to obtain it? Once you achieve what you think you want, will it be enough to truly make you happy?

People have a tendency to talk a good game at attempting to prove what they know or believe to others, but it is more for their own benefit as opposed to those around them. Otherwise, they would do more to consider the consequences of their actions! We live in a world full of the walking wounded, people who are

---

34   www.thoughtco.com/maslows-hierarchy-of-needs-4582571

trying to find their way. Each person with his or her own agenda attempting to fulfill selfish desires. Some are more desperate than others to carve out a perfect place in which to dwell and exist. *While I was with them, I was keeping them in Your name which You have given Me; and I guarded them* and *protected them, and not one of them was lost except the son of destruction, so that the Scripture would be fulfilled* (John 17:12 AMP).

Abraham Maslow[35] introduced his theory in a paper he wrote in 1943 discussing man's motivation and innate behavioral patterns driving individual wants and needs. Maslow used the terms or categories to identify and distinguish between the more extreme to the basic needs of an individual: physiological, safety, belongingness and love, esteem, and self-actualization. People can easily be influenced, controlled, and misled by certain incentives. And, for that reason alone, we should attempt to keep our focus at all times on the Lord to include meditating on His Word, morning, noon, and night. *This book of the law shall not depart out of thy mouth; but thou shalt meditate therein day and night, that thou mayest observe to do according to all that is written therein: for then thou shalt make thy way prosperous, and then thou shalt have good success* (Joshua 1:8).

When a tragedy, like the recent Oregon shooting, happens, we do not take the necessary time to consider all impacted parties to include the antagonist (shooter) and the protagonist (victims). Yes, we are always inclined to be sympathetic to the victims, but we rarely sympathize with the antagonist. Well, yesterday

---

35  www.verywellmind.com/what-is-maslows-hierarchy-of-needs-4136760

evening, upon sitting down to watch television, I flipped through the channels and stumbled across the plea of a father, Ian Mercer, who lost a son, Christopher Harper-Mercer, the shooter. In my opinion, Mr. Mercer lost his son to darkness long before this ordeal; however, he wanted nothing more than to apologize to the world for his son's actions in an attempt to share some insight into his son's life to the best of his understanding.

On the channel I was watching, before the father could state his point, the focus was rather abruptly interrupted and redirected to the commentator who very rudely and with anger in his voice, I might add, criticized the father's love for his son. Can you imagine God's love for us when we repeatedly reject Him time and time again? No matter what, He loves us unconditionally! He does not condemn us and forever leaves the door open for us to return home to Him should we have a change of heart to do so. That is an ultimate example of a gracious and loving father (abba, daddy)! *Beloved, let us love one another: for love is of God; and every one that loveth is born of God, and knoweth God. He that loveth not knoweth not God; for God is love. In this was manifested the love of God toward us, because that God sent his only begotten Son into the world, that we might live through him. Herein is love, not that we loved God, but that he loved us, and sent his Son to be the propitiation for our sins* (1 John 4:7-10).

No, I am not dismissing the actions of the shooter, nor am I overlooking the many who lost their lives during this very senseless killing spree! I am sure, without a doubt, that this young man's life will be turned upside down as many attempt to show how mentally disturbed, confused, evil, and wicked he was to have committed such an unspeakable act. But no one will attempt to explore the root cause of his pain, which triggered such dis-ease to his spirit! Why do I care? *Behold, what manner of love the Father hath bestowed upon us, that we should be called the sons of God: therefore the world knoweth us not, because it knew him not* (1 John 3:1). Because God put him and many others like him on my heart! As I attempted to watch the father to hear his partial presentation, my heart ached and I cried out in agony while clutching at my heart and stomach. There I was in the middle of my living room, yelling and screaming at the top of my lungs while asking God, *why?* Although we are born sinners, we are not born damaged or broken into a world that wishes to consume us. We were innocent until we were corrupted, mistreated, and abused by those who want to silence us. So I have been tasked with a purpose to speak up and out as directed by God to expose injustices in the world. I have been given a platform to speak for those who cannot or are not willing to speak for themselves. I have been allowed to experience great pain and to express that pain explicitly through my testimonies as a vehicle for reaching and connecting with others who are no stranger to pain. With that said, we do not know Christopher Harper-Mercer's story—the complete unadulterated truth—and we probably never will, but God knows the entire truth!

The media often jumps to conclusions to report the news to profit, to boost the ratings, and to set up careers. If you were to compare the information presented by various sources all being broadcast at the same time, you would notice many discrepancies and half-truths. Data is collected, and facts are gathered, but the truth is rarely shared! For instance, we heard this young man was specifically targeting Christians or believers—but once the smoke cleared and witnesses were actually interviewed or questioned, some of them stated he was targeting everybody. Some things are specifically reported or referenced with the hope of influencing a directed result or outcome, such as fear.

How many remember when the *Washington Star*, which was in opposition to the *Washington Post*? Well, consider the tone of the two in how they were different. One was more bias toward the Democratic Party, and the other is more bias toward the Republican Party, while CNN was noted for investigative reporting that gives greater insight into the facts without trying to sway the reader's thoughts or mindsets. I am more interested in knowing what was in the letter that was written by Christopher Harper-Mercer to the police! However, unless I am able to review the letter for myself to know it is the actual product and language as written by Christopher in his own handwriting, we may never know if the contents of the letter are the true version (when and if it is released to or shared with the public). That's why I am most grateful and thankful to Jesus Christ for the Holy Spirit. If we are quick to hear and slow to speak, God often reveals what is hidden through the "Gifts of the Holy Spirit."

> *Understand this, my beloved brothers and sisters. Let everyone be quick to hear [be a careful, thoughtful listener], slow to speak [a speaker of carefully chosen words and], slow to anger [patient, reflective, forgiving]; for the [resentful, deep-seated] anger of man does not produce the righteousness of God [that standard of behavior which He requires from us]. So get rid of all uncleanness and all that remains of wickedness, and with*

*a humble spirit receive the Word [of God] which is implanted [actually rooted in your heart], which is able to save your souls. But prove yourselves doers of the word [actively and continually obeying God's precepts], and not merely listeners [who hear the word but fail to internalize its meaning], deluding yourselves [by unsound reasoning contrary to the truth]. For if anyone only listens to the word without obeying it, he is like a man who looks very carefully at his natural face in a mirror; for once he has looked at himself and gone away, he immediately forgets what he looked like. But he who looks carefully into the perfect law, the law of liberty, and faithfully abides by it, not having become a [careless] listener who forgets but an active doer [who obeys], he will be blessed and favored by God in what he does [in his life of obedience].*

~ James 1:19-25 AMP

When we are hurting, we normally attempt to seek refuge or solace from those we think would be the most understanding or likely candidates to help and save us from our troubles! We are not expecting them to be wolves disguised as sheep who take pleasure in inflicting more pain upon us. Can you imagine finding yourself in a compromising position and feeling helpless or at the mercy of others while your dignity and self-respect are being attacked or stripped away? Do you know what that feels like, to be powerless and holding on for dear life? Upon incurring scars or wounds as casualties of war, the majority of us are not equipped to handle the trauma. We are not familiar with how to address the actions (cruelty) of others as directed toward us at the onset of every incident or inflicted injury to our self-esteem. In fact, society has been more apt in teaching us how to sweep the many offenses against us under the rug (out of sight or out of mind) to forget or pretend that nothing ever happened.

For the most part, those who have been mistreated, abused, or victimized by others have been manipulated into believing that the act of injustice done to them was and is their fault. That, unfortunately, creates a greater impact on the mental psyche while giving the aggressor more control over us and an opportunity for them to continue to do more damage. When this happens, something on the inside breaks, as we die slowly, sinking deeper into the darkness. Our mind does not quietly convert inwardly all at once. No, it happens gradually as we seek avenues for coping with our issues while attempting to simply forget until it becomes unbearable or impossible to push the pain aside anymore. We may even seek to numb our pain by becoming addicts in substituting one problem for another, thus doing more harm to ourselves until we leave this earth or snap and take others into the darkness with us (a permanent death). And then there are others, like me, who lose their focus from time to time but never completely reach the edge of no return while being determined to stay afloat and fight the good fight of faith in knowing and developing a relationship with God. *Thus says the LORD: "Cursed is the man who trusts in man And makes flesh his strength, Whose heart departs from the LORD"* (Jeremiah 17:5 NKJV). Not overnight, but as part of a beneficial process, the closer I allowed myself to get to God, the healthier I become in standing my ground and leaning on the LORD to get me through it all! Today, my focus is different, and I have shifted my way of thinking in an attempt to put God first in my life above my wants and needs. *Beloved, I wish above all things that thou mayest prosper and be in health, even as thy soul prospereth* (3 John 1:2).

In the words of Plumb,[36] from a song called "Lord, I'm ready now!": *I just let go and I feel exposed, but it's so beautiful. "Cause this is who I am!* **I've been such a mess!** *Now I can't care less. I could bleed to death. Lord, I'm ready now. All the walls are down. Time is running out and I wanna make this count. I ran away from you and I did what I wanted to, but I don't want to let you down. Lord, I'm ready now! Lord, I'm ready now.* **I was so caught up in who I'm not!** *Can you please forgive me? I've nothing left to hide. No! No reasons left to lie. Give me another chance. Lord, I'm ready now!* (emphasis added)

---

36  See https://youtu.be/EWN3GDuAMM4 and https://youtu.be/nAsTi8kS2SQ

# THE FINAL AUTHORITY

*And Jesus came and spake unto them,
saying, All power is given unto me in heaven and in earth.*

**~ Matthew 28:18**

February 12, 2017

What I cannot do and refuse to do as instructed by God is to allow myself to get into a dispute with anyone about what God has shared with me. I may attempt to offer more clarity or teaching as directed by God for a greater understanding, but I have also been cautioned by Him not to take the word of anyone else's above what He has already stated to me. I must, however, be open to receiving what He has shared with others to bring confirmation in complementing what He has already spoken to me.

Each person is entitled to his or her opinion, but God's Word is truth and God is Spirit! When He gives us revelation, we should wait until He gives us permission to share it with others. And when we have been released to share that information, it should not be based on our own understanding, but with the mind of Christ from a spiritual perspective. Why? Because there are very distinctive differences between religion, spiritualism, and politics.

When we consider the things of God, we must view the Bible and its content from a place of spirit and truth—outside, above, and beyond our fleshy perspective. The Bible references history: the past, present, and future! We must be willing to receive revelation and interpret it in accordance to God's ways to apply it to our everyday life: past, present, and future. Break it down and dissect it in accordance to the Word of God. Not through your own eyes or heart wiring!

As mentioned above, the Bible is full of history and discloses a great deal of symbolism and parables. God reminded me, sometime ago, that history often has a way of repeating itself. The players are different, but the objective and influence are always the same. They are just packaged differently to throw us off and distract us from the obvious. We keep trying to see it in the natural when we need to use our spiritual eyes. Yes, I know I'm being a little redundant, but I want to emphasize a point. You cannot put God in a box!

*But the Advocate, the Holy Spirit,*
*whom the Father will send in my name,*
*will teach you all things and remind you*
*of everything I have said to you.*

~ John 14:26 NIV

Over a period of **three days**, I had the pleasure of conversing with four sisters in Christ (Mary Bryant, Annette Spivey, Felisha Yancy, and Karyn Collins) concerning the things of God with such intensity and revelation, which they extended to me. Those conversations helped to bring remembrance, confirmation (reinforcement), and introduction as ordained by God. So what am I attempting to point out here? Over a period of three days, the Father, the Son, and the Holy Spirit took part in this discussion to authorize the impartation of what was shared with me!

*Now when Jesus went into the region of Caesarea Philippi, He asked His disciples, "Who do people say that the Son of Man is?" And they answered, "Some say John the Baptist; others, Elijah; and still others, Jeremiah, or [just] one of the prophets." He said to them, "But who do you say that I am?" Simon Peter replied, "You are the Christ (the Messiah, the Anointed), the Son of the living God." Then Jesus answered him, "Blessed [happy, spiritually secure, favored by God] are you, Simon son of Jonah, because flesh and blood (mortal man) did not reveal this to you, but My Father who is in heaven."*

~ Matthew 16:13-17 AMP

Before the title of "president" was used by man to signify the head of government or a nation, there were the words "king" and "pharaoh." In England, the terms "queen," "king," "prince," and "princess" are still being used. But none of those titles is higher than the God I serve, which reinforces to me that **God is second to no one**, regardless of man's position or title of prestige in the earth. So, no matter what it looks like, we must not lose hope or forget who sits on the throne! Take a look at the below information and tell me what sticks out to you: a leader or ruler in ancient Egypt had to be diverse in both religious and political matters. Interesting! Now tell me what religion or being religious denotes to you? When I think of religion, I think of dogma!

> ***Pharaoh*:** a ruler in ancient Egypt, believed to have had the responsibility to lead Egypt in **both religious and political matters.** These dual roles came with distinct titles: "High Priest of Every Temple" and the "Lord of the Two Lands."[37]
>
> The word "pharaoh" is the **Greek** form of the **Egyptian** *pero* or *per-a-a*, which was the designation for the royal residence and means "Great House." The name of the residence became associated with the ruler and, in time, was used exclusively for the leader of the people.[38]
>
> ***Dogma*:**[39] a point of view or tenet put forth as authoritative **without adequate grounds**; something held as an established **opinion.**

---

[37] www.historyhit.com/facts-about-the-pharaohs-of-ancient-egypt/
[38] www.ancient.eu/pharaoh/
[39] www.merriam-webster.com/dictionary/dogma

# A MICROWAVE SOCIETY

May 30, 2017

My mother had a total of five children, and five symbolizes grace. She had two before she met and married my father, and then there were three others to include me. Although my oldest brother and sister were raised by my grandparents in North Carolina, my mother always wanted us to get along and be a family. But as dysfunctional families go, our union wasn't as close as my mother would have liked or hoped. So as the oldest of the three growing up here in the DC area, I didn't really have anyone nearby that I looked up to for guidance or to confide in—even when it came to needing help with homework assignments. And, for other reasons, I regret not having that closeness with my siblings.

If I asked my mother how to spell something, she would always tell me to look it up. I used to get really mad about that and would say often, under my breath, how can I look something up in the dictionary if I don't know how to spell it? And if I ever ran into an issue with a math problem, she would always tell me to read the book. If I said I did, she would simply tell me to read it again until I was able to figure out the solution for myself. There were times when she wasn't around and I would, in secret, have a hissy fit and throw my book or my homework assignment across the room out of frustration. Then, I would hear her say, in the back of my mind, look it up and read it again. I would regain my composure, walk across the room, and pick up my papers and book to begin again.

As time went on, I developed patience for figuring out things on my own and I became very good at completing my homework assignments, including any math problem directed at me, and graduated with honors. There were times when I was the only student in the classroom who had completed the assignment, and I was asked to either help tutor or go to the front to put the answers on the board. I guess you can imagine what that did for my friendships: I didn't have many!

Today, I am so grateful to my mother for her persistence in pushing me to strive and assert myself when it came to research, knowledge, and education. She taught me to never give up or to give in! She taught me how I should approach situations and to never look to others to give me the answers. In addition, she always told me to never expect others to do for me what I should or could do for myself. She also told me to never outstay my welcome or go where I wasn't wanted. So I learned quickly what it was to be independent and alone. I wasn't necessarily lonely; I was appreciative of not needing to be liked, of not needing to follow a crowd or get attention. I simply buried my head in books as a way of escape when I wasn't running off to a friend's house to get away.

In valuing that approach, I seem to have no patience for those who have adapted under the influence of our current culture, which I view as a microwave society. The first microwave was the invention or concept of an engineer named Dr. Percy LeBaron Spencer in 1946 during the time he was employed by Raytheon.[40] It was said his discovery was made when he was experimenting with a form of energy referred to as magnetrons (a.k.a. radiation) used to heat or cook food in less time. In fact, we have grown accustomed to receiving things (answers) in less time without putting forth any time or energy on our own.

Technology such as microwaves, cell phones, calculators, and computers has made us all lazy. Some of us don't even want to take the necessary time to read for ourselves to comprehend a thought or instructions. We have lost our sense of intelligence for being able to identify the main subject and verb in a sentence (the structure of a sentence)! Instead of analyzing one sentence, line by line, at a time for a greater understanding of the content, we run everything together while reading and equate it to the writer lacking the ability to communicate. Drifting backward, we rather have others read for us and then explain it to us while we insist on disputing the information. And yet, we complain about others coming to this country, the United States, who lack an understanding of the English language to be able to read it, write it, or speak it. And what does that make us? Arrogant, hypocrites, or both!

Within the past six months, it has been confirmed to me that our ability to get selected for certain positions has less to

---

40  www.famousinventors.org/percy-spencer

do with our education and knowledge, but more to do with our reputation and association to others. You don't have to take my word for it; just open your eyes to review the evidence that is all around us. There's a growing pattern of ignorance across our nation, and these are the folks we are selecting as our leadership.

**Side note:** How is it possible for an individual to body slam another (bodily harm), get charged for it, and still get elected to a position in the Senate?

**Always remember:** No matter how gloomy things may seem on the surface, there is one who sits up high and looks down below. He sees everything and knows all things! If we abide in Him, He will abide in us. And, you best believe, He is working it all out behind the scenes. Just trust and believe. Read Romans 8:28!

# THE KEY TO HEALING IS FORGIVENESS

*Whenever you stand praying,
if you have anything against anyone,
forgive him [drop the issue, let it go], so that your
Father who is in heaven will also forgive you your
transgressions and wrongdoings [against Him and
others]. ["But if you do not forgive, neither will your
Father in heaven forgive your transgressions."]*

~ **Mark 11:25-26 AMP**

June 9, 2017

Finalized June 12, 2017

Sometime ago, God attempted to teach me that there is a very strong connection between our sin nature—in accordance to the issues of our heart—and our health. But, at the time, I had a difficult time grasping the understanding of what He was trying to tell me until He took my mother home to be with Him.

Sickness is not of God! Sickness and illness are brought on ourselves by our actions based on the choices we make. Said differently, the exercising of our free will concerning how we conduct our lives and give no thought to the consequences of our actions has a great impact on our health, whether we believe it or not. My mother endured a lot of heartache in her lifetime. Like many of us from time to time, she internalized her hurt and pain by holding on to unforgiveness! We, unfortunately, don't realize how unforgiveness opens up a doorway to darkness in giving the enemy permission to attach itself to us to wreak more damage and harm—spiritually, mentally (emotionally), and physically. My mother was attacked by cancer from the inside out. Unforgiveness is like that cancer; and if we don't learn to let go of all the animosity to allow the peace of God to take over, unforgiveness will eat us alive. It is not as important for you to forget the offenses imposed upon you as it is to forgive those who have trespassed against you to be free. Always remember, there are different types of healing. My mother was not healed of her physical cancer, but I can—without any doubt—say she was healed spiritually and emotionally before her spirit left her body.

Directed to the teaching of Dennis and Jen Clark, Releasing the Healer Within, I learned that "**the doorway to the Heart is through the gut!** The gut is the seat of every emotion, and every thought has a corresponding emotion." Your thoughts and your emotions generate energy, and every emotion is linked to an internal and outward expression of that energy, good or bad!

Just as life (blessings) or death (curses) is in the power of the tongue, your emotions dictate, for the most part, what comes out of your mouth on the basis of or influence of your feelings! In other words, your feelings, which are representative of your emotions, are generated by your thoughts. That's why it is important for us to guard our tongue and to be mindful not to speak from the direction of our emotions, especially when we are angry. You cannot easily take back something you have done or said to impose or inflict harm upon another, whether intentional or unintentional! The opposite would be getting caught up in the moment (in the heat of passion) and telling someone "I love you" when you don't mean it. More importantly, we should always be mindful of what type of energy we put out into the universe because we reap what we sow now or later, even down to three or four generations. Put another way, what goes around comes around, or in one word, karma! So what legacy are you leaving? Blesses or curses (sickness and illness)?

Have you ever noted how your emotions affect your behavior to consider the effect those same emotions may have on your health? How often have you heard the following?

1. Laughter is good for the soul.

2. I have to laugh to keep from crying.

3. If I didn't tell you how I was truly feeling, you wouldn't be able to tell by my behavior.

Some of us have gotten extremely good at masking our feelings, but on the inside, we are truly dying and killing ourselves slowly by internalizing every offense. For instance, holding unforgiveness in your heart can be very toxic to your well-being; it opens a doorway to darkness, which is connected to a legion of harmful spirits. And those spirits are released to kill, steal, and destroy your joy, peace, and happiness in any and every way imaginable!

Let me leave you with this: what is the leading cause of ulcers besides overindulgence or gluttony? Stress, worriation, and anxiety! *"Therefore I tell you, do not worry about your life, what you will eat or drink; or about your body, what you will wear. Is not life more than food, and the body more than clothes? Look at the birds of the air; they do not sow or reap or store away in barns, and yet your heavenly Father feeds them. Are you not much more valuable than they? Can any one of you by worrying add a single hour to your life? "And why do you worry about clothes? See how the flowers of the field grow. They do not labor or spin. Yet I tell you that not even Solomon in all his splendor was dressed like one of these. If that is how God clothes the grass of the field, which is here today and tomorrow is thrown into the fire, will he not much more clothe you—you of little faith? So do not worry, saying, 'What shall we eat?' or 'What shall we drink?' or 'What shall we wear?' For the pagans run after all these things, and your heavenly Father knows that you need them. But seek first his kingdom and his righteousness, and all these things will be given to you as well. Therefore do not worry about tomorrow, for tomorrow will worry about itself. Each day has enough trouble of its own"* (Matthew 6:25-34 NIV).

## REFERENCES

> Proverbs 18:21 ~ *Death and life are in the power of the tongue: and they that love it shall eat the fruit thereof.*

> Matthew 15:18-20 ~ *But those things which proceed out of the mouth come forth from the heart; and they defile*

*the man. For out of the heart proceed evil thoughts, murders, adulteries, fornications, thefts, false witness, blasphemies: These are the things which defile a man: but to eat with unwashen hands defileth not a man.*

- Generational Curses: Exodus 20:5, 34:7, Numbers 14:18, and Deuteronomy 5:9

- *Releasing the Divine Healer Within: The Biology of Belief and Healing* (see https://forgive123.com/shop/Releasing-the-Divine-Healer-Within-The-Biology-of-Belief-and-Healing-Intensive-11-CD-Training-Course-p179848536)

# IN THIS SEASON, TRUST AND BELIEF IN GOD ARE VITAL

*There is a time for everything, and
a season for every activity under the heavens.*

~ **Ecclesiastes 3:1 NIV**

July 17, 2017

To quote the upcoming *Emoji Movie*, "discovering who you are is an adventure beyond words!" But in this season and moving forward, unlike any of the previous seasons, there is going to be a tug, a pushing away, a tearing away, and a stripping away (as in Matthew 13:24-30), which will determine who you are for sure! When temptation comes knocking and you are finally given the opportunity to obtain your deepest desire, will you hesitate to consider the source and the consequences of your acceptance? *Blessed is a man who perseveres under trial; for once he has been approved, he will receive the crown of life which the Lord has promised to those who love Him* (James 1:12 NASB).

In the midst of your greatest storm, will you turn your back on God? Will you stand your ground, run and hide, or abandon the ship when faced with your greatest fear? Will you stand strong and firm or quiver and give up? Will you be a Judas?

Do you know what it is to be so close to the edge to feel yourself about to topple over? Have you been there? Well, I have been there many times, and each experience has been more and more intense! It has been an extreme battle to fight or to know when to simply step away or to back up and regain my focus! But you must have an open mind to discern with your heart while allowing yourself to be guided by your spirit to receive your elevation from the Lord. *For since He Himself was tempted in that which He has suffered, He is able to come to the aid of those who are tempted* (Hebrews 2:18 NASB).

Please keep in mind, your elevation or promotion comes from the Lord, not from man, and there is a difference. Each level of elevation also takes you deeper into your purpose for being, and it is in divine alignment with your destiny in comparison to Jeremiah 29:11. When you are well on your way to fulfilling your destiny, the enemy is annoyed and he will attempt to do everything possible to trip you up! *These trials will show that your faith is genuine. It is being tested as fire tests and purifies gold—though your faith is far more precious than mere gold. So when your faith remains strong through many trials, it will bring you much praise and glory and honor on the day when Jesus Christ is revealed to the whole world* (1 Peter 1:7 NLT).

Now, this is important, so pay attention! In addition, just as you get closer and deeper in the Lord (seeking His face and all His righteousness), you find yourself being deeply immersed in the center of the battlefield, in the enemy's camp; therefore, I must emphasize, again, how important it is for you to know and recognize who you are, whose YOU are, where you are, and when you need to pull back to retreat and re-strategize. Notice I didn't say give up or give in! I'm talking about knowing when you need to go back to the well to draw from the living water! I'm talking about refilling and refueling to recharge those drained cells to regain your focus and retreat like David did for a greater perspective of the mission at hand! I'm talking about not giving the opposition any ammunition in your weakened and possibly vulnerable state to use against you, but letting him know that you are a victorious opponent and the battle has already been won by the One who came before you. And you have to believe it yourself deep down in your heart because He said He would never leave you nor forsake you! He himself overcame the world, so you can too, if you are willing to follow His lead and don't cave.

In the early morning of Saturday, July 15, at approximately 8:30 a.m., I was toggling back and forth between 104.1 FM and 105.1 FM to listen to various pastors confirming the above, to include what's happening in this season of challenges and testing. This is a season of intense pressure to see if you will crumble. I don't know about you, but when I find myself down in the trenches—in the middle of the weeds amongst the muck and miry clay—I need to be encouraged. If need be, I need to talk myself through the process to encourage myself.

The next day, Sunday, July 16, while visiting St. Mark's Baptist Church on Underwood Street in the NW part of Washington, DC, I need to know that if He pulled me out of the muck once, would He do it again! I need to feel empowered and strengthened to stand my ground while knowing, He who is within me is far greater than he who is in the world. I need to remember that although I am in the world, I am not of the world and I must not conform to the ways of this world. As a matter of fact, I need to let that mind which is in Christ also be in me as I renew my mind to transform my way of thinking. I'm getting closer to my breakthrough, and the closer I get, the greater the test or the trials that come to correct and perfect! Be forever always ready!

*For we do not have a high priest*
*who cannot sympathize with our weaknesses,*
*but One who has been tempted in all things as we are,*
*yet without sin. Therefore let us draw near with confidence*
*to the throne of grace, so that we may receive mercy*
*and find grace to help in time of need.*

~ Hebrews 4:15-16 NASB

# SUPERNATURAL MANIFESTATION DEFEATING FLESH

*Because of your partnership in the gospel
from the first day until now,
being confident of this, that he who began a good
work in you will carry it on to completion
until the day of Christ Jesus.*

**~ Philippians 1:5-6 NIV**

July 24, 2017

Many days and nights, I cried out to God about the hurting souls, the sick and the walking dead in the world. All the iniquity and the lack of humanity breaks my heart! I find it hard to accept how easy it is for brethren to dwell in the house of the Lord together while professing to be Christians one minute—and, in the next minute, we turn on one another for self-gratification of our flesh just to chase after a false sense of control and a little bit of meaningless success. I wanted, so desperately, to know why the churches weren't doing more to teach, educate, and provide healing and deliverance in the name of Jesus Christ. I kept hearing and repeating the last conversations Christ had with His disciples when He attempted to prepare them for His death, burial, and resurrection. *Jesus said, "I am with you for only a short time, and then I am going to the one who sent me* (John 7:33 NIV). *I came from the Father and entered the world; now I am leaving the world and going back to the Father* (John 16:28 NIV). With tears in my eyes, disappointment and a little anger in my voice, I would consult with God about the lack of miracles, signs, and wonders being performed and shared by those who proclaimed to love Him. Why aren't people sharing their testimonies or the good news of Jesus Christ?

One day, God answered me and said, "What about you?" And I said, "What about me? **Who am I?**" From that day on, I decided to concern myself less and less about what others were or were not doing to focus more on telling folks about a man who is like no other! I wanted to yell from the rooftops about a God who indulges me as He reveals His truth and my destiny according to His will. A man who gives me a voice and a platform to speak and write! A man who still performs miracles and uses willing participants (yielded vessels) for greater works. *Verily, verily, I say unto you, He that believeth on me, the works that I do shall he do also; and greater works than these shall he do; because I go unto my Father* (John 14:12).

He pushes me to see myself through His eyes to build me up. He gives me visions and dreams to develop my faith. He lets me know, often, just how much I am loved by Him! He has unleashed a joy and confidence within me that I had no idea was possible! The more man attempts to brainwash me into believing the worst about myself, the more God convinces me that their approval of me is unimportant. *Thus says the Lord, "Cursed is the man who trusts in and relies on mankind, Making [weak, faulty human] flesh his strength, And whose mind and heart turn away from the Lord* (Jeremiah 17:5 AMP). For it is He who confirms me and shows me just how special I am to Him as well as who I am! So every opportunity I get, I sing His praises, I share and spread the Gospel—no matter what! And, it is my commitment to honor Him by seeking Him above all else to include His righteousness in learning His ways!

Because I, unfortunately, need to see for myself what needs to be seen to be compelled to switch gears, God continues to open my eyes by introducing me to and connecting me with His children who walk and live in the supernatural. On Thursday night at the Arc of Safety, I met *"blind Bartimaeus, the son of Timaeus."* I'm sure you are reading this and asking, "How could that be?" Well, Reverend Dr. Senator C. Anthony Muse apparently received a vision, which led to the bringing together of those who not only believe in that same vision, but they walk in the supernatural as witnesses and *glory containers*. I, unfortunately, missed Wednesday night when a very good authority said she saw the manifestation of raindrops falling on her and someone else minutes before Paul Morton started singing "Open the Floodgates of Heaven and Let it Rain." Oh, how I wished I could have been there to see and receive that blessing! But, I was there the next day and the day after to see and witness what God had for me, the **doubting Thomas**. Speaking to Thomas, *Jesus* *said, "So, you believe because you've seen with your own eyes. Even better blessings are in store for those who believe without seeing"* (John 20:29 MSG).

The second night, Bishop Norman E. Hutchins Sr. spoke about losing his sight as a result of diabetes, which left him blind for five months; the number 5 represents grace. Like many of us, Bishop Hutchins almost lost his confidence, but only for a very short while! He called a friend for sympathy, but that friend led him back to God for encouragement. Thereafter, not once did he stop preaching or believing in God! Similar to JOB, he held on, and one Sunday in the middle of his sermon, his sight was restored. Still battling diabetes, he needed a kidney transplant and flatlined after surgery. That was in 2014, but God revived him, and today he is a walking miracle. On the third night, Bishop Muse himself gave a phenomenal word titled, Who Killed the Church? Oh, my goodness! How can the church cast out demons, heal the sick (mentally, physically, and spiritually), and deliver and set the captives free if it is dead? As referenced by Bishop Muse, just existing with no power to be a witness to witness to others is death in itself! God brought me to Heavens Best Healing and Deliverance Church. Then He brought me to More Than Conquerors, The City of Praise, and The Arc of Safety for a demonstration. So I cannot allow myself to be silent. I cannot allow fear to grip me! I cannot deny the power of Jesus Christ whose DNA flows through me! When will I have seen enough to act and do? When will we step up to do more as a body of Christ?

It is time for us to move out and take our rightful places! God is raising up an army of the undead and endearing. A body of children who know what is truly meant by *Am I Thy Brother's Keeper*! I am ready Lord! Please continue to teach me! Enlarge my territory and send me!! I'll go! Isaiah's Commission: *Then I heard the voice of the Lord, saying, "Whom shall I send, and who will go for Us?" Then I said, "Here am I. Send me!"* (Isaiah 6:8 NASB)

# THE UNPARALLELED STATE OF OUR RACE

*So God created mankind in his own image,
in the image of God he created them;
male and female he created them.*

**~ Genesis 1:27 NIV**

September 9, 2017

Lately, the main topic of discussion seems to be immigration and the need to put up a wall for keeping people who have been termed illegals from crossing over into the United States. But I truly wonder what would have happened to Moses and the children of Israel if a wall was constructed to keep them from escaping Egypt for a better life or way of living in the *promised land* of Canaan! Sadly, we have been royally deceived and encouraged to hate as well as deny others of what we so desperately want for ourselves! We make up excuses to justify our pharaoh like bigotry behavior and tell ourselves we are protecting the United States from the big bad wolf who wants to take our jobs and overcrowd our cities.

The events of history have been changed or rewritten throughout time to give power or leverage to a selective control base, group, or person. Are you aware of how you can change the results of a test in a lab experiment based on the selected control agent to get a desired outcome? In that same context, are you not aware of how easy it is to rig a race or an election? Well, are you not aware that many definitions in the dictionary have been changed based on what the controlling power base wants you to believe? Do you even know that the minds of many have been manipulated within a controlled learning environment (institution or organization); specifically, an *institution of education*?

Yes, education and knowledge are very important! In fact, God references in Hosea how His children are destroyed (ruined) for a lack of knowledge. There is, most certainly, nothing wrong with education, training, and growth when it is associated with integrity! But, if you are familiar with Dr. Carter G. Woodson and his book, *The Miseducation of the Negro*, then you should also be aware of how people can deliberately be misled and taught incorrectly. English, math, and science should be universally unchangeable curricula of study taught at various levels.

God is the same, yesterday, tomorrow, and forevermore. His word is very clear and unchangeable as He encourages us to study to show ourselves approved in rightly dividing the *word of truth* to apply it to our everyday life! But many of us want to pick and choose what we adhere to and abide in! Not many of us are able to effectively apply our education and knowledge to our everyday life to make it work for us, and we have even more difficulty comprehending the Word of God to understand it as intended by God. We, unfortunately, rely on our own intellect by leaning toward our own understanding, which has been shaped by our controlled environment style of education to hinder our growth and acknowledgement of truth. We deny the existence of God, His word, Heaven and Hell while refusing to see what needs to be seen in the belief of many lies to include the ideology or definition of race.

There is a great deal of debate as to the origin of the word "race," which was initially termed to denote livestock and speed. Race, as recognized by modern culture today, widely became the topic of discussion during the existence of slavery to reference human differences or classification of equality and inequality; a subdivision of the human race or species as identified by shared similarities and other inherited traits. However, the Bible refers to differing people in terms, such as tribe, nation, family, and people in accordance to geographical area.

Genesis details the beginning of the world to include the creation of the **human race** on the sixth day; but I grew up believing that the world was comprised of a number of different races, which was and still is being reinforced by our learning institutions and surrounding environment. **Today, I am learning to do my own research and analyze facts to replace what was taught to me by truth in receipt of revelation from the Lord.** My knowledge has evolved to understand that there are various cultures of people throughout the world, and their differences in skin tone were initially (historically) contributed to and determined by their inhabited migration along with their geographical proximity to the equator and the sun. The hotter the sun, the darker the skin tone or the greater presence and development of melanin as a form of protection. The geographical areas with colder climates were responsible for **aiding in the production of less melanin in people and producing lighter skin tones.**

Melanin,[41, 42] produced by cells called melanocytes, is the dark brown to black pigment that gives human skin, hair, and eyes their color. Melanin provides the skin a form of protection from the sun, and the presence of melanocytes increases the production of melanin in response to sun exposure; but, at the same time, the sun can also be harmful. Freckles, which occur in people of all races, are small, concentrated areas of increased melanin production.

Of course, many folks would be more apt to disbelieve the biology and chemistry of the sun as it relates to skin tone, which is very ironic considering the emphasis and importance placed on education. However, like any and everything else, guidance is set and rules are broken at will in accordance to what works for the control base—even if it is wrong! Nonetheless, in the words of Dr. Randy J. Guliuzza, "the Lord Jesus Christ put the human body together to function as a whole. With unsurpassed scientific genius, God designed a complex process—using many different systems—that is capable of generating the protective compound melanin. With power beyond comprehension, He

---

41  www.afrikaiswoke.com/truth-about-melanin/
42  www.webmd.com/a-to-z-guides/what-is-melanin#1

spoke into existence something that requires almost a hundred genes directing hundreds of enzymatic reactions controlling events, which are not arranged in basic linear sequences; but as a vast diverse multidirectional network—with layers of overlapping feedback and control, all acting in a goal-oriented fashion. What an amazing display of His love and glory"[43] for us all!

We, unfortunately, have a lot to learn as it pertains to the fruit of the Spirit, the character of Christ, and the ways of God as true Christians! As one race, the human race, we all are a part of a whole and have yet to realize that a fight against one is a fight against God. He created us all, and everything created by Him is good! We have been out of order for a while, but as encouraged by 1 Corinthians 14:40, *everything should be done in a fitting and orderly way*. He has given us a command to love our neighbors as we love ourselves (Mark 12:31), and we have failed to honor God and His word over and over again! We failed Him in the Garden of Eden. We failed Him in the city of Sodom and Gomorrah. When will we learn to do what is right in accordance to the Will of God? What if the tables were turned? Would we want to be isolated from our brethren and treated the same way?

**Sharing an old Cherokee Indian prayer:** O Great Spirit, who made all races, look kindly upon the whole human family and take away the arrogance and hatred that separates us from our brothers.

---

43  www.icr.org/article/4786

## REFERENCES

**Tribe:**[44] a race or nation, a class or set of persons, especially one with strong common traits or interests.

**Immigration:**

1. The action of coming to live permanently in a foreign country.[45]
2. The movement of non-native people into a country in order to settle there.[46]
3. A person who comes to a country from another to take up permanent residence.[47]

**Race on the Basis of Ethnicity:**

Groups of people who have differences and similarities in biological traits as deemed by society to be socially significant or insignificant. People are treated differently based on our differences.[48]

---

44  The New Combined Bible Dictionary and Concordance, page 426
45  https://en.oxforddictionaries.com/definition/immigration
46  www.collinsdictionary.com/dictionary/english/immigration
47  www.merriam-webster.com/dictionary/immigrant
48  see www.cliffsnotes.com/study-guides/sociology/race-and-ethnicity/race-and-ethnicity-defined; www.jstor.org/stable/30053821?seq=1#page_scan_tab_contents; www.biblestudytools.com/topical-verses/bible-verses-about-equality/; www.news-medical.net/health/What-is-Melanin.aspx; www.icr.org/article/4786; Guliuzza, Randy J., P.E., M.D.; 8/1/2009. "Made in His Image: Melanin, the Sunblock That's Just Skin Deep." *Acts & Facts*. 38 (8): 10-11; www1.cbn.com/cbnnews/us/2017/march/white-pastor-demonstrates-humility-by-washing-black-mans-feet.

# THE SOULS OF MY ANCESTORS

> *"Woe to you, because you build tombs for the prophets, and it was your ancestors who killed them. So you testify that you approve of what your ancestors did; they killed the prophets, and you build their tombs. Because of this, God in his wisdom said, 'I will send them prophets and apostles, some of whom they will kill and others they will persecute.' Therefore this generation will be held responsible for the blood of all the prophets that has been shed since the beginning of the world, from the blood of Abel to the blood of Zechariah, who was killed between the altar and the sanctuary. Yes, I tell you, this generation will be held responsible for it all.*
>
> **~ Luke 11:47-51 NIV**

September 15, 2017

Revised September 25, 2017

God is nothing like any man or person on the face of this earth, past or present! He is a spirit—The Spirit—a ball of energy or life force that existed long before the world took shape and He created people to inhabit the earth. I believe many of us conveniently forget that it is because of Him that we exist and not the other way around! So don't get it twisted! Genesis 1:26-27 AMP states, *Then God said, "Let Us (Father, Son, Holy Spirit) make man in Our image, according to Our likeness [not physical, but a spiritual personality and moral likeness]; and let them have complete authority over the fish of the sea, the birds of the air, the cattle, and over the entire earth, and over everything that creeps* and *crawls on the earth." So God created man in His own image, in the image* and *likeness of God He created him; male and female He created them.*

**God is the divine and ultimate Creator of the universe and everything within and outside of it!** Christ, The Son is the image of the invisible God, the firstborn over all creation. For in him all things were created: things in heaven and on earth, visible and invisible, whether thrones or powers or rulers or authorities; all things have been created through him and for him (Colossians 1:15-16 NIV). The invisible or the intangible, which also represents the supernatural, and the visible or tangible, which also represents the natural, are under the command of God! Nothing happens or takes place without His permission, although we think that it is us who are in control of everything! No, not true at all, and we will be held accountable for every action! There is a Divine Order to it all, which, unfortunately, is not considered or acknowledged by the human race as intended and laid out by God!

We are tri-part beings made in His image, spirit first and foremost without a physical form or appearance. Spirit is neither male nor female but has the ability to assume both identities to be able to interact effectively with one another. It is the outer shell, which is termed the flesh, that houses our spirit-man to give us a physical form and presence on the earth within this dimension known as the physical or natural realm. But we have the ability to exist in both dimensions simultaneously and at the same time, the natural and the supernatural realm! Inverting everything, we tend to believe that the natural realm is more real than the supernatural realm, but it is the other way around. **The natural realm cannot and would not exist if it were not created out of the supernatural.** The supernatural, which is the natural dwelling or habitat of the spirit, existed first and foremost before the dimension we call Earth; and the natural (physical existence) can easily be voided or wiped out by the supernatural—which is also referred to as being the spiritual realm!

At a very early age, long before developing a deeper knowledge or awareness of injustices in the world, I had an unexplainable burning and ache in my heart for those who were mistreated, abused, or taken advantage of by others. As time went on, I felt a growing intense loathing for slavery, racism, and chauvinism as if I were—at one time or another—present and existing during periods in history when my ancestors suffered greatly. Until recently, I never understood the connection, but then God began to reveal and unlock truth concerning history repeating itself and generational soul ties that bind through blood, soul, and spirit on the basis of Godly (healthy) or ungodly (unhealthy) relationships.

Without form, as *spirit beings*, we are more alike than we are different! Limitless to walls, doors, or windows that cannot contain us and are connected to a divine and greater source (a three-strand cord), which cannot be easily broken. In fact, 1 John 5:5-8 speaks of witnesses in the earth (the blood, the water, and the Spirit) and in Heaven (the Father, the Word, and the Holy Spirit), which reads: *Who is he that overcometh the world, but he that believeth that Jesus is the Son of God? This is he that came by water and blood, even Jesus Christ; not by water only, but by water and blood. And it is the Spirit that beareth witness, because the Spirit is truth. For there are three that bear record in heaven, the Father, the Word, and the Holy Ghost: and these three are one. And there are three that bear witness in earth, the Spirit, and the water, and the blood: and these three agree in one.* That's divine unity!

Now, let's go a little deeper! Are you familiar with the story about Cain and Abel? Cain thought he could hide the offenses he committed against his brother, Abel. In Genesis 4:10 NIV, the Lord said, *"What have you done? Listen! Your brother's blood cries out to me from the ground.* Little did Cain know about the power of the blood to speak in the earth from beyond the grave and above the ground to be heard! Yes, the blood speaks, and it has a testimony! Deuteronomy 21:1-9 declares that *the righteous blood cries out for vengeance,* and Deuteronomy 32:35 declares *vengeance is the Lord's*; therefore, He will make it right!

So today, in the year 2017 and beyond, the blood of Abel still cries out! And through God who is my Lord, Master, and Savior, not only am I connected to my ancestors but many others who are able to speak and share their pain which is relative to mine.

The pain of being singled out, rejected, and ostracized on the basis of jealousy, skin color, gender, appearance, and social class while being told—over and over again—that certain conditions and mindsets from times past no longer exist when that is further from the truth! Pain is not always easy to ignore! And, somehow, unfortunately, people want you to believe that pain can easily be ignored, pushed aside, tucked away, and swept in a corner. But, sometimes, that same pain is revived by God for a purpose!

Jesus' pain was evidenced by Him taking the weight of our sins unto Himself to save us from ourselves! In my case, He uses pain to sear deep within my subconscious mind as well as my consciousness that which no man can make me doubt through fear, manipulation, or intimation! Ultimately, God uses *pain* in my life to unleash (reveal) reality through *revelation*! He uses it to teach me the nature of being a burden bearer in demonstrating the realness of His connection to us all and the power of intercession for His glory! Many nights, I lie awake and cry in agony in hope of change for a better tomorrow as I pray myself to sleep for my soul and yours.

If we only knew and truly realized just how much we are connected to one another—above and beyond our outer appearance—would we do better at treating one another with greater respect in putting ourselves in the place of one another? "Teacher, which is the greatest commandment in the Law?" Jesus replied: "'Love the Lord your God with all your heart and with all your soul and with all your mind.' This is the first and greatest commandment. And the second is like it: 'Love your neighbor as yourself.' All the Law and the Prophets hang on these two commandments" (Matthew 22:36-40 NIV).

# NO MORE APOLOGIES!

*For with much wisdom comes much sorrow;
the more knowledge, the more grief.*

~ **Ecclesiastes 1:18 NIV**

October 3, 2017

Revised October 25, 2017

The world as we know it has been shifting, changing, and evolving for a while! Actually, throughout history, the changing events have been impacted by a very volatile spiritual warfare being waged for centuries with us (human beings/mankind) right smack in the middle of it. Contrary to popular belief, this fight is as real as Heaven and Hell! It is not a game; however, it is a test of wills and an unveiling of truth and positioning! Many of us are lost, drifting out to sea, and have been blinded by the darkness because we have simply failed to take heed to God's Word. Driven by our flesh and the need to fit in to be counted amongst those we believe are in control, we only pay attention to that which is temporarily placed in front of us, and we, sadly, take the bait of the enemy to distract us while we pretend to stay afloat! In this season, you will no longer be able to fake it until you make it!

Like the weather which is seasonal, change is seasonal, and we must be willing to discern what is taking place—at all times—if we are expected to be victorious at honoring God! Said differently, we must *exercise wisdom* to know what is happening in the atmosphere in being an aide and not a hindrance to the movement of God. Remembering always that it is impossible to serve two masters, we must stay in our lane even if others around us do not understand or agree with the position we are taking: a position we have been instructed to take by God if we are true followers of Christ! Therefore, it is extremely important for me to hold my position in not allowing man's unrighteous behavior and desire of my time or his antics to cause me to stumble in disobedience to what is expected of me by God.

Not long ago, I was called into a meeting to discuss my behavior based on antics of he-said-she-said, which was far from the truth, and my side of the story was never a welcoming factor. So, in cases like this, there is always an underlying agenda of cat and mouse with the potential to back you in a corner to overpower you—if you don't know who you are! Nonetheless, in the mind of my **antagonist**, I'm sure she meant well when she said she wanted me to be successful, but success does not look the same for everyone. Especially, if your **success** is contingent upon you playing a role that does not line up with your **personality, character, integrity**, or more importantly, **your God-appointed position** (a.k.a. your God assignment). In fact, within certain controlled environments, your successfulness is defined or measured by your willingness to conform to an existing culture—one representative of a larger piece of the puzzle on the playing field of life. And the reality of it all is, there are "only" two major opposing forces or sides that really matter: good vs. evil, light vs. darkness, righteousness vs. unrighteousness, and Yahweh vs. Lucifer.

Performing and carrying out tasks as directed is not an issue if it does not require breaking a set of guidelines (polices and regulations) of systematic order to encourage operating outside of the will of God for my life. Unfortunately, many folks have grown accustomed to demanding and getting what they want when they want it and how they want it with no inverse impact as a warning of wrongdoing! But, that same adage does not apply to everyone, even if you are put in an unfair position in being expected to follow orders (do as you are told and do not question your superior) and you succeed at carrying out their agenda. According to certain standards, using you to accomplish their agenda, you are considered to be invaluable and disposable (replaceable) as you are put in position to take the blame or the fall should a discovery of wrongdoing come to light even if you were ordered/delegated to execute the task.

In this season, the real you to include the side that inspires or influences you will be exposed! You will no longer be able to pretend or simply follow orders of an unrighteous request! When you are able to see clearly, how do you adjust or adapt to an environment or culture that uses a military structure (Babylonian Empire) on the basis of a chain of command order (the spirit of elitism) as a strategy aided by intimidation (coercion) and manipulation to force people into submission? Especially when those same practices could very well threaten to degrade, humiliate, and violate civil liberties to incorporate a form of oppression and bullying being carried out by appointed taskmasters in doing harm to others. In this season, much will be uncovered with the right mindset (or Issachar anointing) to study and analyze your environment!

## A PERSONAL TESTIMONY & DECLARATION

As a Black female, born in 1960 and living in America where sexism and racism is just as widely practiced today as it was in 1619 and, unfortunately, striving, I will no longer attempt to make apologies for who I AM! I will no longer sit quietly because I AM forbidden to speak the truth about my experiences, called my reality, in an atmospheric double-standard culture that still wishes to silence me and feels I AM only suited for positions others have reserved for me. Why? Because, although the movie *Hidden Figures* speaks of a past time, 1961, those events as depicted are still a reality for some of us. Some have since made a vow to rebel against certain stereotypes only to be labeled difficult. Some are stuck in the past out of fear of rejecting oppression. There are others who don't even have a clue or could not care less as long as they are not directly impacted and are allowed to partake in some of the spoils!

What keeps me level-headed and moving forward although my heart has been wounded by double-minded ungodly worldly practices is my attachment to God, Abba Father; I will make no excuses for my spiritual belief because it makes you feel uncomfortable! What about my discomfort when I AM expected to turn the other cheek and you repeatedly attempt to degrade me and strip me of my dignity while saying you too are a Christian, but you still believe that there is no place for my God in government when there would be no government if it were not for Him? Yes, I AM aware of the Word of God to include how scripture is sometimes taken out of context to promote personal and selfish gain. Just as there is a time and place for everything under the sun, I AM not being instructed by God—in this season—to turn the other cheek!

I serve an all-powerful and all knowing God who is the Creator of us all! It is that same God who is challenging us to love one another as Christ loves the church. It is that same God who will judge us all accordingly in the end. He is that same loving God whose breath encompasses our being. He is a part of me and I AM a part of Him; there is no separation between the two of us. Where I go, He goes, and where He goes, I will go! For Him I live and for Him I die. No more apologies!

> *Then I heard the voice of the Lord, saying, "Whom shall I send, and who will go for us?" Then I said, "Here am I. Send me!" And He said, "Go, and tell this people: 'Keep on listening, but do not understand; keep on looking, but do not comprehend.' "Make the heart of this people insensitive, their ears dull, and their eyes dim, otherwise they might see with their eyes, hear with their ears, understand with their hearts, and return and be healed." Then I said, "Lord, how long?" And He answered, "Until cities are devastated and without inhabitant and houses are without people and the*

land is utterly desolate, the Lord has removed [His] people far away, and there are many deserted places in the midst of the land. "And though a tenth [of the people] remain in the land, it will again be subject to destruction [consumed and burned], like a massive terebinth tree or like an oak whose stump remains when it is chopped down. The holy seed [the elect remnant] is its stump [the substance of Israel]."

~ Isaiah 6:8-13

## FOOD FOR THOUGHT

- All life should be considered valuable!
- Not everyone signed up for or enlisted in the military. The draft ended long ago. There should be a sense of mutual respect—one to another—regardless of the position (from employer to employees to supervisor), race, gender, age, etc.

## REFERENCE

- https://youtu.be/AH5myTDN48w

# REALLY?

*Do not be anxious about anything,
but in everything by prayer and supplication
with thanksgiving let your requests be made known to God.*

**~ Philippians 4:6 ESV**

November 17, 2017

I talk to God, often, about *everything* and I very seldom leave anything out! I know without a doubt that He knows my heart, but it has been extremely important to me to openly express my feelings to include just how disappointed I am with people and their unethical value system within an increasingly unstable world system fueled by hate and indifference. I'm sitting, observing, and digesting it all in disbelief of blatant defiance and double standards. I actually see what others don't think I see to understand what the truly arrogant don't care if I see or not! Why? Because to them, I simply don't matter! *He who sows injustice will reap [a harvest of] trouble, And the rod of his wrath [with which he oppresses others] will fail* (Proverbs 22:8 AMP).

Each and every person in this world as created by God is equally important to Him. He does not diminish your value based on your age, gender, race, or profession. In fact, the title or the position you hold has no bearing on what He thinks of you! God encourages us to not only have confidence in Him, but in ourselves as well, to know and appreciate our worth. However, not to the point of us disregarding the worth and importance of each other. Romans 12:3 MSG states, *I'm speaking to you out of deep gratitude for all that God has given me, and especially as I have responsibilities in relation to you. Living then, as every one of you does, in pure grace, it's important that you not misinterpret yourselves as people who are bringing this goodness to God. No, God brings it all to you. The only accurate way to understand ourselves is by what God is and by what he does for us, not by what we are and what we do for him.* Simply expressed another way, the King James Version states, *For I say, through the grace given unto me, to every man that is among you, not to think of himself more highly than he ought to think; but to think soberly, according as God hath dealt to every man the measure of faith.* And yet, many of us attempt to take advantage of others based on an unwritten, unlawful, and unmerited value system in thinking that we have every right to assert inappropriate power and control in the name of who we think we are! Not true!

If you were to access the Office of Personnel Management's website to review the topic of classification, you would see how positions are weighted to determine salary and importance. However, in the same manner in which the desired outcome of performance ratings is manipulated, the writing of various position descriptions are also manipulated and devalued in association with the person occupying the position. Have you ever noted how an individual is regarded in a particular position as people fade in or out of that same position? Men and women in the same position and title are oftentimes paid on a different scale in the same manner as the pay scale differs according to the race of an individual, even today. Historically speaking, men have been paid significantly higher wages than most women in various cases while Caucasians have been paid significantly higher wages than people of color performing some of the same tasks; and sometimes, people of color are expected to do more and work harder for much less! I am sure that many reading this will be quick to tell me that what I see is incorrect, but I know from experience working within a human resources environment that my observation is right on point! I'm simply not expected to speak about what I see and I'm even less expected to write about it! *He who justifies the wicked and he who condemns the righteous, Both of them alike are an abomination to the LORD* (Proverbs 17:15 NASB).

Women, like African Americans during slavery, have been encouraged and conditioned to know our place, to speak only when spoken to, and to be mindful of what to say or how to behave for fear of being met with great retaliation and limited in various job categories or fields—even after obtaining the right education. Nonetheless, women have attempted to address the disparaging differences in how they have been treated and devalued in comparison to men for quite some time, but their cries for change and justice have continuously fallen on deaf ears.

Do you remember the woman who attempted to get the courts to appeal on her behalf for a restraining order against her domestically violent husband while the presiding judge, a man, dismissed her urgent plea? Not long after that, her husband, in retaliation, tracked her down at a cell phone company in Clinton, Maryland, where he threw gasoline on her and set her on fire. Currently, in the news, women—and some men who have found themselves to be in the same position—are coming forward to openly speak out about the abuse (sexual assault and harassment) they have suffered and endured at one time or another.

To paraphrase a tweet by Rose McGowan concerning her claims of sexual abuse, she stated many were aware of what she had experienced, but she was encouraged to keep her mouth shut and toe the line if she wanted to succeed in her career as an actress. How many people within your surrounding environment are aware of the injustices committed against you? But, because you objected to the violations committed against you, your acquaintances, known and unknown, have turned on you and treated you as if you had the plague or had done something wrong? Yes, it hurts! And, overtime, you push onward to *grin and bear it* while becoming numb to it all! For that reason alone, I understand why she took the money. No one wanted to listen or sympathize with her enough to take her side in attempting to address her claim. So, yes, she took the money for the pain, suffering, and humiliation, which I'm sure still did not justify the act committed against her. Why? Because a small resemblance of justice did not prevail until now, long after others came forward to vindicate her truth as they share their "me too" stories! Does anyone remember Anita Hill?

In the words of James Brown, "this is a man's world, but it wouldn't be nothing, nothing without a woman or a girl." Women have been the glue in various aspects or arenas throughout history, in the home, office, or boardroom, while maintaining (still standing) and enduring all types of abuse and receiving very little credit for holding families together. We are daughters of the Most-High God, He who sits up high and looks down low upon us all! Please don't think that He has tossed us aside and forgotten just how precious we are to Him. *Finally, be strong in the Lord and in his mighty power (Ephesians 6:10 NIV).* Timing is everything, and things are being revealed (uncovered) and brought to the surface! This is just the beginning! Be still (Psalm 46:16)!

## REFERENCES

1. www.wusa9.com/news/local/military/i-said-no-20-times-military-rape-victims-speak-out/491460321

2. www.essence.com/news/litesa-wallace-sexual-harassment-black-women-government

3. www.cnn.com/2017/11/16/politics/settlements-congress-sexual-harassment/index.html

4. www.washingtonexaminer.com/treasury-has-paid-nearly-1m-in-settlements-for-harassment-and-other-claims-just-this-year/article/2641021

5. www.washingtonpost.com/investigations/how-the-military-handles-sexual-assault-cases-behind-

closed-doors/2017/09/30/a9df0682-672a-11e7-a1d7-9a32c91c6f40_story.html?utm_term=.c13fbb987b3a

6. www.nbcnews.com/news/us-news/sexual-assault-reports-u-s-military-reach-record-high-pentagon-n753566

7. http://abcnews.go.com/US/pentagon-releases-data-sex-assault-reports-made-military/story?id=51227443

## RECOMMENDED READING

1. *The Discerner: Hearing, Confirming, and Acting on Prophetic Revelation* by James W. Goll

2. *The Prophet in the Wilderness* by Apostle Ken Cox

# FREQUENCY

*Let this mind be in you,
which was also in Christ Jesus.*

**~ Philippians 2:5**

March 29, 2018

How many times have you encountered folks who weren't speaking your same language? I don't mean literally as if you were speaking English and they were speaking French! I mean two "perfect" English-speaking adults on a different page, channel, or *frequency*. No matter how much you may have in common, you often find yourself being at odds with another individual feeling as though you are at battle or war because they simply don't understand you! Why can't we simply agree to disagree while accepting the fact that we are wired differently in our thinking or viewpoints? Not everyone you meet, come to know, and love will see things from your perspective. All you can do is pray and move forward!

## DIFFERENT SCALES

When you think of musical notes, each sound resonates at a different scale or vibration to the tune of a frequency. In fact, there are generally two different radio bandwidths: AM (amplitude modulation) and FM (frequency modulation). Each has varied degrees of stations at various positions on a turning or tuning scale based upon the transmission and reception of a signal. The transmitter, a radio (or TV station), broadcasts a signal by pulse radio waves with around 50,000 watts of power. One turn to the right or left can align you with one station or another. If you land in between two stations, you could possibly be out of alignment or off balance to receive static. As *spiritual beings* housed in a body, we are generally a ball of vibrating energy, particles of floating atoms that solidify (come together) to form tissues of flesh. And we are capable of vibrating at a negative or positive frequency to encourage healing or dis-ease.

When I think of God and what He is doing in my life, the word "frequency" comes to my mind! Being in tune and vibrating on the right frequency keeps me in perfect alignment with my Heavenly Father to hear and receive His wisdom, knowledge, and understanding of things such as this! It is that same frequency which helps me to understand and realize, without apology, the level of thought to which my mind is able to comprehend the importance of a *divine connection* and staying on track.

To fulfill my *divine purpose* on Earth, the ultimate reason for my existence in being fully liberated, I must denounce all worldly teaching and fear to think and live my life like Christ.

The above scripture reads, *Let this mind be in you, which was also in Christ Jesus,* to push beyond the barriers and through the force field which is intended to alter or disrupt my frequency! Without question, I am encouraged by John 15:7 AMP, which states, If you remain in Me and My words remain in you *[that is, if we are vitally united and My message lives in your heart],* ask whatever you wish and it will be done for you. My petition to the Lord is simply to stay on the right frequency step by step! What about you?

> *Think of yourselves the way Christ Jesus thought of himself. He had equal status with God but didn't think so much of himself that he had to cling to the advantages of that status no matter what. Not at all. When the time came, he set aside the privileges of deity and took on the status of a slave, became human! Having become human, he stayed human. It was an incredibly humbling process. He didn't claim special privileges. Instead, he lived a selfless, obedient life and then died a selfless, obedient death—and the worst kind of death at that—a crucifixion. Because of that obedience, God lifted him high and honored him far beyond anyone or anything, ever, so that all created beings in heaven and on earth— even those long ago dead and buried—will bow in worship before this Jesus Christ, and call out in praise that he is the Master of all, to the glorious honor of God the Father.*
>
> ~ Philippians 2:5-11 MSG

## FOOD FOR THOUGHT

David was an anointed musician who danced and played the harp. He was actually a psalmist who was described by 1 Samuel 16:18 AMP: *One of the young men said, "Behold, I have seen a son of Jesse the Bethlehemite who is a skillful musician, a brave and competent man, a warrior, discerning (prudent, eloquent) in speech, and a handsome man; and the* LORD *is with him."*

# A REBEL 4 CHRIST!

*Praise be to the LORD my Rock,
who trains my hands for war, my fingers for battle.
He is my loving God and my fortress,
my stronghold and my deliverer,
my shield, in whom I take refuge,
who subdues peoples under me.*

**~ Psalm 144:1-2 NIV**

May 21, 2018

All of my life, I have been trying to find out where I fit! I struggled on a daily basis to get along without having to change who I was created to be while attempting to find myself and learn my purpose. Through the trials and tribulations of the ups and downs, I actually discovered who I AM!

**The Faith of the Centurion:** *When Jesus had entered Capernaum, a centurion came to him, asking for help. "Lord," he said, "my servant lies at home paralyzed, suffering terribly." Jesus said to him, "Shall I come and heal him?" The centurion* replied, "Lord, I do not deserve to have you come under my roof. But just say the word, and my servant will be healed. For I myself am a man under authority, with soldiers under me. I tell this one, 'Go,' and he goes; and that one, 'Come,' and he comes. I say to my servant, 'Do this,' and he does it" (Matthew 8:5-9 NIV).

Within a certain age eligibility timeline, I contemplated joining the military and later decided against it—but with good reason! I simply cannot align myself with others to take their side against another person or thing outside of it being morally or spiritually right! In a political, military-driven work environment, many people are not selected and placed in positions at various levels and then promoted because they particularly are qualified to perform the tasks in question. They are simply chosen on the basis of their willingness to follow orders or to carry out any command without question. I was actually told by one manager that he didn't have to know or be qualified to perform the duties of those he supervised. He just needed to know who to delegate the tasks to and get the job done. So here's my question: how is he able to accurately evaluate those he supervises if he does not know the exact layers of each element and the timeline involved in accomplishing the delegated tasks?

Although I have been renamed by many of those I come in contact with on the job as **difficult or trouble** because I refuse to sacrifice my soul for the sake of my career or lack thereof, my greatest challenge isn't following orders. It's about following the command of those who lack the integrity and character of Christ to take ownership and full responsibility as a leader concerning what they delegate to others! In an HR environment, I am expected to know policies, rules, and regulations, adhering to them and relaying them to others in the name of double standards while being denied details, promotions, and growth opportunities. And I witness this type of leadership on a daily basis as it is also done to others! In some cases, I am expected to ignore certain guidelines to fulfill tasks on behalf of others in the name of entitlement and privilege.

I could never understand how easy it is for people to abuse and mistreat another human being while directing more love and kindness toward their pets and other animals! No, I am not saying that it is okay to mistreat or abuse animals! I am saying that it is not okay to redirect a greater sense of honor and respect toward animals than you do toward human beings. Order is important, and God is love! Are we not instructed through Matthew 22:39 to love our neighbors as we love ourselves?

**God is about divine order and He encourages spiritual excellence!** Spiritual excellence incorporates character and integrity! God does everything decently and in order while expecting us to do the same. Like the centurion, but unlike many others, I understand the order of chain of command and I honor God's position as the head of the government and the world! The government sits on His shoulder; He is above Earth, Heaven, and Hell! All authority comes from Him to others based on our positioning as ordained by Him!

When I think about the Lord, I feel overwhelming joy in my heart, which brings tears to my eyes! I reverence Him with all my heart and soul! I am thankful and grateful for who He is to include what He has done in my life. Why would I not have intense passion and compassion for someone who sacrificed Himself for me in showing me love and encouraging me to love others unconditionally through the pain and their animosity or hatred for me. Through His example, He has shown me how to love my enemies and still honor my calling while pushing to and beyond the upsets in life to live! I gladly worship Him in spirit and in truth secretly and openly for all of the world to see! No, I cannot go along to get along if it goes against God's divine order! The last will be first, the first will be last, and a table will be prepared!

# YOU CAN MOVE PAST THE PAIN!

*For I reckon that the sufferings of this present time are not worthy to be compared with the glory which shall be revealed in us.*

**~ Romans 8:18**

July 2, 2018

We all were created with a purpose for a purpose! I pray each and every person on the face of the earth at some point in their life—before it is too late—will grow to understand and live out their purpose in fulfilling God's plan for their life and move past their pain! *For I know the thoughts that I think toward you, saith the LORD, thoughts of peace, and not of evil, to give you an expected end* (Jeremiah 29:11).

Your first connection to this world is family and then it is the connection or associations you develop with others along your life journey! Unfortunately, your path may not always be clear of pain and strife. I remember, not long ago, a family member once told me that I wasn't living in the real world, but she was sadly mistaken. People, to include family and friends, may not always understand you, but that most certainly doesn't mean you don't live in the real world. It simply means, it's possible you connected to something far greater than what this world can offer you. In fact, through the Word of God, there is liberty and hope, which encourages that although we are in the world, we should not allow ourselves to be consumed by the world. And yet, there are many who not only get lost in the world, but they, unfortunately, lose their souls to it.

This world and the people in it have caused me so much pain over the years. The intensity of my pain was so great at times that at one point I didn't think it would be possible to go on with my life to move beyond the pain. Then I discovered the realness of God through His grace, mercy, and love for me. A love far greater than any personal encounter I have ever had with another individual to include family in my lifetime. *The LORD is nigh unto them that are of a broken heart; and saveth such as be of a contrite spirit* (Psalm 34:18).

In the midst of my pain, God gave me the opportunity to know His unconditional, unchanging, unselfish, uncondemning kind of love that grows, heals, nurtures, and lifts you up! *He healeth the broken in heart, and bindeth up their wounds* (Psalm 147:3). I was able to develop an unimaginable relationship with God to know and understand my reason for being which unlocked my purpose and an insurmountable amount of explosive joy in my heart!

This joy opened my eyes! A joy that compels me to choose a life with God and for God beyond my own ambition! It compelled me to want to know more about a God who loved me so deeply that He would sacrifice His only begotten son so I could live and have joy abundantly. A God who touched my heart and compelled me to want to love others and forgive those who hurt me. A joy so compelling, it pushes me to want to give others the benefit of the doubt more times than I feel I ought to! But the most amazing thing is I refuse to harbor pain in my heart. I refuse to allow the pain caused by others to overtake me and render me helpless. Through God's love, I have learned that there is purpose in my pain and He holds my heart while I live in this world until He takes me home!

# THE REAL WORLD

*Jesus answered: "Watch out that no one deceives you. For many will come in my name, claiming, 'I am the Messiah,' and will deceive many. You will hear of wars and rumors of wars, but see to it that you are not alarmed. Such things must happen, but the end is still to come. Nation will rise against nation, and kingdom against kingdom. There will be famines and earthquakes in various places. All these are the beginning of birth pains.*

**~ Matthew 24: 4-8 NIV**

July 7, 2018

Revised December 14, 2018

**The evil that we do!** Unfortunately, in the natural order of civilization, human beings born in the flesh on Earth, in this real world, are sinful by nature! Their hearts are naturally wicked, and their actions (lawlessness and transgression) toward others are just as evil! *The heart is hopelessly dark and deceitful, a puzzle that no one can figure out. But I, God, search the heart* *and examine the mind. I get to the heart of the human. I get to the root of things. I treat them as they really are, not as they pretend to be* (Jeremiah 17:9-10 MSG). So when God reveals to you the heart of those around you, believe it!

Before Adam and Eve had eaten the fruit from the forbidden tree in the Garden of Eden, they were not yet mortal, although they were living a physical life. Their spirits were housed in physical bodies made from the dust of the earth, and they were living a spiritual life because they were always in the presence of God! They resided in the Holy of Holies, and because they disobeyed "God's only commandment" not to eat of the tree of the knowledge of good and evil, they fell from grace! This egregious act made them vulnerable to evil and changed the outcome of their future and ours, which put us in a more rebellious state of mind. So they were sent from the Garden of Eden into the world.

After the fall of Adam and Eve, all of humanity became corrupt and drifted further away from the Lord in deed and in action. *This people draweth nigh unto me with their mouth, and honoureth me with their lips; but their heart is far from me. But in vain they do worship me, teaching for doctrines the commandments of men* (Matthew 15:8-9). After the war in Heaven, Satan and his minions (fallen angels) were tossed down to Earth (Revelation 12) where they wreaked unspeakable havoc on all of humanity through their sinful influence! Therefore, just as sin came into the world through one man and death through sin, so did death spread to all men because all have sinned (Romans 5:12) and all have fallen short of the glory of the Lord (Romans

3:23). But, through *free will*, we are given a choice to follow the Lord or Satan. In doing so, we have been given an option to choose life and prosperity or death, adversity, and destruction! And yet, God still grants us grace and mercy to get it right!

The real world, unfortunately, is ruled by man, and we consistently choose destruction in pleasing our flesh over doing what is morally right. *Now the works of the flesh are evident: sexual immorality, impurity, sensuality, idolatry, sorcery, enmity, strife, jealousy, fits of anger, rivalries, dissension, divisions, envy, drunkenness, orgies, and things like these. I warn you, as I warned you before, that those who do such things will not inherit the kingdom of God* (Galatians 5:19-21 ESV). Too often, I have heard this nation (a.k.a. America, the United States) was founded upon Godly or Christian Biblical principles! But lately, more than ever before, I have pondered over these most important questions:

1. Which god? The God of Heaven or the god of Hell?

2. Are we reading the same Bible?

3. Do we realize that the root word in "Christian" is "Christ," which denotes Christ-like?

4. Have we read and studied the Bible to know who Christ was to understand that He was and is a person of character, integrity, and love for all?

5. Do we understand that our actions have consequences?

Based on everything I have witnessed and experienced in my life, this nation has exhibited and encouraged anything other than Biblical principles in regard to the children of God! And many of us have fallen into a trap by taking the bait in how we, unfortunately, interact with one another! I never wanted to believe that people do harm to others intentionally and deliberately or that they were willful and disobedient because they actually made a choice to do so! I wanted to believe that they didn't know exactly what they were doing. But, somewhere in the scheme of things, they could have stopped long enough to consider the heart of those they inflict undue hardship upon as if they were considering themselves.

Over the years, within a human resources environment at the federal, state, and private levels, I was positioned by God as a witness. Too often I observed the abuse of power and war being waged as EEO violations were freely being committed by those in position of power simply because they could and it gave them pleasure! All things can be handled differently and with compassion! You call it business; I call it shameful (see Zephaniah 3:5) and pure evil! That which is done in the dark will soon come to light!

*Judge me, O God,*
*and plead my cause against an ungodly nation:*
*O deliver me from the deceitful and unjust man.*

~ Psalm 43:1

# WHAT IS ENDURANCE?

*For everything that was written in the past
was written to teach us,
so that through the endurance taught in the Scriptures
and the encouragement they provide we might have hope.*

**~ Romans 15:4 NIV**

July 23, 2018

Endurance, in my opinion, is the will to stay in the race! No matter the situation of being faced with adversity time and time again, it is the drive and determination to keep going against all odds, making a conscious effort to see something through from the beginning until the end in victorious defeat of meeting the desired outcome.

Adversity, unfortunately, is a part of life, and each person handles it differently! Many of us are not necessarily strong because we want to be; we are strong because we have to be! However, Proverbs 24:10 NIV states, *If you falter in a time of trouble, how small is your strength!* So, we have decided—to the best of our abilities—not to allow adversity to keep us bound and held in captivity in keeping us from achieving our God-ordained purpose.

A number of us have experienced trials and tribulations, causing us insurmountable, deep-rooted pain! Pain we didn't believe we would ever be able to escape until Jesus showed us the way. *He healeth the broken in heart, and bindeth up their wounds* (Psalm 147:3).

Enduring until the end is about overcoming adversity and pushing beyond the pain in becoming whole and healthy again. It demonstrates a willingness to "fight the good fight of faith" in the midst of conflict to take hold of the external life to which we were called by witnessing and encouraging others to believe and have faith. *Jesus said unto him, if thou canst believe, all things are possible to him that believeth* (Mark 9:23).

Deciding not to keep silent in allowing your experiences to get the better of us. Deciding to overcome through your testimonies (Revelation 12:11) to allow healing to take place in yourselves and others. Too often we suffer in silence and fail to see the power of our pain to help others. *So let those who are suffering according to God's will entrust themselves to a faithful Creator by continuing to do what is good* (1 Peter 4:1 CJB). Pain, whether emotional or physical, can be conquered with the right mindset and determination. *Nay, in all these things we are more than conquerors through him that loved us* (Romans 8:37).

> *Don't interfere with good people's lives; don't try to get the best of them. No matter how many times you trip them up, God-loyal people don't stay down long; Soon they're up on their feet, while the wicked end up flat on their faces.*
>
> ~Proverbs 24:15-16 MSG

---

ENDURE or ENDURANCE:

1. to abide or to bear up under pressure (suffering)

2. Continuing Christian commitment in the face of difficulty.[49]

STRONG'S CONCORDANCE:

- Hebrew: *ko•ach se•vel*[50]

    > **5281** - **ko•ach** is strength and **se•vel** is to bear, to suffer, and burden, putting them together makes up the modern Hebrew expression "endurance." It translates as "the strength to suffer, to carry a burden."

- Greek: *hupomoné*[51]

    > **5281** – a remaining behind, a patient enduring

---

49  www.biblestudytools.com/dictionary/endurance/
50  https://hebrew.jerusalemprayerteam.org/endurance/
51  www.biblehub.com/greek/5281.htm

# POST-TRAUMATIC STRESS DISORDER (PTSD)

April 11, 2019

Finalized April 15, 2019

During a session with Margaret Lilly Simmons of Lilly Acupuncture & Wellness on Wednesday, April 10, she asked me a series of questions that led to a discussion about post-traumatic stress disorder (PTSD). Amazingly enough, I have dealt with and endured a great deal of disappointment and pain in my life over a number of years. I actually remember telling God, "Please let me get over one disappointment, trial, and tribulation before you hit me with another one!" My trials were taking place one after the other, and the tribulations were mounting! I seriously wondered how I was coping and staying afloat through it all. Ironically, if I didn't share my story, no one would ever know the depth of my pain to understand who I am today. So after sharing some intimate details with Margaret, she not only apologized for her line of questioning, but she thanked me for trusting her enough with my story to allow her to treat me.

Honestly speaking, I felt a little chatty—or, to be exact, overly chatty—in my mind! But God has been teaching me and instructing me about the importance and purpose of transparency. Society, unfortunately, teaches us to suppress all of what is thrown at us unless specific individuals are able to control the outcome to receive credit for the building up or breaking down of our character. Our opposition (enemies), those who attack us and oppress us, want us to keep quiet and never reveal our feelings to include the impact of their actions toward our overall well-being, the impact to our physical and mental health. And, whether we refuse to accept it or not, there is an **intricate** connection. Truth, unfortunately, is not respected, but denial and lies are encouraged!

Many people don't want to be held accountable for or believe just a little bit that there may be a connection or distinct correlation between an individual's overall health and the impact of our environmental (atmospheric) experiences. Someone once stated, "You didn't grow up in the (deep) South to experience racism and have such a passionate concern, yet you are able to articulate the pain as though you were not only present during that era but slavery too!" My ancestors lived it, and their DNA runs through my veins! Yes, we are living in a different era, and the current year is 2019, but the mindset of people in how we interact and disrespect (as well as bully) one another hasn't improved all that much! Pain is pain, no matter the era! Some of us have simply gotten better at ignoring it or choosing other alternatives to numb the pain while others look away. Look at how high the suicide rate has climbed amongst adults and children to include the increased use of opioids!

People, oftentimes, want us to be personable, but only when and if it benefits them. For instance, a former supervisor wanted me to believe I was either antisocial or racist because I opted not to engage during social events within the workplace. But what about the mental torture to me? How can you feel comfortable and personable with folks who care nothing about you as a fellow human being? People talk at you but never to you while plotting your demise (failure) in the name of business to benefit themselves at all costs. In many cases, their only reason for wanting you to be a part of a social event is to gather intel they can use against you later. Some social events are used to foster a false sense of trust as well as reinforce the breakdown of hierarchy in setting boundaries between the leadership and the help. Or perhaps your presence was needed to ensure they didn't have to go far to look for you at the conclusion of the event when it was time for you to be volunteered as part of the cleanup. Yes, it sounds morbid, but it's true! No, not everyone looks down upon you in treating you so inhumanely, but it puts you on guard to want to protect yourself! At work, on the street, around family and friends, you see the similarities as it is being taught universally. And you wonder why people are so stressed out! There is an end and a limit to mostly everything!

So what was the million-dollar question, in summary, as asked by Margaret Lilly Simmons? *Do you think you have healed [emotionally]?* That was so profound! Why? Because she made me understand how emotions are trapped in our blood to cause stagnation! With stagnation comes blockage. With blockage comes the interruption to the flow of circulation! Nonetheless, my response was, "Yes! Today, I am able to give my testimony without crying or falling apart." But as I think about it, is that really a viable sign that I am "A-okay"? My pain simply didn't disappear or go away! Have I constructively dealt with the issues of my offenses, or was I simply managing? But to treat my symptoms, which started the second week of February 2019 and manifested within my body as an intense headache with cranial pressure and numbness on the left side of my face causing bleeding from my left nostril, she needs to know the root cause and extent of my physical and mental injuries not visible to the naked eye. In other words, what am I holding in or compressing?

After Wednesday, my conversation with Margaret Simmons in addition to the conversations I have had with Dr. Marcia Boyce Levi make so much more sense to me now! These women, who are medical professionals, don't just treat the physical body, they treat the invisible wounds and scarring imposed upon the spirit, the whole person. **Our DNA is imprinted in our blood and our experiences, which affect our emotions and create memories. Those memories evolve and take shape by getting coded in our blood along with our DNA. As offenses pile up, big or small, they strike at the core of our existence to add weight that needs to be released.** That which has not been settled can be reawakened by similar offenses (new ones) to trigger old memories of emotional pain and trauma.

PTSD is often thought of and associated with combat fatigue, but many of us are experiencing a different kind of war. The battle of life and (chronic) physical or mental stresses leading to spiritual warfare is real! As outlined in something I read, symptoms of PTSD may result in the following: withdrawal, nightmares, unwanted memories of trauma, avoidance of situations that bring upon unpleasant reminders, anxiety (panic attacks), and depression. What wasn't mentioned is high blood pressure, temporomandibular joint (TMJ) dysfunction, temporal arteritis, and the possibility of a stroke and heart attack.

**To elaborate, healing is not just about addressing the visible scars!** Your experiences, trials, and tribulations concerning how you *process* information as a coping mechanism have a direct impact to your health. You may see yourself as being strong, as so do I, but the constant hits of compounded emotional trauma created by stressors leave an impression on your body. **Being burdened and stressed sends signals to the brain that something is wrong.** Enzymes are *secreted* in an attempt to heal the body, but there is no evidence of a foreign object or invasion that needs to be evicted or eradicated. When triggered by stress, an enzyme attacks a synaptic regulatory molecule in the brain. High blood pressure develops. The development or presence of inflammation is also a sign of dis-ease in your body that is often ignored. In some cases, the immune system triggers inflammation as a healthy response or reaction indicating the presence of injury or infection. The accumulation of inflammation causes greater damage over time if not treated accordingly.

Things have most certainly taken a turn within the workplace. Nothing is as it was when I graduated from high school and thought about integrating amongst the more mature working class while continuing my education. There was the feeling of being a part of an extended family of team members who pulled together to encourage one another. Today, there is an unspoken display of **ownership** as if you were purchased at an auction to be used as disposable damaged goods at will. You are told you should be grateful to have a job regardless of the unrealistic expectation. And there is a growing awareness of turf wars and under-the-table, back-alley deals being waged with people as pawns. Too many people are getting caught in the cross fire as they become casualties of war. They are getting hurt or destroyed and tossed to the side or thrown out with the bathwater to be replaced by the next unsuspecting hire unless they are brought in based on association (nepotism). No matter the position as dictated by the world's way of conducting business, there is a *divine order* and expectation under the son!

Signs, discussions, and training concerning "insider threat" are on the rise. As defined, an insider threat is a threat to an organization that comes from people within the organization to include current and former employees, contractors, and business associates who have been privy to inside company business and operational information. But what about the malicious insider threat to employees as directed by the organization, thus contributing to the presence of PTSD within employees? What about the need for change concerning employee relations to deal with and to eliminate the bullying? What about streamlining the manner in which the offices (or organizations) are structured to reduce the stress of employees?

## REFERENCES

**Nepotism**: the practice among those in positions of leadership with power and/or influence of recruiting and favoring relatives and friends.

## LINKS

1. www.cnn.com/2019/04/12/entertainment/ariana-grande-ptsd-brain-scan-instagram-trnd/index.html

2. www.ptsd.va.gov/understand/what/ptsd_basics.asp

3. https://youtu.be/zwibgNGe4aY

# GOD IS MY SOURCE AND MY STRENGTH

## THERE'S HOPE IN FRONT OF ME!

*My flesh and my heart may fail,
But God is the rock and strength of my heart
and my portion forever.*

**~ Psalm 73:26 AMP**

July 8, 2019

I never thought or imagined sharing myself with others so intimately, but God blesses me and gives me the strength as well as the voice to be open and honest (transparent) about my journey in an attempt to reach others. We all are struggling or have struggled in one fashion or another. We all haven't always been on top or on the right path!

    I am someone who has struggled with staying afloat and is forever fighting to stay on track to keep her flesh under subjection. I am someone who knows pain to recognize pain in others, but I am also someone who knows *unconditional love* and forgiveness are a saving grace for healing. Someone who, in spite of her pain, also has joy in the knowing, deep down in my soul! Someone who has sought refuge in knowing Jesus and developing a relationship to know He exists for herself. Someone who believes and has faith in the supernatural beyond the natural. Someone who refuses to give up or give in to this world system! *In the World, but not of the World!*

I have, unfortunately, met many people who are hurting and/or have checked out! People who are trying hard to maintain and hold on to hope. People others have dismissed or have tossed to the side and condemned. I know what it is like to be condemned and rejected or left out in the cold! Some of my sisters and brothers need to know that they are not alone. They need to know that someone understands and is not afraid to disclose her testimonies no matter what others may or may not think and believe! I'm not afraid of looking foolish or weak to those who do not understand my mission to grab hold of the hand that needs to be held, extend a hug, a listening ear, or a simple "hello"!

We have to stop telling people to man up (or woman up) and show a little compassion where and when it is needed. We simply don't know just how close to the edge is the edge for a soul that has been wounded! When you have done all that you can do, God will let you know when you have done enough to move on to the next and the next and the next for someone else to step in. One plants and another waters. As one waters, another may be sent to nurture. As one nurtures, another may be sent to mentor. But it should all be done in love!

## REFERENCES

- www.youtube.com/watch?v=O5GFiDdGGGM
- www.youtube.com/watch?v=pgJFUW3VenY

# UNTIL NOW

*Now faith is the substance of things hoped for,
the evidence of things not seen.*

**~ Hebrews 11:1**

September 9, 2019

Updated October 5, 2020

On July 27, 2019, Minister Hannah Forney of Applied Faith Ministries International gave an on time word from the Lord; and what a glorious word it was too! She had no idea as to what I was going through or how much I needed that word! The title, Until Now!, and scripture tells us that **Faith Is Now**! Not tomorrow or yesterday, but **now**! As I mature in the word to know and to appreciate who God is, it is, often, just important to be quiet while God is intervening on your behalf. In fact, Psalm 46:10 tells us to Be still, and know that HE IS GOD: He will be exalted among the heathen, and He will be exalted in the earth. Prior to September 8, 2019, for approximately six months, I was more quiet than usual. There are times when you must guard your tongue! And I was very careful not to speak much, share much, write much, or post much on social media until the time was right! **UNTIL NOW!**

Not everyone has your best interest at heart, and not everyone knows how to process information to make the right decision for handling what is disclosed to them with maturity. And not everyone is in position, spiritually, for praising God when news is not favorable! We normally celebrate and praise the Lord when things are going well. No, this is not a criticism; it is an honest observation! God said to call those things that are not as though they were (Romans 4:17), and when you petition the Lord to act on your behalf (showing you favor), you say thank You and move forward with *an attitude of Thanksgiving* in believing that it is already done! Not many may understand that concept! Let's take a look at Isaiah 55:8-9, which states, *For my thoughts are not your thoughts, neither are your ways my ways, saith the* LORD. *For as the heavens are higher than the earth, so are my ways higher than your ways, and my thoughts than your thoughts.*

For that reason, when I receive news from my doctor concerning my health, I take it seriously; but it is not the *final* diagnosis. In other words, I refuse to claim that outcome as my final word until I hear from the Lord! **God is my Master Physician, and He has assured me that He is fighting for me.** God is very specific! He said, if I abide in Him, He will abide in me! And I made my decision some time ago—no matter what— to choose Jesus as my saving grace! Therefore, I AM tethered to Him like He is tethered to me! I AM SOUL'D OUT, and nothing can separate me from my *first love*! My faith, belief, and trust in Him remains *high*! I cannot (and must not) allow surrounding voices of possible doom and gloom (naysayers) to negate what God has done and is doing in my life!

*I am the Vine, you are the branches. When you're joined with me and I with you, the relation intimate and organic, the harvest is sure to be abundant. Separated, you can't produce a thing. Anyone who separates from me is deadwood, gathered up and thrown on the bonfire. But if you make yourselves at home with me and my words are at home in you, you can be sure that whatever you ask will be listened to and acted upon. This is how my Father shows who he is—when you produce grapes, when you mature as my disciples.*

~ John 15:7-8 MSG

**PRAISE REPORT:** First came the letter from my primary care physician stating that there were some abnormal test results and she needed me to make an appointment to see her right away. But, me being me, I didn't act quickly; so my doctor attempted to contact me by phone on my cell and at work. Unfortunately, I was moved, but not overwhelmingly. Isaiah 53:5 AMP states, *But He was wounded for our transgressions, He was crushed for our wickedness [our sin, our injustice, our wrongdoing]; the punishment [required] for our well-being fell on Him, and by His stripes (wounds) we are healed.* It was important for me to remember that!

Upon making the appointment and following through, I learned there were three concerns, so I made additional follow-up appointments to see various specialists to confirm the outcome of the results. While waiting, I was hearing and receiving instruction from God. I was already using ginger oil on my legs and other parts of my body for inflammation, but I was also hearing, from God, to rub it on my stomach. In addition to using the ginger oil, I was told to rub frankincense oil on my breast and across my chest. Some nights, I mixed the ginger and frankincense oil together. Making my way to each appointment, it all fell into place!

1. There was the presence of a mass or lump on my right breast, which turned out to be benign! It was a fluid-filled cyst or pocket, which was easily drained.

2. For quite some time, for a person who was already at a full stage of menopause, there was some abnormal menstrual bleeding and spotting, and the tests revealed polyps as well as some calcified fibroids or tissue mass. A hysteroscopy was performed, and the results yielded a benign outcome as well!

3. The third I am still waiting to confirm, but I am also hopeful of a glowing report. Why? Because He said so!

---

Added October 5, 2020

God worked this out too! The appointment to see a pulmonary specialist took place on Friday, October 4, 2019.

There is a saying that "no news is good news," but, according to the pulmonologist: "Although there is a mass (or nodule) present as referenced by the CT scan, it is so small that we are unable to operate to get a sample of the tissue to be biopsied at this time." He encouraged me to pay attention to any persisting symptoms as they (may or may not) develop and to get another CT scan in six months to a year to see if it is growing or shifting in any way.

The inconclusive diagnosis was a little annoying, but I do understand. He called in a couple of prescriptions for the cough, the dryness, and my asthma, but because I am a little apprehensive when it comes to prescription drugs, as explained to him, I will research each and seek to narrow an herbal substitute, if possible, with assistance from Dr. Levi, who is my nutritionist and chiropractor. He said he understood and asked me to follow up.

The good news is, I wasn't in any pain. The doctor couldn't hear any abnormality in my breathing, no obstruction, blockage, or wheezing in my lungs or chest, which means there was a presence of fluid. And, I haven't seen any bleeding (or as much as I did initially) when I cough. There's a slight tickle, and the cough is annoying, but God has assured me that all is well!

It's a process as I move toward complete *divine healing* with faith. So I won't complain!

Since day one of my existence, according to my mother, I have had a number of health challenges. Starting with February 2019, there has been one health issue after the other, but I was determined not to lose my cool over it, although I was a little frustrated about many things coming to light all at once. However, I was really starting to understand the true meaning behind Matthew 22:14: *For many are called, but few are chosen.* In addition, Luke 10:19 (paraphrased), which states, Behold, I give unto you power [or authority] to tread on serpents and scorpions, and over all the power [or authority] of the enemy: and nothing shall by any means shall hurt you, was also ringing in my ear! God has a plan for my life. A plan that involves prospering me, not to harm me, and I must always remember that no matter what and push forward!

## FOOD FOR THOUGHT AND ENCOURAGEMENT

I would like to encourage you to review and study all the herbs mentioned in the Bible. Do you know why the **Three Wise Men** specifically chose frankincense, myrrh, and gold? Have you considered the spiritual significance of each item? When I asked God what herb represents gold in my case, He said *ginger*!

# LONG-SUFFERING

*After you have suffered for a little while,*
*the God of all grace [who imparts His blessing and favor],*
*who called you to His own eternal glory in Christ,*
*will Himself complete, confirm, strengthen, and establish you*
*[making you what you ought to be].*

**~ 1 Peter 5:10 AMP**

December 31, 2019

There is absolute beauty and purpose in everything that God does or allows! You simply have to be willing to move outside of yourself (your flesh and ego) to see (discern) through the Holy Spirit to understand the lessons (training and discipline) to embrace the strengthening of your core that's being built up from the foundation (root) to stand tall on solid ground.

When it is all said and done, no matter what may come, you will be able to stand for eternity, leaning on the Lord as His spiritual warrior. We all want the blessings and the anointing along with the power of the Holy Spirit, but lack the staying power for long-suffering. We want to give up before the finished work is complete. Quality is perfected, and it goes hand in hand with being tried, tested, confirmed, and elevated! Let God qualify you for the positioning through the process of long-suffering so you don't crack under pressure!

## THE NINE FRUITS OF THE SPIRIT

*But the (9) fruits of the Spirit [the result of His presence within us] is [1]love [unselfish concern for others], [2]joy, [inner] [3]peace, [4]patience or longsuffering [not the ability to wait, but how we act while waiting], [5]kindness, [6]goodness, [7]faithfulness, [8]gentleness or meekness, [9] temperance or self-control (restraint). Against such things there is no law* (Galatians 5:22-23, combination of the AMP and KJV with emphasis added).

Jesus was described as being meek. He was also mistaken for being weak or submissive in accordance to the world's view of Him. But not so! He drew strength from the Father, and when He was submissive, it was to God! He exemplified **power under control** and He was in total control of Himself! He knew what to do, when to do it, and how to do it for getting the best results and responses for all within His environment.

*Meekness*: an attribute of human nature and behavior. It has been defined several ways: righteous, humble, teachable, and patient under suffering, long-suffering willing to follow gospel teachings; an attribute of a true disciple.[52]

---

52   https://iblp.org/sites/default/files/pdf/meekness.pdf

# PASSION

*A tranquil heart is life to the body,*
*But passion is rottenness to the bones.*

~ **Proverbs 14:30 NASB**

May 21, 2020

Revised July 7, 2020

Back in 2009, God revealed to me the intensity of a mother's love for her son in comparison to her level of grief for him when he was killed. As deeply as she loved, she grieved. You could say that her heart broke, and a little piece of her died with him; and she has felt the hurt of his passing many days since then! Each and every person loves, grieves, and hates at different degrees of intensity based on their passion for life, living and dying.[53] To the same extent, each person learns, evaluates, and understands information at different stages or phases of their mental development!

---

53  Living without dying to self is death. Living and dying to self is living.

Passion is an emotion of great intensity and desire, as it is processed through different phases of mental development. Many of us are relentlessly driven by burning desire (our wants and needs) as demonstrated through our actions. We can be so passionate or headstrong about a particular topic of interest that no one can tell us anything differently, show us anything differently, or teach us anything evidenced by truth and facts contradicting our faulty way of thinking, which is fueled by negative influence and ignorance!

Many of us are also driven by ambition, which goes hand-in-hand with desire. Ambition and desire can be viewed as a need to succeed and advance in any area (personal or career related) even if it means joining forces with others (good or bad), which tests our resolve or willingness to be ruthless to accomplish what we want!

## EXAMPLES OF PASSION AND DESIRE

1. King David and Bathsheba: Displaying an abuse of power in relation to a hierarchy of chain of command, David is driven by lust for another man's wife. David was willing to sacrifice his own soul to covet that which was not his and sent (ordered) Bathsheba's husband (Captain Uriah) to a mission of war to clear the way for him (David) to make advances toward Bathsheba. When Bathsheba learns that she is pregnant with David's child, David plots to send Uriah to bed Bathsheba as a cover-up attempt. When that fails, he arranges and orders Uriah to the front lines in battle with the hope that he would be killed. When he receives word of

Uriah's death, he plans to wed Bathsheba to save her from a fate of being shunned, stoned, and killed for committing adultery. Once they are married, the baby is born with complications and dies (see 2 Samuel 11).

2. Muhammad Ali: When the United States drafted Muhammad Ali in the Vietnam War, he refused, was sentenced to jail, and was later released. Ali was very passionate about his belief in not going to war with a country that had done no harm to him personally. In fact, he spoke of a government that was instrumental in allowing great disrespect and continuous mistreatment to him and many others who looked like him on the basis of skin color and was now knocking at his door and expecting him to fight for them. He spoke of the racial injustice, discrimination, and violation of civil liberties by a country that wanted him to war on their behalf, and yet, they did not value him the same to see him as a human being to grant him equality! When I myself had learned of his story, it caused me to have a greater sense of respect for a man who was willing to take such a strong stand for what he believed! It was a display of passion (unselfish,[54] selfish,[55] or selfless[56]) for the life of others. (Read about his life story to learn about the essence of this man beyond his boxing career.)

---

54  https://dictionary.cambridge.org/dictionary/english/unselfish
55  https://dictionary.cambridge.org/dictionary/english/selfish
56  https://dictionary.cambridge.org/dictionary/english/selfles

## THE PASSION OF CHRIST

If and when you take the time to read and study the Bible for yourself, you will note the clarity of its truth. It speaks of two major dimensions—the natural and the supernatural—with each having subdimensions within itself. All being linked to God, the Father, the Son (Yashua, Jesus Christ of Nazareth), and the Holy Spirit, who are one! It all began with our Abba Father, the Creator, who had a *divine purpose* in aligning the dimensions to include each and every inhabitant and positioning through the Son and the Holy Spirit. God foresaw and foreknew every aspect of that which has taken place and has yet to take place, the beginning and the end as predestined by Him.

God loves us very deeply with intense and controlled passion! He does not waver in His emotion nor does He use it as a bartering chip. He made a conscious decision to love us unconditionally and to save us from ourselves. He has given us countless opportunities to get ourselves into position to be reconciled back to Him, *divine alignment* to live righteous and Holy. But we insist on attempting to remove God out of the equation and cutting Him out of our lives after He sacrificed His only begotten Son!

Yashua, with great passion, honored His assignment of suffering. Through His sacrifice (birth, life, death, and resurrection) of unselfishness, He took the weight of our sins upon His shoulders by standing in the gap to restore life back to us. Like Moses before the birth of Yashua, we are also expected to stand in the gap for others to pray and intercede on their behalf in the honor and continuation of Yashua's life through the Holy Spirit (see Luke 23:34, Hebrews 7:25, Psalm 106:23, Ezekiel 22:30, 1 Timothy 2:1-2). And we must not forget about Esther (see Esther 8).

## PERSONAL WILL

We keep making excuses and justifications for doing things our way! We can no longer sit quietly on the sidelines doing nothing and saying nothing as children of the Most High God who are being called, chosen, and pushed out front to fight the good fight of faith! We have simply gone through the motions for far too long without giving any real thought to the motives of our actions and not take any responsibility.

Like robots, day in and day out, we routinely conduct our lives as conditioned to believe outside of the Word of God, to think and act with such zeal and vigor! Holding on strongly to a disdain for self as we direct that same behavior toward each other. We refuse to challenge ourselves to penetrate the inner core of our synapses to encourage a reevaluation of our reasoning process for objectively considering all of what we were taught (brainwashed) to believe incorrectly! Even as Christians who are supposed to be committed to following Christ as He follows God the Father, we refuse to relinquish control to view the world through God's eyes.

What if we allowed ourselves to be just as passionate about God and His word as He is about us? What if we believed and trusted God with all of our heart, mind, and soul to unite as one spirit to accomplish God's will on Earth as in Heaven? Can you imagine the unity and the love to generate healing as we demonstrate immeasurable miracles, signs, and wonders from and for one to another, not leaving anyone out? How glorious would that be?

## REFERENCES

- Predestine(d): determine an outcome or course of events (actions) in advance by divine will or fate.

- www.passionofheart.co.uk/room-of-no-exit/jewish-struggle-with-daemonic/hebrew-word-for-passion/

- www.passionofheart.co.uk/wound-of-existence/heart-is-deep/truth/anger-sadness/hebrew/

- https://youtu.be/3UNuPcuRjao

# ARROGANCE, IGNORANCE, AND FEAR!

*"For My thoughts are not your thoughts, Nor are your ways My ways," declares the Lord. "For as the heavens are higher than the earth, So are My ways higher than your ways And My thoughts than your thoughts."*

~ Isaiah 55:8-9 NASB

June 20, 2020

Revised October 14, 2020

As stated, many times before, people are a product of their environment and upbringing. Our environment normally influences our thought and behavioral patterns through our experiences, education, and interactions with others. Our experiences along the path of our mental development when we are young or old directs our actions. A part of our environment and experiences also has to do with the culture in which we have been exposed to in grooming our growth and understanding or lack thereof from a place of fear, ignorance, and arrogance! Some of us are stuck[57] in our heads in a certain mindset, which is contributed to a time period, event, or position from trauma or faulty thinking. Too often, we refuse to inventory our way of thinking to catch up, grow, take responsibility for our actions, repent, and change to reform for the betterment of our souls.

God is not the author of evil, confusion, or strife! He encourages love and unity; and He has blessed us with free will! The mindset to know right from wrong and the ability to choose who we will serve based on the condition of our hearts! We have, unfortunately, conformed to the ways (pulse), principals (leadership), and principles (guidance) of this world system, which encourages falling in line whether right or wrong and not questioning the motives or the outcome. We have become overly comfortable and conditioned to accept the norm in not being expected to challenge any injustices regardless of the circumstances. And the law through the judiciary system has been written and used in many cases as a justification for numerous civil violations and the spilling of blood. *Ye that love the LORD, [should] hate [ALL matter of] evil: He preserveth the souls of His saints; He delivereth them out of the hand of the wicked* (Psalm 97:10).

Today, we are at a turning point! We must acknowledge the ignorance and arrogance of our thinking, which has been fueled by darkness to generate fear in keeping us bound! There is a fork in the middle of the road, and the sky is breaking open to reveal the light, forcing the acceptance of truths—which can

---

57  stuck: strong hold, bound

no longer be dismissed or denied if we are to move forward effectively! Truth and trust cannot be built on a lie! Inadequate structures and strongholds are being exposed and torn down to deconstruct, rearrange, and bring order based on truth. God wants to bless us for our obedience and give life. It is not his intent to bring us any harm, but there are also consequences for our disobedience. Lucifer, the falling angel who is our enemy, wants to curse us and destroy life. In fact, John 10:10 refers to him as a thief whose main objective is to come steal, kill, and destroy. We have an opportunity to overturn curses by resisting the temptation and manipulation of the enemy and follow the leading of the Lord to release blessings in our lives, our loved ones, and the land, and to generate healing for us all!

## REFERENCES

1. **Ignorant/ignorance** - lacking knowledge, information, or awareness about a particular or specific thing; uneducated, unsophisticated; discourteous, rude, obnoxious.

    a) *Having the understanding darkened, being alienated from the life of God through the ignorance that is in them, because of the blindness of their heart* (Ephesians 4:18).

    b) *For they being ignorant of God's righteousness, and going about to establish their own righteousness, have not submitted themselves unto the righteousness of God* (Romans 10:3).

c) *For I would not, brethren, that ye should be ignorant of this mystery, lest ye should be wise in your own conceits; that blindness in part is happened to Israel, until the fulness of the Gentiles be come in* (Romans 11:25).

2. **Arrogant/arrogance** - pompous, haughty, overbearing, and prideful; condescending; someone who displays a behavior of being prideful and full of themselves; thinking more highly of themselves; unwarranted self-importance to the position of entitlement or privilege.

    a) *For I say, through the grace given unto me, to every man that is among you, not to think of himself more highly than he ought to think; but to think soberly, according as God hath dealt to every man the measure of faith* (Romans 12:3).

    b) *Talk no more so exceeding proudly; let not arrogancy come out of your mouth: for the LORD is a God of knowledge, and by him actions are weighed* (1 Samuel 2:3).

    c) *The fear of the LORD is to hate evil: pride, and arrogancy, and the evil way, and the froward mouth, do I hate* (Proverbs 8:13).

## SCRIPTURE

1. For blessings, see Deuteronomy 28:1-14.

2. For curses, see Deuteronomy 28:15-68.

3. *But now, having died to what bound us, we have been released from the law, so that we serve in the new way of the Spirit, and not in the old way of the written code* (Romans 7:6 BSB).

# LEAD WITH INTEGRITY, NOT DISCRETION!

> *Then Peter opened his mouth, and said, Of a truth I perceive that God is no respecter of persons.*
>
> ~ **Acts 10:34**

January 28, 2014

A word that I have heard more often lately than I care to within the human resources arena is *discretion*. If discretion was used by management or those in positions of authority "fairly" across the board in granting or disapproving an employee's or person's ability (rights) to be held accountable or exempted from adhering to a rule, regulation, policy, or law, then, I believe, I would be okay with it being used or exercised as freely as it is! But the use of it tends to give a false sense of empowerment in granting or denying favor in a senseless and somewhat corruptible or an ironically legalistic way. When you really think about it, it is quite contradictory to the purpose for creating laws, regulations, polices, or rules—especially if these policies (etc.) are broken on a whim or at will on the basis of how a person is feeling at the time. In essence, you could say it is more connected to emotion rather than reasoning, which can be quite counterproductive and sends mixed signals to those within an environment who are watching and observing.

As children of God, those who proclaim to be *Christians* or *believers*, we are called to be greater examples! We have to be careful not to send mixed signals regardless of what is allowed or practiced unfairly by others around us. We are held to a higher standard, and it is our responsibility to teach that standard in accordance to how we live our lives—meaning, as children of God, we are expected to uphold every command or word of God. We are expected to study the word of God, live our lives in accordance to the word of God, teach the word of God, and spread the Gospel according to the mindset of God in honoring His ways, not in accordance to the ways of the world! We should not be straddling the fence or cutting corners in allowing what is done in the world to compromise our right standing (position) with the Lord.

Always be mindful of your *salvation* to include the *price* that was *paid* by our Savior in freeing us from bondage to our *sin nature*. God's Word is very clear! He is very precise and specific about what He expects. He has granted us all free will. He has given us a choice to do the right thing. No science in any area of business as taught by the world system should be allowed by you to compromise your salvation. The line is very thin with all intensive purposes to deceive you. The traps are strategically set to confuse you into thinking that you are doing the right thing because you have been given the authority to exercise your discretion over one from another. But, if that right thing falls outside of the Will of God for your life as a believer, then that thing which you have been convinced, deceived, and influenced into thinking is right is actually wrong in the eyes of God, regardless of what area of business is attached to it. Managing and supervising people can still be exercised with a Spirit of Excellence in following the example or pattern given to us by God. That example is Jesus Christ. The character we should be studying and following is His which is linked to the Nine Fruits of the Spirit. What fruit are you bearing? Lead with integrity!

*But the fruit of the Spirit*
*is love, joy, peace, longsuffering, gentleness, goodness,*
*faith, Meekness, temperance: against such there is no law.*

~ Galatians 5:22-23

## SUGGESTED READING

*A Call for Character: Manifestation of the Sons of God*

Author: Greg Zoschak

ISBN-978-1-6024741-1-6

# WHAT IS TRUTH?

*And ye shall know the truth, and the truth shall make you free.*

**~ John 8:32**

November 18, 2011

Revised October 14, 2020

The number one question these days has to be, "What is truth?" And depending upon who you ask, I'm sure their definition of truth would be entirely different from yours. Should you consider to take the opportunity to study and show yourself approved by rightly dividing the Word of Truth (the Holy Bible which is the Word of God) you may, just possibly, learn to embrace and accept what many believe to be the only truth. But first you have to be willing to believe (in your heart) in the power and existence of the Father, the Son, and the Holy Spirit (Ghost). Then you must walk in faith, thus leaning to that truth and hope against all hope that all things are possible with and through Him who has the authority to give man dominion on earth. And whatsoever is true is also righteous, void of man's interpretation or personal views (opinion).

That which is perceived as truth by one may not speak to another's truth. For most truth to be real to them, they have to experience it, touch it, or see it. However, the fact that one has not experienced a certain truth for themselves does not mean it is not true. Nonetheless, because the mental psyche is very powerful and delicate, we must take into consideration the experiences one has encountered. By acknowledging the experiences of others, it attempts to aid in understanding how and why an individual thinks in the manner in which they do to be able to objectively introduce another truth. If you are not willing to humble yourself and your approach, (absent of the Spirit of Offense, but gentle), you have only served to impose more damage to that person's mind, meaning you will never get through to them to offer any guidance if guidance is necessary!

People are a product of their upbringing. Their behavior, mannerisms, and actions are all dictated by the influences (people, places, and things) within their environment. What they have been exposed to or the lack of exposure in certain areas contributes to their way of thinking. Some are honest about their lack of knowledge in certain areas, while others may attempt to overcompensate through their actions in pretending to know what they do not know. Some are very resourceful at making attempts to research and learn out of interest to educate themselves, while others become very comfortable with their state of mind and avoid change at all costs. The overcompensators tend to fall in this last category. They are the ones who tend to exert their power and authority (earned or unearned) very disrespectfully through bullying to lord over you.

## HOW DO YOU DEFINE ACCOMPLISHMENT?

Prior to and without the revelational knowledge of God, I saw my life and the things of this world through the eyes of man with rose-colored glasses. Then I learned I cannot love the world, see it clearly, and have no desire to please God. How can I aspire to meet man's objectives, which are more subjective in nature and serve to honestly—with the greatest of integrity—please God at the same time? Everything within me is calling me to live my life much differently and in absolute truth and freedom of what is projected around me.

# THE UGLINESS INSIDE

*Beloved, follow not that which is evil, but that which is good. He that doeth good is of God: but he that doeth evil hath not seen God.*

~ 3 John 1:11

March 23, 2014

Today, we see a great display of misalignment, division, and power play amongst those who see themselves as gods at the helm of our less-than-organized governmental structure. As the position of who is in power changes, so does the direction of certain laws that have been put into place to further separate those "who have" from the "have nots." Decisions are made at the top level with the false misrepresentation of the common good just to lift someone higher amongst the ranks of their perceived plateau in being recognized (reputation) as one of the elite, all while dictating and delegating downward in demonstrating (and teaching) inappropriate examples of leadership for others to follow. A society based on nothing but selfishness and greed, therefore, further lacking in *unity*, puts us in a constant state of war by those in positions of power and leadership against the weak. However, that does not particularly mean that those in positions of power and leadership are strong. It just simply means that they have the backing or support of the major players who have been instrumental in dictating the rules that have been set in motion to control the less fortunate.

> *But I urge and entreat you, brethren,*
> *by the name of our Lord Jesus Christ,*
> *that all of you be in perfect harmony*
> *and full agreement in what you say, and that there*
> *be no dissensions or factions or divisions among you,*
> *but that you be perfectly united in*
> *your common understanding*
> *and in your opinions and judgments.*
>
> ~ 1 Corinthians 1:10 AMPC

Amazingly, we live in a world that encourages education that is only recognized and deemed acceptable (glorified or taken seriously) depending upon society's standards of where that knowledge should be obtained (e.g., Ivy League institutions with a big name). As mentioned before, man views himself and others according to their position, title, and net worth in exercising power over others in deeming who he thinks should be considered worthy, important, and of value in the name of a false validation system. However, no matter the name or the recommendation, education (knowledge) is nothing if it is not applied accordingly. And yet, with all that so-called intelligence (smarts) and credentials (whether it be an associate's, a bachelor's, a master's, or a doctorate degree), we still fail miserably at being human beings to examine truth and lead with integrity for all. Instead of evolving to create a better universe for the future of our existence, we have gone in circles to reproduce the past with the same results. Still living in and conspiring with darkness, we have never really changed our mindsets! We have only changed our outer **image** to successfully disillusion ourselves and others into thinking or believing change has occurred with no evidence of change. We simply continue to ignore the problems by making excuses not to see what needs to be seen in making a difference.

> "What's the use of a carved god so skillfully carved by its sculptor?
> What good is a fancy cast god when all it tells is lies?
> What sense does it make to be a pious god-maker
> who makes gods that can't even talk?
> Who do you think you are—saying to a stick of wood, 'Wake up,'
> Or to a dumb stone, 'Get up'?
> Can they teach you anything about anything?
> There's nothing to them but surface.
> There's nothing on the inside.
>
> ~ Habakkuk 2:18-19 MSG

Throughout my existence, I have seen the needs of children being pushed aside by the world's "ugliness" as they are continually being victimized and trampled on over and over again in the name of politics and used as pawns. If you were to take the necessary time to conduct your own research to include the history of this nation, you will see we have never put children first to consider their well-being. Ironically, as adults, we are still refusing to accept we are nothing more than children in a grown-up body attempting to work out our own unresolved issues from our childhood. Playing dress up, we do not even regard each other with the same level of expected humanism and compassion! Have we truly considered the clear message we are sending to children in accordance to our actions? What we are really saying to them is this: nothing matters, them or the human race! We are demonstrating we have not placed any value upon them to care one way or the other about what happens to them as human beings in a world that's dictated by an "anything goes" principle! At least not until the situation escalates "out of control" to the point of us no longer being able to ignore the obvious! Never being proactive, but reactive at best, to salvage an *image* in the name of damage control! What about developing character?

*Deceit is in the heart of them that imagine evil:*
*but to the counsellors of peace is joy.*

~ Proverbs 12:20

Here's the thing! Children are a precious gift to you from God. You have been blessed to create life through an earthly process as ordained and allowed by God. Although birthed through you and to you, they do not belong to you. They have been entrusted to you to nurture and to lead or guide toward the Father until they become of age to choose wisely on their own. Each and every experience (good, bad, or indifferent) is absorbed and imprinted upon their hearts. Those experiences become a matter of life and death to the soul, thus strengthening or weakening the SPIRIT. The mind, if not fully equipped to handle those experiences, could interfere with the child's spiritual growth, which formulates into baggage. If that baggage is not properly addressed or sorted out, it can easily be transported into adulthood to continue to grow, fester, and possibly overflow and spill out. Are you familiar with the phrase "children having children," meaning those who are having children lack the maturity to raise them, or "once an adult, twice a child"? If we learn wrong, we teach wrong, and then we develop or grow prematurely, thus spreading darkness and compiling casualties along the way. In the same manner as those who grow into adults lacking the ability to compartmentalize their emotions and being easy to implode, thus unleashing their rage upon others and letting out the ugliness from within!

*And God saw that the wickedness of man*
*was great in the earth, and that every imagination*
*of the thoughts of his heart was only evil continually.*

~ Genesis 6:5

Many people, unfortunately, do not believe in "Heaven or Hell" enough to take God seriously and to acknowledge His word. And why would we? Most of us do not believe in God who is the Father of all creation, that Jesus Christ (Yahweh in the flesh) is God's only begotten Son who came to Earth to save us from ourselves, or that the Holy Spirit (the Comforter, Counselor, Helper, Advocate) was sent by the Father to teach us all things and to remind us of everything! Because we are deeply loved by Him and connected to Him by spirit! One Spirit, one Body, three different entities or persons (many members), all with a different function, but the same common goal and denominator! And it is imperative for us to strive to obtain the same heart that is in Christ Jesus (and Christ-like compassion for one another)! Nonetheless, your disbelief or unwillingness to repent (*express sincere regret or remorse about one's wrongdoing or sin to change within your heart*) does not negate the existence of who God is or the fact that we are supernaturally surrounded by influencing spirits, angels, and demons (fallen angels) every day!

The Bible gives us many references of that from Genesis to Revelations to include angels ascending and descending from Heaven to Earth as depicted in Jacob's dream (see Genesis 28:12). Just as we are told that the devil, as a roaring lion, walketh about (to and from), seeking whom he may devour (see 1 Peter 5:8). Scriptures, the word of God, holds much truth of what to expect even if we refuse to regard it. So, keep in mind, our actions have consequences and we will be held accountable for every action, seen or unseen by the necked eye! God is all knowing and He sees everything! He feels everything! That which is imprinted upon our hearts is imprinted upon His heart! That which concerns Him should concern each of us!

> *But what saith the answer of God unto him?*
> *I have reserved to myself seven thousand men,*
> *who have not bowed the knee to the image of Baal.*
>
> ~ Romans 11:4

In January of 1988, Michael Jackson's song "Man in the Mirror" soared to the top of the singles chart. I truly wonder how many people actually listened to the lyrics to understand its true meaning. How many of us have truly taken a nice, long, objective look at ourselves in the mirror to see the person or persons (**legion**) looking back at us? In conclusion, I would like to leave you with this and take a quote from the TV show *Grimm*: under certain conditions, whatever is "evil" in men's nature seems to always come to the front (surface). They say that the eyes are the widows to the soul! What if you were able to see into the soul of a person to know who they truly are beneath the surface? Skin deep beyond the flesh, bone, and marrow! Beyond the masks people so tightly keep pulled down over their faces to conceal their real identities. What if no matter how hard we try to conceal who we really are from the outside world, it only serves to keep us from acknowledging who we really are on the inside to avoid having to deal with our unresolved issues (great or small) later? The greater the issue, the bigger the stronghold! If we are not careful or are not willing to be truthful with "at least" ourselves, these issues or demons from our past hurts can manifest to release the ugliness inside to do extensive damage to ourselves and/or others. Nonetheless, eventually, each and every person will have to face their own insecurities (and demons) if they truly wish to be set free.

*And oppress not the widow,*
*nor the fatherless, the stranger, nor the poor; and*
*let none of you imagine evil against his brother in your heart.*

~ Zechariah 7:10

**An excerpt from an unknown source referred to as A WISE MAN:** *Crime and violence within the community are the glaring problems that overshadow many other problems that go unseen because they are hidden within our hearts. Cultural differences and problems are in our workplaces, our churches, and government. These cultural differences are taught in our homes, schools, and within our communities. Jesus went against the norm because He didn't allow the culture in which He lived to restrict Him from demonstrating love amongst all people. Jesus didn't place limits in how He cared for others based on their belief systems or preferences. He loved all!* Are your cultural differences getting in the way of God using you as a resource to touch the lives of others? Jesus loved lepers, thieves, drunks, tax embezzlers, and crooked religious leaders. Could the real problem live within us? It's time we all put our differences aside and come together to make a difference.

*Wisdom resteth in the heart of him that hath understanding: but that which is in the midst of fools is made known.*

~ Proverbs 14:33

# POETIC JUSTICE

*Be still, and know that I am God:
I will be exalted among the heathen,
I will be exalted in the earth.*

**~ Psalm 46:10**

March 12, 2015

Revised March 17, 2015

Why does she keep singing that same old tune? *He who covers and forgives an offense seeks love, but he who repeats or harps on a matter separates even close friends* (Proverbs 17:9 AMP). If things are really as bad as she says it is, why doesn't she just get another job and move on? Why continue to subject herself to enduring such an environment? She just needs to put it all behind her and try to *forget* it all! But no—she keeps drudging up her past and playing the victim! *Blessed are those who are persecuted because of righteousness, for theirs is the kingdom of heaven* (Matthew 5:10). When God plants you in a particular location on assignment, it is not as easy as people may think to flee, especially if you want His perfect will for your life!

*And be not conformed to this world:*
*but be ye transformed by the renewing of your mind,*
*that ye may prove what is that good,*
*and acceptable, and perfect, will of God.*

~ Romans 12:2

The pen is mightier than the sword! Prior to 2010, God gave me a command in the form of an assignment to write. An instruction to put my testimonies on paper and make it plain! I was simply told my life was an open book, I was a living testimony, and I had no secrets. I was being called to live a life of full **transparency**. In following through with His command, He blessed me with the title of my first book, *What Do I Do With My Pain?*, which He gave to me through a friend (a very dear spiritual sister, Mary Bryant). From that point onward, God has been revealing to me the importance of that pain within my life to include why He has allowed the many trials and tribulations I have encountered from birth with purpose. In the same manner in which we are given life with a purpose, everything else surrounding our life is planned out with purpose for God's *definitive glory*.

*But the God of all grace,*
*who hath called us unto his eternal glory by Christ Jesus,*
*after that ye have suffered a while,*
*make you perfect, stablish, strengthen, settle you.*

~ 1 Peter 5:10

Getting through the *process* of those ups and downs, also known as trials and tribulations, does not feel good at all and may vary according to each individual. However, the process is necessary to bring you to an expected end. And there is a surefire method for receiving your *breakthrough*, walking in the *spirit* and not according to your flesh, adhering to the word of God and believing in your heart that He will not leave you nor forsake you as He strengthens you! While in the midst of your storm, you are the most vulnerable, and the enemy will stop at nothing to use whatever leverage he can to enslave you and keep you bound. The lower you sink in despair, the harder the enemy hits you to include influencing those around you to strike an even greater blow to your self-esteem. But no matter how great the cost of your pain, you must not waver (falter) in your faith, have any kind of doubt, or distrust in the Father regarding His plan for your life. *He delivers the afflicted in their affliction and opens their ears [to His voice] in adversity* (Job 36:15).

A long way away from being perfect, there have been times when I doubted not only my strength but God's love for me. Before regaining my footing or composure from one trial, there seemed to always be another one hitting me around the corner to knock the wind out of my sail. Just when I thought the tide was low, it would rise again when I least expected it. *But He said, "The things which are impossible with men are possible with God"* **(Luke 18:27 NJKV)**. Forgetting and putting things behind me was no longer an option. Why? Because forgetting only set me up for falling for or pulling me into another trap. In fact, the enemy loves it when we are forgetful. But 1 Peter 5:8 instructs us to *[b]e sober, be vigilant; because your adversary the devil, as a roaring lion, walketh about, seeking whom he may devour.*

## A HARD TRUTH

Watching movies like *Roots*, *The Butler*, and *12 Years a Slave* as a form of entertainment, without feeling enraged on some level, is simply not an option for me! So although I support them, I cannot watch them, especially when the demons depicted in movies like those are a reminder of my present truth. How can I forget the history of this nation as it encompasses the history of my ancestors in viewing me today as it once did? How can I forget the pain of being singled out on the basis of my skin color to include my gender in being a woman in a male-dominated world? Even in this day and time, certain positions are still being reserved for women and Blacks, while other positions are considered to be off limits regardless of your education, skill level, and ability to execute the tasks in getting the job done. Sure, to throw off suspicion or in an attempt to disprove the obvious, there's a sprinkle here and there of women, people of color, and Black men in certain positions with the greatest visibility. But are they really allowed to showcase their true talents or exercise power, control, and authority in a position or role justly earned? I'm sure President Obama would have something to say about that!

> *But what saith the answer of God unto him?*
> *I have reserved to myself seven thousand men,*
> *who have not bowed the knee to the image of Baal.*
>
> ~ Romans 11:14

In a previous writing, titled "The Ugliness Inside," I stated, "Instead of evolving to create a better universe for the future of our existence, we have gone in circles to reproduce the past with the same results. Still living in and conspiring with darkness, we have never really changed our mindsets; only our outer *image* to successfully disillusion ourselves and others into thinking or believing change has occurred with no evidence of change! We simply continue to ignore the problems by making excuses not to see what needs to be seen in making a difference." So each day I get up, I am constantly reminded of the darkness in this world as contributed by many soulless and unrighteous actions of people displaying unfruitful characteristics and no integrity. *But the fruit of the Spirit is love, joy, peace, longsuffering, gentleness, goodness, faith, Meekness, temperance: against such there is no law* (Galatians 5:22-23).

See, here's the thing! Spirit is neither male nor female and it has no color (or ethnicity). If the restart of civilization (the human race) began with just Noah and members of his family, are we not all from the same race, thus made in the image of He who has created us? *In Him we also were made [God's] heritage (portion) and we obtained an inheritance; for we had been foreordained (chosen and appointed beforehand) in accordance with His purpose, Who works out everything in agreement with the counsel and design of His [own] will, so that we who first hoped in Christ [who first put our confidence in Him have been destined and appointed to] live for the praise of His glory! In Him you also who have heard the Word of Truth, the glad tidings (Gospel) of your salvation, and have believed in and adhered to and relied on*

Him, were stamped with the seal of the long-promised Holy Spirit (Ephesians 1:11-13 AMPC).

## FORGIVENESS

O Eternal One, aren't You looking for truth and integrity? You struck them, but they did not flinch. You destroyed them, but they did not yield to Your correction. They wouldn't change their ways. They have set their stony faces against You—defiant and determined, refusing to repent (Jeremiah 5:3 VOICE). Although preached and taught differently, *forgiving is not about forgetting!* On the contrary, one doesn't necessarily have anything to do with the other; one or the other can simply exist or cease to exist with or without the other—meaning you can easily forgive without forgetting. You can also forget and not forgive. Or you can simply forgive and forget just the same, depending upon the circumstances as commanded of you by God. But for me, as ministered to me and commissioned to me by God, to forgive is about remembering and embracing your sin nature to include that of others in appreciating how far you have come. It is about learning and growing on your way to healing the wounds to your soul as caused or inflicted by those sins (and others). It is about overcoming and conquering your experiences and greatest fears on the road to being victorious. Remembering and not forgetting is an attempt to ensure "I" do not run the risk of repeating past mistakes or revisiting certain situations in finding myself to be still bound in any way by my afflictions.

> *And Jesus prayed, Father, forgive them,*
> *for they know not what they do.*
> *And they divided His garments*
> *and distributed them by casting lots for them.*
>
> ~ Luke 23:34 AMPC

Discerning your surroundings is the same as being sober and vigilant to be able to see near and far in the spirit. Being forgetful about the previous lessons, trials, and tribulations you have encountered is the same as being ignorant to the truth. What if Jesus was not equipped to recognize Lucifer in the wilderness? What if He had forgotten about what took place in the Garden of Eden to discern his true nature? What if He had forgotten about bearing the sins and the hurt of the world upon His shoulders to include His death, burial, and resurrection? Would that also equate to Him forgetting about His purpose: being born to die?

If my pain and suffering are not in vain, why would it be necessary for me to forget my spiritual journey on the road toward fulfilling my God-ordained purpose? If I, who has asked God to use me for His glory in allowing me to be a vessel, were to forget my afflictions, how would I be able to minister to others to aid them in their afflictions? *For thou, Lord, art good, and ready to forgive; and plenteous in mercy unto all them that call upon thee* (Psalm 86:5). For His mercy endureth forever! And He blesses me with grace and Christ-like compassion for those who have pained me while calling upon me to bless them and not curse them in prayer.

Forgiving those who have trespassed against me brings healing to my soul. Harboring ill feelings does nothing but induce bitterness and harden my heart. Also, I heard the voice of the Lord, saying, whom shall I send, and who will go for us? Then said I, Here am I; send me (Isaiah 6:8). But, before that can happen, to be an effective vessel, I must die to my flesh each and every day to be in right standing and in perfect alignment with the Lord to include me rebuking any and all anger threatening to stand between me and the *Will of God* for my life. And for my sake and yours, I must be like Peter who asked, *"Lord, how oft shall my brother sin against me, and I forgive him? till seven times? Jesus saith unto him, I say not unto thee, Until seven times: but, Until seventy times seven"* (Matthew 18:21-22).

# SECOND TO NO ONE

*And Jesus came
and spake unto them, saying,
All power is given unto me in heaven and in earth.*

~ **Matthew 28:18**

January 31, 2017

Revised February 2, 2017

Are you taking notes and seeing what is happening all around us concerning our government? To stay on course, I normally make it a point not to focus on the news. Truth be told, I have a next-door neighbor who keeps me abreast of everything before I get in my front door, mainly because she knows I'm not the least concerned so she feels it is necessary to make me aware.

Well, yesterday, I simply explained: Our new president is who the people wanted; they made their choices, and now we must live with it, respect it, and embrace the decision whether we agree with it or not! Clearly, the people wanted a *dictator-*

*ship* rather than a *democracy*. They wanted a *king* rather than a *leader*. Surely you know the difference. If not, look at all the other nations for a comparison and tell me what do you see? When you get the opportunity, please read 1 Samuel 4.

Yes, I know many would argue with me to say this is not what the people wanted and God doesn't make mistakes! So, let me start by saying, CORRECT! God doesn't make mistakes nor does he need our permission or approval for anything He does. And His word is very clear! His ways are not like our ways, and our ways are not like His. But if we believe and trust who He is, then we must also set our minds to stand on His word. Romans 8:28 states, *And we know ALL things (not a few or some, but all things) work together for the good of those who love God and are called in accordance to His purpose.*

If you truly believe that God is all powerful, all knowing, and everywhere all at once or at the same time, then what's the issue? Can't He turn any situation around according to His will? Does He not have the power to allow or disallow that which takes place? Now, let's go a little deeper! Yes, it is clear the visible vote as it pertains to the electoral in comparison to the public side offers a great deal of disparity. But have you considered the invisible vote? The hearts of the people!

We value *reputation* and give no thought to the true meaning of *character* or *integrity*. We talk about image and only give credence to the illusion of it all while giving no thought to the real substance. Why? Because we would gladly accept the imitation only to abandon and avoid the real McCoy! Do you see the irony of it all? And yet, we still refuse to change! We refuse to return to our first LOVE. He is second to no one, and the government sits on His shoulders!

## WATCH AND PRAY WITHOUT CEASING!

> *For to us a child is born, to us a son is given, and the government will be on his shoulders. And he will be called Wonderful Counselor, Mighty God, Everlasting Father, Prince of Peace. Of the greatness of his government and peace there will be no end. He will reign on David's throne and over his kingdom, establishing and upholding it with justice and righteousness from that time on and forever. The zeal of the LORD Almighty will accomplish this.*
>
> ~ Isaiah 9:6-7 NIV

We have to learn how to apply the word of God to our everyday life and act on it accordingly by walking it out in FAITH!

# THE WAR IN THE EARTH

*And they overcame him by the blood of the Lamb and by the word of their testimony, and they did not love their lives to the death. Therefore rejoice, O heavens, and you who dwell in them! Woe to the inhabitants of the earth and the sea! For the devil has come down to you, having great wrath, because he knows that he has a short time.*

**~ Revelation 12:11-12 NKJV**

May 11, 2017

Spiritual warfare is more real than people wish to acknowledge. It all began in Heaven when Lucifer convinced one-third of the angels, under the influence of the *spirit of rebellion*, to help him overthrow God—but his plan backfired. So he, along with his minions, was tossed out of Heaven and cast down to Earth. However, the war didn't end there; it simply transitioned to Earth and the *influence* of evil to include a personal vendetta was unleashed on the world. And as referenced in Bishop George Bloomer's book, *Spiritual Warfare*, "Hell-inspired maneuvers are being executed all around us"; but you do not have to give in to it. Unfortunately, however, we just refuse to see or to accept truth to conduct ourselves accordingly as the sons and daughters of a mighty God who has given us dominion over the earth to take back our territory! We have to stop straddling the fence and being intimidated by the spirit of fear. *For God did not give us a spirit of timidity or cowardice or fear, but [He has given us a spirit] of power and of love and of sound judgment and personal discipline [abilities that result in a calm, well-balanced mind and self-control]* (2 Timothy 1:7 AMP).

We have to stop playing with the devil in allowing him to decide our fate. Therefore, *first and most importantly, we must, seek (aim at, strive after) God, His Kingdom and His righteousness [His way of doing and being right—the attitude and character of God]. Then all your other needs will be met as well [these things will be given to you]* (Matthew 6:33)! When God sends us out into the darkness to represent Him as Ambassadors of Christ in carrying out our purpose and God-appointed assignment, we must reign (hold the royal office and rule as king or queen). We must not only hold our position but conduct ourselves as soldiers of war on a mission as rightful stakeholders. If you have been chosen by God to go out on the battlefield, then you must know that He has equipped you with all of what is needed (His wisdom, His knowledge, and His understanding) and strategic infantry (the Armor of Christ) for the victory.

So what are you afraid of? *"No weapon formed against you shall prosper, And every tongue* which *rises against you in judgment shall. This* is *the heritage of the servants of the* Lord,

*And their righteousness* is *from Me,"* Says the LORD (Isaiah 54:17 NKJV). Know who you are and claim your victory! You can do all things through Christ who strengthens you.

# SOMETHING IS MISSING!

*Praised be God,
Father of our Lord Yeshua the Messiah,
compassionate Father, God of all encouragement
and comfort; who encourages us in all our trials,
so that we can encourage others in whatever trials
they may be undergoing with the encouragement
we ourselves have received from God.*

**~ 2 Corinthians 1:3-4 CJB**

November 6, 2017

Revised November 11, 2017

Things are happening all around us—like never before—to get our attention and to encourage change! But not just on the outside, from the inside out! Due to constant interference, we have allowed iniquity to cloud our judgment and push us further away from God. We have allowed our desire to succeed out of a place of power, control, and greed to override our sense of Godly principles, which have, unfortunately, been replaced with worldviews. Society, unfortunately, creates the culture, and culture dictates the pace or norm regarding what is acceptable. Culture is also responsible for dictating where and how value is placed, and limitations are being weighed regardless of moral righteousness. God doesn't see just one viewpoint. He has a standard and considers each individual to be of equal value and importance to extend compassion toward us all!

More often than not, many words have been redefined to make its meaning less significant and subjective. The word *compassion* in our present-day culture as defined in many dictionaries denotes to show pity. In another, it states sympathetic pity. But it is much more than that and needs to be reevaluated in how it should be applied! What about putting yourself in the place of God to view compassion more along the lines of showing love or extending love one to another; simply to love and show mercy? What about an act of passion and simple co-suffering or bearing the burden(s) of another to intercede (pray) for each other?

Words should not be redefined to remove the intent of uniting people to care one for another about their mental and physical states. There is a great difference between man's narrow-minded definition and an action of compassion—especially when we should have Christ-like compassion, one toward and for another! We all want compassion, grace, and mercy, but when it comes to extending the same toward others, there is a very serious disconnect. We must do more to show love to one another in the same manner in which love is directed toward us from God.

**COMPASSION:** If someone shows kindness, caring, and a willingness to help others, they're showing compassion.

- Greek

    > 4697 - splagchnizomai (pronounced splänkh-ne'-zo-mi)

    1. to be moved in the inward parts; deep within your soul to include your heart, lungs, liver, etc.

    2. properly, to be moved as to one's bowels, hence, to be moved with compassion, have compassion (for the bowels were thought to be the seat of love and pity): absolutely[58]

- Hebrew

    rahamim originating from the word rehem or racham meaning womb.

    > 7356[59] – racham (pronounced rakh'-am): womb, to be **deeply** (and sincerely) moved with passion

People are hurting, and something is missing! Take time to ask questions and make yourself available to lend an ear or a hand, a simple hello and occasional conversation to encourage hope. Speak life, liberty, hope, and faith!

---

58   www.blueletterbible.org/lang/lexicon/lexicon.cfm?t=kjv&strongs=g4697&ss=1
59   http://biblehub.com/hebrew/7356.htm

> *Master,*
> *which is the great commandment in the law?*
> *Jesus said unto him, Thou shalt love the Lord thy God*
> *with all thy heart, and with all thy soul, and with all thy mind.*
> *This is the first and great commandment.*
> *And the second is like unto it,*
> *Thou shalt love thy neighbour as thyself.*
>
> ~ Matthew 22:36-38

## THE CONDITION OF THE HEART

During a WORD at a work Bible study session as presented by Michael Vernon Kelsey Sr. of New Samaritan Baptist Church, he asked if it was easier or harder to do the right thing. I don't think that I will ever forget that experience. The responses were very interesting, but what he did not know about me was the number of conversations I have had with God concerning that very same thing. In fact, I used to question God often about the **heart** He gave me. A **heart** I did not appreciate because it would not allow me to treat people as unjustly and unkindly as they were compelled to treat me. After each and every cruelty I suffered at the hands of others, I would think of what I wished I had said or done in response to their grave inhumanity toward me. But God, through the conviction of my **heart**, would not let me as I struggled to understand why it was so difficult for me to commit a wrong act even if it was justified. As time went on and I spent more time with God in seeking His face, He would speak to my **heart** and reveal many things to me. The choices we make help to determine the condition of our heart.

In 2 Chronicles 16:9, it says, *For the eyes of the Lord run to and from throughout the whole earth, to shew himself strong on behalf of* them *whose heart is perfect toward him.* And, in Proverbs 4:23, it says, *Keep thy heart with all diligence; for out of it are the issues of life.* This includes what we think about, care about, and what we choose to do and where we choose to go. What causes an individual to quickly lay down his or her spiritual duties and embrace the fleeting things of the world? Their hearts!

> *Search me, O God, and know my heart:*
> *try me, and know my thoughts:*
> *And see if there be any wicked way in me,*
> *and lead me in the way everlasting.*
>
> ~ Psalm 139:23-24

Galatians 6:4-5 MSG teaches us to *Make a careful exploration of who you are and the work you have been given, and then sink yourself into that. Don't be impressed with yourself. Don't compare yourself with others. Each of you must take responsibility for doing the creative best you can with your own life.* But God, I guess what I do not understand, or am not able to find it in my heart to believe, is how easy it is for one individual to turn their back on a cry for help from his brother or sister! How is it possible for people to be consciously aware of what they know in their hearts is an immoral act and turn a blind eye to it all while denying the existence of what they see or know to be a true injustice? How is it possible that they complain about an injustice being done to them, but allow themselves to be influenced to commit that same wrongful act to another and possess no moral compass for **repentance**? I find it to be so difficult to fit in or to go along for the sake of getting along with those who seem to have no problem doing that which I know goes against what God commands of me (or all of us, for that matter) to be and to do! I cannot in good faith sit idly by the sideline and witness injustice being done to others as well as myself and do nothing in making my objection known. For it is important for me to be faithful to God concerning what I have been called to do and be! Therefore, I want to scream from the top of my lungs and say, "No more! Enough is enough! How dare you!"

> *[He that is] first in his own cause seemeth just;*
> *but his neighbour cometh and searcheth him.*
>
> ~ Proverbs 18:17

*

> *You shall not repeat or raise a false report; you shall*
> *not join with the wicked to be an unrighteous witness.*
> *You shall not follow a crowd to do evil; nor*
> *shall you bear witness at a trial so as*
> *to side with a multitude to pervert justice.*
>
> ~ Exodus 23:1-2 AMPC

# REFERENCES

- www.biblestudytools.com/dictionary/compassion/
- http://markmayberry.net/wp-content/uploads/bible-study/2007-09-09-am-MM-Compassion-Long.pdf

# THINGS ARE UNFOLDING!

*For to be carnally minded is death;*
*but to be spiritually minded is life and peace.*
*Because the carnal mind is enmity against God:*
*for it is not subject to the law of God, neither indeed can be.*

**~ Romans 8:6-7**

November 30, 2017

Revised October 14, 2020

Approximately eight years ago, many criticized Rev. Dr. Jeremiah Wright concerning statements he made about the United States to include the disparaging acts of terrorism it has committed without any remorse against others in the name of politics. Many things are and have been done in secret and swept under the rug in the name of greed and self-interest on behalf of the elite until it mysteriously comes to light. And then and only then, when folks get caught, in some cases—according to the American way, a not very heartfelt apology is given and money is thrown at the situation, here and there—in an attempt to soften the blow of intentional indiscretions! But no real lessons have been learned, and much of the same behavior of playing god with a flair for immorality and arrogance is being practiced over and over again. In fact, those in positions of power don't often denounce self; their misguided ways of thinking and prejudice views, to rule and lead objectively on behalf of every concerned citizen while still referring to themselves as being Christians or believers of God and Christ. How is that?

John 20:27 states, *My sheep hear my voice, and I know them, and they follow me.* Ironically, no one took into consideration the position Rev. Dr. Jeremiah Wright held, nor equated him to his biblical namesake in carrying out his assignment to speak a word of warning and truth. We hear truth and see the evidence of what has been spoken and still deny it! Would that be due to a feeling of entitlement (arrogance) or ignorance? We seem to have an extreme problem with acknowledging and accepting truth if it does not spring forth from and through the vessel we deem as having great importance or value based on who they are (lack of association as having privileged status, image, and gender)! Truth is truth and has no lesser meaning if it flowed from a donkey, a burning bush, or a baby out in the middle of the wilderness! And if God chooses the vessel, who are we to deny their importance or value to include the validity of the message? As education goes, the recipient of credentials from a historically Black college and university (HBCU) or an Ivy League affiliate like Harvard University, which still didn't seem to matter in the case of Barack Obama, should tell us that other factors do indeed exist as well!

When Marion Barry was the mayor of the District of Columbia, many people failed to value his position or him as an individual, but he never stopped trying to make us aware of truth in speaking of what was to come. For instance, he attempted to tell us about a plan to make the District of Columbia a *moat* surrounded by toll roads! Sure, those who are not paying attention are laughing at my statement. Is not the District of Columbia surrounded by water, which was nothing more than a swamp itself? And what is the definition of a moat? The start of Highway 66 as a toll road in and out of the district is just the beginning—although that plan did not turn out so well! So I guess there was much truth to what Marion Barry had to say, long after his 2014 death!

*Look at where we are today, you are trusting in deceptive words that are worthless* (Jeremiah 7:8)! That which had become the norm—not because it was right but because we allowed our flesh and righteous indignation patterned after the ruler of Hell and darkness to take hold of our minds into thinking we are king, judge, jury, and executioner. We have been challenged and tested as a nation all across the nations, and yet we still refuse to acknowledge the errors of our ways to repent and incorporate change even though things are unfolding all around us. Well, that's the definition of arrogance for you! The evidence of immorality that has been forever present is at an all-time high. *But the natural [unbelieving] man does not accept the things [the teachings and revelations] of the Spirit of God, for they are foolishness [absurd and illogical] to him; and he is incapable of understanding them, because they are spiritually discerned and appreciated, [and he is unqualified to judge spiritual matters]*

(1 Corinthians 2:14-15 AMP). And that which many have attempted to ignore is being pushed out in the open for all to see! You may want to continue to disregard truth, but that which is done in the dark always comes to light to be revealed (uncovered) in due time! **Timing is everything and, in this season, things are unfolding!**

To that end, divine promotion and positioning come from God; much of what takes place is allowed by Him even if man thinks he is the one in control. No, God is in control and He has the final say! As God's so-called sheep, we have continuously ignored and rejected the teachings of God's word to justify our own will within a nation we state was founded upon godly (or Christian) principles while picking and choosing how justice shall prevail! Remember, many are called, but few are chosen! So which God are you serving? My God is no respecter of persons. He is the same God who places value and importance upon me to flow through me to deliver this message!

*"Get yourself ready! Stand up and say to them whatever I command you. Do not be terrified by them, or I will terrify you before them. Today I have made you a fortified city, an iron pillar and a bronze wall to stand against the whole land— against the kings of Judah, its officials, its priests and the people of the land. They will fight against you but will not overcome you, for I am with you and will rescue you," declares the Lord.*

~ Jeremiah 1:17-19 NIV

Sin and unrighteousness always have consequences whether you believe it or not! You cannot continue to play ignorant to your actions in believing you are right when you are immoral. *For the wages of sin is death, but the gift of God is eternal life in Christ Jesus our Lord* (Romans 6:23 NIV)! And the letter of the law without the Spirit kills! *Those who trust in themselves are fools, but those who walk in wisdom are kept safe* (Proverbs 28:26 NIV).

## REFERENCES

Suggested scripture reading:

- 1 Samuel 4
- Romans

Links:

- https://m.huffpost.com/us/entry/6761840
- https://plus.google.com/+AnnGwenMack/posts/Yy1zfmyi5hH

# THE STORM IS RAGING!

January 14, 2018

Open our eyes and heart O'Lord! You've whispered to me, The Calm Before the Storm, but in reverse! I hear you loud and clear: The Storm Before the Calm! The weather, disasters, and upheaval we are having are our own doing! They are a physical manifestation of our unrighteous "indignant" output! It is the collective *energy* within the atmosphere fighting back to cleanse itself of all the toxicity (iniquity) that we have imposed upon it. It is a warning that we continue to overlook, and this is just the beginning! The signs are obvious, but no one is paying attention *to the shift*!

**Energy is fluid and flows very freely. It gives life to the living and the dead. Spirits are a form of energy. Other different forms of energy include kinetic, potential, thermal, gravitational, sound, elastic, and electromagnetic.**

As seasons change, so does the shift within the atmosphere! For quite some time now, there has been a shift according to the influence of the power base on Earth. That influence which has been more negative in nature has unfortunately attempted to interfere with people's civil liberties (human rights), thus giving more power to darkness. But it has an expiration date! That which is done in the dark will soon come to light! Those positioned on the wall must stay in place!

# INTEGRITY

*No one calls for justice; no one pleads a case with integrity.
They rely on empty arguments, they utter lies;
they conceive trouble and give birth to evil.*

~ Isaiah 59:4 NIV

June 3, 2018

What is integrity? The justification for the termination or removal of folks from their positions these days—throughout the government—is "lack of candor." But, unfortunately, the entire world system, it's total dichotomy[60] and economy have been flourishing on the basis of a lack of candor. What is the definition of candor? Honesty, openness, and truthfulness!

---

60  Division into two usually contradictory parts or opinions; schism.

> INTEGRITY
>
> ▸ Perfection, sincerity, ***truth***, honesty
>
> ▸ Rigid (strict and concise) adherence to a code of behavior or conduct; probity (the quality of having strong moral principles; honesty and decency)
>
> > Truth
> >
> > Hebrew, Strong's #571; emeth (pronounced eh'-meth): firmness, faithfulness, truth
> >
> > Greek, Strong's #225; alétheia[61] (pronounced al-ay'-thi-a) that candor of mind which is free from affectation, pretense, simulation, falsehood, deceit. More to the point as in straightforwardness, divine truth revealed to man

God is very specific, and His word references "in the world, but not of the world"! *They sent their disciples to him along with the Herodians. "Teacher," they said, "we know that you are a man of integrity and that you teach the way of God in accordance with the truth. You aren't swayed by others, because you pay no attention to who they are* (Matthew 22:15 NIV). God is a God of order, and He has a standard! He is the principal of the world who is very strategic about His expectations for us all! He has laid out a set of principles covering character, integrity, *responsibility*, and *accountability*. You could say, God has developed laws

---

61  https://biblehub.net/searchgreek.php?q=integrity

governing His principles, which do not change to accommodate those in position of power and control; and no one is exempt. Although He is known to extend mercy and grace, we all will be held accountable to the same standards on the day of judgment.

> *But you will receive power when the*
> *Holy Spirit has come upon you,*
> *and you will be my witnesses in Jerusalem*
> *and in all Judea and Samaria,*
> *and to the end of the earth.*
>
> ~ Acts 1:8

God sends out His troops to scout out the land and to report back to Him! In the same manner, like Nehemiah, He appoints many of His children to sit on the wall, as watchmen, to pray and intercede on behalf of others! Little did I know, God had purposely positioned me, like many others, in the earth to witness and observe how things are being done in accordance to this world system, but not to adapt and participate unlawfully in an ever-changing system, as part of a growing culture, void of integrity. All too often, people in positions of power with the control to redefine principles at will get bigheaded and operate under the guidance or leadership of a dictatorship. When there is no connection to the true and living God in their life, they fool themselves into believing that they are the god of this world and they are exempt from holding themselves accountable to the same of scrutiny that they attempt to rule by! But, in the end, *for it is written, As I live, saith the Lord, every knee shall bow to me, and every tongue shall confess to God* (Romans 14:11).

When I think of the art of politics, I think of anything and everything but candor in noticing an increase of a lack of integrity and corruption. The audacity to campaign for or to consider legalizing pedophilia (or paedophilia) says it all! And people refuse to understand that very thin line of sexual perversion and sin, which is why some men feel they are entitled to a woman's body to commit rape with no remorse or accountability! People are being persuaded and influenced to get on board with any and everything outside of the Will of God! As those who proclaim to be Christians, we must be mindful of God's Word, God's teaching, God's expectations, and God's heart! Where is the integrity, and why have you allowed the world's way of doing things to spill over into your heart? Judas, *after these things I heard something like the great* and *mighty shout of a vast multitude in heaven, exclaiming, "Hallelujah! Salvation and glory (splendor, majesty) and power (dominion, might) belong to our God;* BECAUSE HIS JUDGMENTS ARE TRUE AND RIGHTEOUS. *He has judged [convicted and pronounced sentence on] the great prostitute (idolatress) who was corrupting* and *ruining* and *poisoning the earth with her adultery (idolatry), and* HE HAS IMPOSED THE PENALTY FOR THE BLOOD OF HIS BOND-SERVANTS ON HER" (Revelation 19:1-2 AMP).

Overcoming sinful attitudes and behaviors starts with *genuine repentance*, which has three aspects or parts:

1. *Conviction* – The Holy Spirit will reveal the areas in which we have sinned and convict us of wrongdoing. Through scripture, the Spirit shows us God's standard

and what needs to change. Repentance begins with understanding where we have gone astray.

2. *Contrition* – The next step, grieving over our iniquity, is followed by confession to the Lord. Genuine sorrow arises from the knowledge that we have sinned against Him. In a different context, human unhappiness often comes from being caught misbehaving. Other times, we are miserable because of where our choices led us or feel ashamed that people know about our sins. True contrition is followed by humble confession.

3. *Commitment to Act* – Real repentance is complete when we wholeheartedly pledge to turn around our old behavior and move toward righteousness. God knows we will not live perfectly, but He looks for a surrendered heart that diligently seeks to obey Him in living holy.

## CORRUPTION

Forms of corruption vary, but include bribery, extortion, cronyism, nepotism, patronage, graft, and embezzlement. While corruption may facilitate criminal enterprise such as drug trafficking, money laundering, and human trafficking, it is not restricted to these activities. The activities that constitute illegal corruption differ depending on the country or jurisdiction. For instance, certain political funding practices that are legal in one place may be illegal in another. In some cases, government officials have broad or poorly defined powers, which make it difficult to distinguish between legal and illegal actions.

Definition of corruption via www.bing.com

- dishonesty for personal gain; dishonest exploitation of power for personal gain
- depravity; extreme immorality or depravity
- undesirable change; an undesirable change in meaning or another error introduced into a text during copying (displaying) past actions

Definition of corruption via www.businessdictionary.com

- The act of wrongdoing on the part of an **authority** or powerful party through means that are illegitimate, immoral, or incompatible with ethical standards
- Often results from patronage and is associated with bribery

www.infobloom.com/what-is-political-corruption.htm

- Political corruption: A general term that refers to instances where appointed or elected government officials, from judges to legislators and police, fail to uphold the law in a fair and balanced manner.

https://www.sciencedaily.com/terms/political_corruption.htm

- Political corruption: The use of legislated powers by government officials for illegitimate private gain. Misuse of government power for other purposes, such as repression of political opponents and general police brutality, is not considered political corruption. Neither are illegal acts by private persons or corporations not directly involved with the government. An illegal act by an officeholder constitutes political corruption only if the act is directly related to their official duties.

- Worldwide, **bribery** alone is estimated to involve over one trillion US dollars annually. A state of unrestrained political corruption is known as a **kleptocracy** (alternatively *cleptocracy* or *kleptarchy*), literally meaning "rule by thieves."

# CULTURE

July 11, 2018

Culture, unfortunately, has been known to dictate character (attitudes and personality), customs (practices), and norms. As a child of God, a born-again believer in Christ, you are expected to forego any culture that does not line up with the expectation of our Lord. We are in a different dispensation from the day of old ways. Stop using culture as an excuse!

## MARRIAGE AND CULTURE

While attending a recent conference, a statement concerning culture was addressed and the Holy Spirit within me hit me in my gut in disagreement! Today, He gave me some clarity, and we must always be vigilant and sober as to what we cosign on. Everything may not always be on point, so it is important for us to know the Word of God to include His expectations for our lives. One husband and one wife with God in the mix! God is about order, and He has a standard regardless of the culture being recognized by various ethnic groups in a geographical area! What was doesn't have to be what is now! As daughters of the Most-High God, we must be careful not to be too gullible[62] or anxious to get married in accepting anything! He who finds a wife finds a good thing and favor with the Lord! I am expecting my husband to love me as Christ loves the church—if he is a true man of God! And, we all (male and female) should be mindful to wait on the Lord to bless and sanctify our union of Holy Matrimony in accordance to His will!

## ORGANIZATIONAL CULTURE

Organizational culture, whether right or wrong, is the personality of a department, division, agency, or organization. Culture is comprised of the prejudices, assumptions, values, norms, and tangible signs of people and/or members within an organization as well as their personal behaviors (idiosyncrasies). Depending upon how observant one is or how close one may be to situations being displayed or experienced within an organization, a person does and is able to soon sense the particular culture of an organization. Culture is taught, enforced, and reinforced over time and varies according to the change in leadership as to what is allowed and by whom.

> *Dear brothers and sisters, if another believer is overcome by some sin, you who are godly should gently and humbly help that person back onto the right path. And be careful not to fall into the same temptation yourself. Share each other's burdens, and in this way obey the law of Christ. If you think you are too important to help someone, you*

---

62  Being gullible is not a negative trait. It speaks to the CONDITION of your heart, but use WISDOM to protect your heart!

*are only fooling yourself. You are not that important. Pay careful attention to your own work, for then you will get the satisfaction of a job well done, and you won't need to compare yourself to anyone else. For we are each responsible for our own conduct. Those who are taught the word of God should provide for their teachers, sharing all good things with them. Don't be misled - you cannot mock the justice of God. You will always harvest what you plant. Those who live only to satisfy their own sinful nature will harvest decay and death from that sinful nature. But those who live to please the Spirit will harvest everlasting life from the Spirit. So let's not get tired of doing what is good. At just the right time we will reap a harvest of blessing if we don't give up. Therefore, whenever we have the opportunity, we should do good to everyone—especially to those in the family of faith.*

~ Galatians 6:1-10 NLT

Negative organizational culture, if not challenged, can thrive, fester, and poison a previously healthy environment. Why? Because practice makes perfect, and most people become comfortable with their wrongdoing or sin nature. This type of unhealthy culture may be distinctly difficult to express for some, but everyone knows it when they recognize it. However, through fear and intimidation, they may not choose to acknowledge it openly or speak up or out about it. Because many people find it easier to go along to get along, thus giving no thought to accountability or responsibility! Once it gets into the heart of an individual, it takes root and grows like a virus or toxic substance flowing through the air to reach its full contamination potential. As people move onward from one organization to another, somewhat like those who are indoctrinated and deployed by the military from post to post, they take that same mindset and culture with them to be pushed upon or forced on others wherever they go. Because my driving force is the word of God in carrying out His mission and mandate for my life, I cannot allow my mind to take hold of what my heart through God does not approve. This is why I keep holding out for the hope and belief that not all people are without a righteous soul to do good and not evil—regardless of their atmospheric (environmental) influences!

*For there is no faithfulness in their mouth;*
*their inward part is very wickedness; their throat is*
*an open sepulchre; they flatter with their tongue.*

~ Psalm 5:9 KJV

*The LORD saw how great the wickedness of the human*
*race had become on the earth, and that every inclination of*
*the thoughts of the human heart was only evil all the time.*
*The LORD regretted that he had made human beings on*
*the earth, and his heart was deeply troubled. So the LORD*
*said, "I will wipe from the face of the earth the human race I*
*have created—and with them the animals, the birds and the*
*creatures that move along the ground—for I regret that I have*
*made them." But Noah found favor in the eyes of the LORD.*

~ Genesis 6:5-8 NIV

# STRUGGLING TO UNDERSTAND

*Blessed are those who find wisdom,
those who gain understanding.*

**~ Proverbs 3:13 NIV**

October 22, 2018

Finalized October 3, 2020

What in the world is going on? When we read the Bible, which is the word of God, we should treat that information as being sacred—**undisputable, undeniable truth**! There are a number of people claiming to be Christians or believers who are not adhering to the word of God, and they are being seduced by worldly desires. The Bible discusses two opposing forces at war since the beginning of time: light and darkness! Although we are granted free will, we are to choose a side and stay in position! Through my quest for truth, I am being encouraged to seek knowledge, wisdom, and understanding of God as to the nature of the two opposing forces in taking **an unmovable stand**. It is up to me to seek out as much information as available and as divinely possible for me to wrap my brain around for a **solid supporting argument**. But I am also encouraged not to get into a combative argument or dispute with anyone concerning the word of God. Should you desire to learn the truth, I am instructed to direct you back to the word of God to help you develop your own conclusion and a relationship with God.

What disturbs me or vexes my spirit is knowing that there are so many of us in and out of church who have made a decision to choose light over darkness, but we are falling hard and fast into traps. Why? You must not play with fire by putting yourself into a situation that will subject you to temptation! The two leading causes of our temptation seem to be money and lust! The Bible is very clear about both and attempts to teach us wisdom and guidance on how to prepare ourselves for not being deceived.

> Money: *For the love of money [that is, the greedy desire for it and the willingness to gain it unethically] is a root of all sorts of evil, and some by longing for it have wandered away from the faith and pierced themselves [through and through] with many sorrows* (1 Timothy 6:10 AMP).

God does not speak against us having or obtaining money as long as it is not on the basis of ill-gotten gain! He eludes to us being willing to do any and everything unethically to beg, borrow, and steal to have it. For example, being so much in love with money or the idea of having monetary wealth that you would be willing to sell your soul and compromise your salvation to get it.

- Lust: *For all that is in the world—the lust and sensual craving of the flesh and the lust and longing of the eyes and the boastful pride of life [pretentious confidence in one's resources or in the stability of earthly things]—these do not come from the Father, but are from the world* (1 John 2:16 AMP).

The Spirit of Lust along with the Spirit of Greed seems to be taking center stage in being a cultural immoral phenomenon that's easily accepted and not questioned. Many, like pastors, are also falling prey as they themselves are tempted to engage in lewd and lascivious behavior to include adulterous affairs and children out of wedlock. America has a massive child-adult marriage issue, which is, in my opinion, nothing but another name for pedophilia. Did you know that marriage involving children under the age of eighteen is considered to be legal in approximately forty-nine US states? And why is this not being contested when the legal drinking age is twenty-one? Within the military or armed forces, there has been a history of both men and women being sexually abused and afraid to speak up or out about the assault! Is rape a modern-day weapon of war or a historical pattern of one person (the oppressor and the abuser) attempting to prove and exert physical and mental control over another as a psychological tool of terrorism? It is animalistic! Large amounts of money are being exchanged from hand to hand for payment of sexual favors and/or sexual trafficking of women and children. When there is a threat of a possible scandal being exposed, some of the victims are paid to keep quiet about any unsavory acts committed against them. The Catholic Church has been known to secretly pay off families for their abuse of children, for many to keep quiet about what may or may not have happened to them. Look at the direction of the state of the world!

*Then when lust hath conceived, it bringeth forth sin: and sin, when it is finished, bringeth forth death.*

~ James 1:15

**The *spirit of denial* is a very powerful thing!** *Do not deceive yourselves. If any of you think you are wise by the standards of this age, you should become "fools" so that you may become wise* (1 Corinthians 3:18 NIV). Unfortunately, many people refuse to see or to accept the obvious as displayed by a growing unhealthy and immoral pattern of events. Principles are principles and, for some, the truth is too hard to swallow. So they walk around in darkness refusing to see the light, meaning some may see or feel what others do not. If you are following Christ, you need to take a stand for Kingdom Principles. Those who usually follow the crowd normally get lost in the crowd and, soon after, get left or pushed to the side by the crowd.

*One person considers one day more sacred than another; another considers every day alike. Each of them should be fully convinced in their own mind.*

~ Romans 14:5 NIV

# THE GOVERNMENT SHUTDOWN

*I'll never forget the trouble, the utter lostness, the taste of ashes, the poison I've swallowed. I remember it all—oh, how well I remember—the feeling of hitting the bottom. But there's one other thing I remember, and remembering, I keep a grip on hope: God's loyal love couldn't have run out, his merciful love couldn't have dried up. They're created new every morning. How great your faithfulness! I'm sticking with God (I say it over and over). He's all I've got left.*

**~ Lamentations 3:21-24 MSG**

January 24, 2019

God keeps talking to me about visibility, and since August 20, 2018, I began taking notes! To see or not to see—that is the question and an unfortunate issue of people as dictated by the American culture to avoid the truth! When something is made visible for all to see, should I assume that integrity and fairness in the name of righteousness is being honored when it isn't? Why shouldn't I give more credence to that which is hidden and unsaid when it impacts me? Why should I allow deceit and a lack of candor to dictate what I know to be true?

The government shutdown is about more than a wall at the border. It is about a history of bigotry, a test of wills, and the ultimate control for power to act out idiosyncrasies. It has very little to do with the working-class folks who suffer in the cross fire except to prove a point. Like a military admiral or general far from the action of the battlefield pulling the strings in deciding who goes to war and when!

People stand divided by their differences, affiliations, and beliefs in a political party whose fight is about securing their own personal self-interest of elitism. Loyalty, these days, seem to have nothing to do with credibility or doing the right thing! And yet, every four years, we flock to the polls to cast our votes for people running for office that we know very little about while failing to conduct important research into the character of those we choose to represent us with little to nothing in common.

Do they believe in God to love humanity enough to put us ahead of their ambition? Do they know about our struggles, trials, and tribulations to hold our family together to pass laws and policies to aid in protecting the family unit? What about better and affordable healthcare or housing for all? Why is the social security and pension of the elderly taxed so high when they already paid dues? Do they even know what it means to be paid a minimum wage or less for hard labor while having to stretch finances from pay day to pay day or work numerous jobs to make ends meet? Why do we continue to put our faith in man, people who see themselves as being above us to condemn us to a lesser fate? Why does education or the welfare of our children seem to be less important with every passing moment?

In the history of politics, we are always thrown something to tip the scales to direct who we should vote in or out of the White House for fleeting agendas. Before Woodrow Wilson took office, the establishment of the Department of Labor (DOL) was reluctantly signed into operation on March 4, 1913, by President William Howard Taft. Based on my research, William Howard Taft, a Republican, was the 27th president of the United States and the 10th chief justice of the United States serving in both positions at the same time. What does that look like to you? Talk about a conflict of interest! Hypothetically, that's like having a neo-Nazi, grand wizard of the KKK, or a white supremacist sitting in the chair as president and serving as a chief justice. I'm just saying! With an open mind, you have to be able to see how it all falls in place. For instance, our current president, Donald Trump, announced on June 21, 2018, his future plans to merge the Department of Labor and the Department of Education into a single agency to be named the Department of Education and the Workforce. Interesting! And folks keep trying to tell me that history doesn't repeat itself! Really! There can't be an impact if there is no *shift*!

Many things are done for visibility with no intent to honor the integrity of doing what is truly right, camouflaged to give the illusion of creditworthiness and a caring heart! Only that which is right for the moment in the interest of the power base to stay on top of the food chain and to remain in full control while being completely out of order. On paper, under the disguise of visibility, there are many written policies and laws to give us the hope of a fair and equal playing field. However, are the Fair Labor Standards Act, the Family and Medical Leave Act, the Americans with Disabilities Act, and the hiring practices and other protections for veterans being honored and enforced accordingly? No! So would the merging of two agencies and a face-lift improve anything to promote positive change? Wait for the impact!

The Fair Labor Standards Act (FLSA) was written into law in 1938 to encourage order, structure, and fair labor practices such as implementing normal working hours, ensuring minimum wage, establishing overtime guidelines, encouraging equal pay, and performing record-keeping. They are also supposed to be responsible for extending guidance in the area of workman's comp! But, if you ask those who have been victims of workman's comp, what do you think they would tell you? Why are there so many civil lawsuits and employment-related grievances? Why has our current president and his administration threatened to eliminate union representation for federal government employees? Impact! If you ask a whistleblower if they were really protected when they assumed they were doing the right thing, what would they tell you?

Where is the justice to protect us from the man-made evil? I used to think that justice was obtainable by everyone or for everyone, but over the years, in the world of human resources, I have seen and witnessed more than I care to in how people are bullied, abused, oppressed, and simply disregarded with the aid of policies and laws. However, shifts in the atmosphere, culture, and economic climate have been adjusting and restructuring for a while. Organizational and revolutionary change can occur very quickly or slowly, but things are always transitioning. For those of you who don't understand what I mean, let's consider revolutionary and societal change over the years throughout history: from slavery to indentured servitude; from a demand for manual labor to machines and technology replacing people; from the agrarian (agriculture) to the industrial age and the importance or purpose of each person in position of power as the head of our government to big corporations controlling our governments. It's all connected! To date, there is a spiritual shift happening, and we have to be willing to get in position and stay there to see it all play out to ride the wave of the impact! Focus!

God is mapping it all out, remapping and restructuring! He is putting things into divine order, and He is watching us through the process. Are you crumbling under pressure due to the weight of all that is happening around you, like the government shutdown? Are you willing to hold your ground and pull together (unite) to come to the aid of others? Are you watching with your spiritual eyes to discern the change in the season to brace yourselves for the impact? Are you readjusting and readapting to analyze where your loyalty lies? Have you started to shift your priorities to move closer to the Lord? All over the United States, people are showing acts of kindness and love. In Tennessee, Yassin Terou, a Syrian refugee who co-owns a falafel shop in downtown Knoxville, is offering free food to anyone affected by the government shutdown. The sign inside the restaurant reads:

*WELCOME!*

*All sizes. All colors. All cultures. ALL RELIGIONS. All types. All beliefs. All people SAFE HERE at Yassin's Falafel House.*

God, the Father of us all, is love, and He is our greatest representative! It is He who we should direct our trust and seek guidance from the Holy Spirit in weighing our decisions and options! He will NEVER leave us, forsake us, or lead us astray! Open your eyes! Pray for our government! Pray for those in leadership! Pray for those in position of power! Pray for the nation! Pray for the land to be healed. Pray without ceasing!

*Well done thy good and faithful servant!*

~ Luke 4:18

## VISIBILITY

1:  the quality or state of being visible

2a: the degree of clearness (as of the atmosphere or ocean); specifically, the greatest distance through the atmosphere toward the horizon at which prominent objects can be identified with the naked eye

2b: capability of being readily noticed

2c: capability of affording an unobstructed view

2d: PUBLICITY

3:  a measure of the ability of radiant energy to evoke visual sensation

## PUBLICITY

1: the quality or state of being public

2a: an act or device designed to attract public interest; specifically: information with news value issued as a means of gaining public attention or support

2b: the dissemination of information or promotional material

2c: paid advertising

2d: public attention or acclaim

# MARTIAL LAW

March 5, 2019

For a while, I have been hearing "Martial Law" in my ear, over and over again! Until yesterday, while talking to a friend, I never really said what I was hearing out loud. The fact of the matter is, we, as a society—a country—the United States, have been traveling down this road for quite some time, and the evidence of that is all around us. A definite example is the "do as I say and not as I do" behavior and actions of many in positions of leadership. The lack of knowledge of many in positions above us to lead us with integrity to include the deafening knowledge of many of us who are asleep and have been for centuries.

Last week, one of my coworkers walked over to my desk and said, "I thought with *all* the changes in leadership that things would get better." It took everything within me not to laugh. I could see that she was genuinely hurting and trying to make sense of what was now becoming a reality for her. And the fact that she saught me out was a milestone!

Like the movie *The Matrix*, she was becoming "unplugged." Her eyes were opening to all of the upheaval within her immediate surroundings and it was causing her some distress! In fact, she was chosen (based on image) to fit in and to be rewarded handsomely like many others in her position. I'm sure it was also believed that she would simply fall in line and do exactly what she was told in being oblivious to seeing behind the *illusion* (the great deception) longer than two years. Most people are kept in the dark for at least five (grace) to seven (completion) years before they start to wake up! On an average, it takes some eight (new beginnings) to nine (birth) years unless they are continually being seduced by receiving things gratifying to their flesh to keep them preoccupied. It takes others much longer to wake up because they could care less either way and they are extremely lost or overpowered by complete darkness! But I am hopeful! *That which is done in the dark will soon come to light!* (See Luke 8:17.)

In such an environment, people are changed around and shuffled all the time. The change is not to improve the current status or situation. The change is to find the most suitable personality for moving in the direction of what has already been set in motion to continue without rocking the boat until the task is fully accomplished. You might even say, that which has been revealed on the surface (for visibility only) is merely a *diversion* to keep you preoccupied and ignorant to the real plan operating behind the scenes. You don't see the real work until it is too late for you to have any impact to interrupt (protest) the progress.

Many of us just haven't been that smart (knowledgeable) enough to see the picture clearly. We are so busy trying to dispute what we are really seeing with our own eyes while putting our hope in people who have been put in place to destroy us. Yes, I know! Right now, you are attempting to identify me as being negative, cynical, and a conspiracy theorist. Are you familiar with Hosea 4? The entire chapter is very clear and speaks to our current actions as a race—human beings! In particular, Hosea 4:6 is very plain: God states, His children perish (are destroyed) due to a lack of knowledge!

So what is Martial Law? Martial Law is a military regime or operating tactic to create robots and puppets, it is the intent of government to rule people or a nation by enforcing military law as a way of control, positioning the masses to follow orders without questioning the actions or motives of those at the helm imposing the commands—right or wrong! Realigning the opposition to get them in line to meet the objectives of the elite to rule by accomplishing their self-interests for greater wealth. I have witnessed many ambitious people make great sacrifices to climb to the top for a piece of the pie, until it was no longer advantageous for them to be used, at which point they become the threat. So they get moved or shuffled around again and again to a more suitable position in the corner or on the sideline. Some, out of frustration or embarrassment, simply quit and move on—but not before their eyes are truly opened to what they refused to realize initially!

They actually get retired until they actually retire! Some may even become collateral damage, and a plan is put in place to simply destroy them by attempting to discredit them. According to Martial Law, as it is being operated today, all people—if they are no longer useful and don't get in line—become the enemy of the state, a nation, or the existing culture! Also known as "insider threat." Are you? No! You simply are an out-of-the-box thinker who wants equality! An educator or motivator who believes in bringing (ushering) others out of the dark into the marvelous light. A soldier on a spiritual mission for the Lord! A citizen of the Kingdom of God!

I challenge you to research "Martial Law" for yourselves and pray for the world!

# YOU ARE MORE THAN

> *Beloved,*
> *I pray that in every way you may succeed and prosper and be in good health [physically], just as [I know] your soul prospers [spiritually].*
>
> **~3 John 1:2 AMP**

March 28, 2019

You are more than what you do! Never let people define you or limit you on the basis of what they have limited you to do and be! **It took me a while to stop putting any importance in what people think of me.** In ministry, we call this being delivered from people! I am more than what they know or want to believe about me. What I do is only a part of or aspect of who I am! If only they knew who I really was, they would be more afraid of me than they are already! Why? Because, in spite of what people think, I AM still growing and striving to be the best me according to the *will of God* for my life!

People limit you on the basis of their fear of you. The fear of your knowledge or capability to be greater than what they want to believe is the opposition that creates the barriers and challenges surrounding you! If people are not able to control your growth to take credit for your success, you become less important to them! Why? People need to feel more important than what they are! We, as human beings, creatures of habit, crave validation! Some of us need others to put us on a pedestal to feel appreciated and valued. Unfortunately, society (the basis of this world system) teaches us and encourages us to fear one another on the basis of our differences, whether it be, to name a few: skin color, facial features, age, sexual orientation, gender, disability, or religious beliefs. We are generally led to be competitive in our thinking than we are encouraged to work together (coexist) to accomplish and achieve success as a human race all created by the same source.

We are taught and encouraged to hate when God advocates for love. We tell ourselves that we are Christians who know God while living our lives contrary to the expectations of our ABBA Father. People have actually said to me—to my face—while attempting to tear me down and challenge my love for God and others, "but Ann, I am a Christian. I believe!"

As individuals, children of the Most-High God, we are all operating at various levels! Various levels of immaturity. Various levels of spiritual immaturity in need of growth. Various levels of growth. We let our ambition to rise to the top as dictated by the world to interfere with our spiritual growth. In fact, some of us have stopped growing and we don't even know it! And we allow others with their limited mindset based on separation from the truth to validate what God is doing through us to get us to our destiny in Him by limiting our own growth. STOP IT!

We have stopped reaching to be our best self as created by God because we have replaced our humanity with ambition and material possessions on the basis of a world-induced consciousness. We have allowed people who think they have arrived based on their titles, financial status, and privilege but are absent of the love of God to speak over our spirit. And at one time or another, I was allowing this same world system and people to convince me to see myself through their eyes in accepting the value they placed upon me. As shared and told to me approximately seven years ago within my current workplace in a closed door (one-on-one) meeting, "If a person doesn't like you they can be your worst enemy to hold you back (put limitation upon you); but, if they like you, they can be your best ally to help you grow and receive success to be promoted in your career." Now, what I learned on that day is, your credentials, skills, or abilities to perform don't matter. Who you are as a person or individual doesn't matter! Your integrity, or character for wanting to do what is right, doesn't matter. Being liked or disliked and misjudged is what matters! Wow, but it all matters to God!

Today, I am content with seeing myself through the eyes of God. Today, I am content with following Jesus as He follows God. Isn't that the true definition of being a Christian? Attempting to be Christ-like! Believing in a higher power is about reaching high enough to raise your level of consciousness to see yourself, not as man sees you, but by taking into account what needs to be changed to be the best you as created by God! For me, it is about pleasing God and soaring to greater heights in my spirituality. You can't break or block the flow of what God has ordained, anointed, and positioned to prosper!

# JUSTICE OR JUST US!

July 14, 2019

In 2010, after breaking my leg in four places, my then-supervisor wrote a memorandum to a department head (lead manager) addressing and targeting approximately five employees with medical issues and/or a disability who she thought would present a problem by failing to be high performers, in accordance to their definition.

Being one of the five, it was suggested that I be demoted and/or terminated due to the injury I had sustained on February 20, 2010. In an attempt to further justify the supervisor's reasoning for targeting me, she also questioned my mental state by saying she felt I was unstable. Unstable because I had started to speak up against the injustice that I was seeing within a human resources environment to include a culture of workplace bullying! And now was the time for them to deal with me by making me an example and taking advantage of the opportunity to shut me up and put me in my place!

When one of the five named in the document discovered the information lying out on the copier for all to see, she decided each employee named should receive a copy to be made aware of its existence as well as the threatening situation. So a calendar invite was sent out to each of us and upon our arrival to this meeting, we not only received a copy of the memo, but there was some discussion about us joining forces to establish a class action suit against the agency and the author of the document. However, I needed to decline! Why? Because God was talking to me and teaching me about the importance of not jumping so quickly to seek justice in man's court of law where there is no fairness or respect for right or wrong. An arena where the truth is sometimes heard, but twisted consistently to make the innocent look guilty; and the guilty is freed! This truth is currently being played out and witnessed all around us. So justice, as it should be referenced, is always never really granted freely and accordingly. It's more about which side is the most convincing!

Many of the innocent are tried and convicted on the basis of fabricated and trumped up charges by those who have been sworn in to uphold the law. Attorneys and judges alike have the final say based on who should be benefited, compensated, and protected from having to do any time even if they are guilty. Much of the decision to prosecute is tied to a person's influential status and association to the elite for a desired outcome. And God forbid they desire to make you the sacrificial lamb in the name of politics toward their own best interests. *For the tyrant will come to an end and the scorner will be finished, Indeed all who are intent on doing evil will be cut off—Those who cause a person to be condemned with a [false] word, And lay a trap for him who upholds justice at the [city] gate, And defraud the one in the right with meaningless arguments* (Isaiah 29:20-21 AMP).

## TIMING IS EVERYTHING!

People, unfortunately, don't believe that the Father, the Son, and the Holy Spirit (Ghost) are real to allow themselves to develop a relationship with the Lord! They refuse to go deeper in allowing the comforter to play a very important role in their lives. God has been guiding me and revealing Himself strong in my life to understand the importance of being obedient to His word and His voice to know that timing is everything!

When that memo resurfaced as part of a lawsuit by one of the five through the federal government mediation process, an investigator was told that the memo was nothing more than a fabrication for attention to target the supervisor. From there, in an attempt to lessen the liability to the agency, a plot was underway to name me as being the one who fabricated the memo. Before they were successful in attempting to unlawfully destroy me to be set up to take the fall, the sacrificial lamb, God, through the Holy Spirit, the one and only comforter, made me completely aware of their plans. I was hurt, frustrated, and devastatingly angry! *Be ye angry, and sin not: let not the sun go down upon your wrath: Neither give place to the devil* (Ephesians 4:26-27). It was hard for me not to shout from the rooftop to all and anyone who would listen: I know your plan, but it is not going to work!

God cautioned me and directed me every step of the way on how and when to confront the situation. I drafted a memo of my own to address and confront the three in command who were directly responsible for carrying out the plan against me, from the immediate supervisor up! I kept quiet about what I knew to be true, holding on to my confrontational memo and my tongue for approximately a little over a year until God told me to move forward! Upon receipt of a notice to make myself available for questioning by the Office of the Inspector General and Office of the General Council on behalf of the plaintiff and the agency, I was released by God to release my correspondence to the three!

Many are naive and brainwashed to take questionable sides! Did they clear my name? Probably! Probably not! Was anything placed in my personnel file or taken out to ensure my name and status were not linked or unlawfully tied to any misconduct? I have no idea! Did I receive an apology, verbal or written? Of course not! It was difficult for them to look at me! They were surprised to know I knew what I did for a while and was still able to present myself as nothing other than respectable. I came to work every day as pleasant as usual and carried out every task delegated to me, as expected of me by my Father in Heaven! Shortly afterwards, the investigator/agency council who met with the department head and was given the untruthful information about me, resigned or retired! But not before taking my hand and making direct eye contact to thank me for my hard work and service! He knew the information was bogus, but his hands were tied, and I'm sure he was tangled and caught in a web of deceit in his position for a lot longer than he could stand or take! In a chain-of-command environment, people are too often expected to follow orders and do so blindly!

I once was blind, but now I see clearly! I had aligned myself with the Lord, and it is He who cleared my name, feels my pain, walks with me, protects me, and showers me abundantly with His love! All is documented with Him on His heart in Heaven! Everything should be done in accordance to the will and timing of God! No man or nothing should be more important to you than God! Nothing in your life should take His place! We are living in a world of darkness, and people, unfortunately, are allowing themselves to get sucked in. Think about it! What I described above and worse is happening all around us all the time in a world where we are led to believe that justice will prevail! Yes, justice will prevail with the Lord as your saving grace! Which side are you choosing? My mind has been made up! I'm sticking with my saving grace, the Lord, who is on my side! Divine justice can only be obtained from and through the Lord! Timing!

# THERE IS EVIL IN THE WORLD!

*Be ye therefore perfect,
even as your Father which is in heaven is perfect.*

~ **Matthew 5:48**

April 27, 2020

Revised May 29, 2020

Whether we want to believe it or not, there is evil in the world! Some of us are awakened to the truth while many of us are still sleeping, stumbling in the dark, and extremely lost. With blinders on, many of us have become comfortable in our ignorance to allow ourselves to be controlled by iniquity like puppets as we believe what is being dictated and refusing to change. Unfortunately, many delight in refusing to see truth while seeking a justification for holding on to their old narrow-minded ways of thinking. And yet, all around us, things are coming to a head like an erupting volcano!

The more things change, the more they stay the same! That green-eyed monster continuously attempts to raise its ugly head while others find it more and more difficult to escape the seduction of his charm! So although the circle of darkness widens as the faces change and boundaries are pushed, the agenda throughout history remains the same. We keep trying to remove God from the equation in taking His place while digging a deeper hole to bury our humanity. Ignoring God and His existence to include who He is always leads to a downward spiral; and we as a race of people—traveling on different paths to destroy the world and all in it—have been out of control for a very long while!

**God is pure love, and He encourages each of us to love one another—no matter our nationality or culture—while challenging us to let go of the hate!** Instead, we took Him out of our schools, homes, and churches. We even told ourselves that there was no room for Him in business, government, or a work environment as a whole to avoid taking Him into consideration in how we treat others or conduct business. And we wonder why things are falling apart!

True *obedience* comes through faith and not fear! The world uses fear to force obedience through evil means for acquiring our wants. God uses love to encourage obedience and to increase our faith and belief in Him to follow Him as He supplies our every need and we never want for nothing! When we are willing to make a conscious decision to reconcile ourselves back to Him *in divine alignment* with Him—body, mind, and spirit—our hearts line up with His will and His ways as our spirits join His!

Through this process, we are open to change as we *transform* from the inside out and osmosis takes place in shedding the old spirit man to be renewed.

Like a person who is introduced to and falling in love for the very first time, you are willing to denounce yourself to follow the lead of another. But this isn't just anyone! This is God, our Heavenly Father, the creator of us all! He doesn't play with your mind or your heart to speak sweet nothings in your ear. He doesn't take your love or your heart for granted in taking advantage of you. He doesn't speak empty promises to seduce you into being naughty or nice, and He is able and willing to honor **every promise** ever made. He doesn't leave you in a lurch to take a fall while hiding in the shadows. He stands by your side in the light and is ready to catch you when and if you should fall.

God is worthy of your undivided attention and your open decision to choose Him exclusively above and beyond the evil one! Try Him! Seek Him! Say yes to His will and say yes to His ways! Let go of what you think you know to be true and allow God through the *revelation of the Holy Spirit* to teach you and guide you!

> *I am not ashamed of the gospel, for it is the power of God for salvation [from His wrath and punishment] to everyone who believes [in Christ as Savior], to the Jew first and also to the Greek. For in the gospel the righteousness of God is revealed, both springing from faith and leading to faith [disclosed in a way that awakens more faith]. As it is written and forever remains written, "THE JUST and UPRIGHT SHALL LIVE BY FAITH." For [God does not overlook sin and] the wrath of*

*God is revealed from heaven against all ungodliness and unrighteousness of men who in their wickedness suppress and stifle the truth, because that which is known about God is evident within them [in their inner consciousness], for God made it evident to them. For ever since the creation of the world His invisible attributes, His eternal power and divine nature, have been clearly seen, being understood through His workmanship [all His creation, the wonderful things that He has made], so that they [who fail to believe and trust in Him] are without excuse and without defense.*

~ Romans 1:16-20 AMP

# CHAIN OF COMMAND: NEW LEVEL, NEW DEVIL

*Woe to you, because you build tombs for the prophets, and it was your ancestors who killed them. So you testify that you approve of what your ancestors did; they killed the prophets, and you build their tombs. Because of this, God in his wisdom said, "I will send them prophets and apostles, some of whom they will kill and others they will persecute." Therefore this generation will be held responsible for the blood of all the prophets that has been shed since the beginning of the world, from the blood of Abel to the blood of Zechariah, who was killed between the altar and the sanctuary. Yes, I tell you, this generation will be held responsible for it all.*

**~ Luke 11:47-51 NIV**

June 2, 2020

Finalized June 7, 2020

On a weekly basis, lately on Wednesdays and Fridays, I am extremely blessed to receive medical attention from a **highly anointed doctor**. Displayed on the wall of one of her treatment rooms is a sign which reads, "There is no process which does not require time." This is very true; we must also be committed to taking an active role in doing our part in allowing the process to work effectively in acceptance of change. For instance, you cannot simply reach an expected improved outcome without acknowledging what changes are needed and then be committed to the implementation of those changes throughout the process in an associated amount of time for that time to be meaningful!

With each planned attempt to advance to the next plateau or stage in my chosen career of interest, I have encountered many challenges or roadblocks called people. People with no real objective (motives) or justifiable reasoning for their actions of transgression to block me other than the position and power they occupy to impact an environment or the lives of those around them. Just because they can!

Encouraged by today's culture, abuse of power is an acceptable normal managerial style of leadership. In my current place of work, I have witnessed a great deal of unchecked behavioral patterns of bullying (aggression). Within this same environment, many are bullied into bullying others to prove that they are worthy candidates for advancement opportunities. Not everyone is selected or chosen based on their skill level, but their willingness to fall in line and follow orders whether right or wrong. Their ability to be pushed (up, down, or around) and groomed to fit a certain role regardless of the position they choose for themselves or, in many cases, chosen for them. This is the ultimate example of a chain-of-command-driven culture of leadership style with a *drill sergeant* flair! For instance, I was told, "our [the organization's] need for administrative support is far greater than your need to succeed in your career" and steps (called reassignment and reclassification of my position) were put in place by the leadership to ensure that! Now, of course, if I don't like it, I am always free to leave and find another job versus them being committed to doing the right thing with the same amount of fairness as extended to others put in line for training, promotion, and advancement! And my continued presence or unwillingness to leave doesn't mean I like it. It simply reflects my desire to be a good soldier.

If you consider a pyramid business model, which is unlike a true pyramid, it resembles the practice of a chain-of-command hierarchy (military culture), which represents a level or levels of authority from the top down (descension) or the bottom up (ascension). People at the top, normally, delegate or bully down with or without integrity, and you may never actually see or be able to acknowledge the real puppet master(s)!

Nonetheless, in such an environment, you are expected to do what you are told and to know your place at all times to avoid a citation or label of being insubordinate, difficult, incompetent, and possibly more on the basis of control to support the argument or justification for the ruling of leadership. Some of us simply want more power and control than we deserve to feel important. And there is nothing wrong with feeling important, but character and how you develop it is the central key!

With mixed emotions, in review of the recent state of affairs affecting our nation across the world, I am reminded of the nature and impact of a storm before the calm in which *change* takes place. Throughout history, there has been a pattern or evidence of inner conflict exploding from the inside out in the form of corrosive energy like pollution being dumped in the atmosphere upon all of us! When greeted with such energy, you can choose to adapt to it or exercise a greater sense of character for setting a higher standard. Those who are in a position of power to lead and guide our countries with integrity have not stepped up to the plate in divine form and fashion with the love of God and wisdom in their hearts to work together in unity for righteousness—although many have claimed to be believers. Believers of what? Good or evil? That is the true question! Actions tell all!

War is being waged on a larger scale, which includes an increase of smaller and individual turf wars happening on the side. There is a great divide across our nation (geographically across the globe as a whole), in churches, households, cultures, and Congress. Our judicial system is flawed and is extremely broken! The theme of the day has always been to divide and conquer in any way necessary without conscience and moral consideration of the pain and civil violation of others as we continue to avoid change in the name of losing our humanity and selling our souls to the highest bidder!

Change can be positive or it can be negative as dictated by the roles or positions of leadership with the power to enact change. Change can be welcomed or it can be despised and forced. For change to be effective, the existing culture, which has dictated and set the stage for how things have progressed (or regressed in many cases) and been allowed to thrive negatively, for so many years, must objectively be evaluated and considered in how it has impacted others. There are varied degrees of evil operating from one end of the spectrum to the other.

My inner struggle to stay grounded is real! My fight to hold back my anger in review of all of the injustices is real! My pain from the impact of life's trials and tribulations is real! But my hope in God based on my commitment to be a soldier in His Army is also real! His *unconditional love* for us all is true and it is as real as it gets with no comparison to anything else! Because of His faithfulness, I am able to push through as my *witnessing* increases and my faith grows in holding on! I'm praying for the wherewithal to continue to endure with *grace*!

God sits up high and looks down low. God is nothing like any man or person on the face of this earth, past or present. He is the ultimate and Divine Commander and Chief. He has the last and final say about everything. From His throne, judgment is coming and it will be made and directed upon us all: Jew, Gentile, believer, non-believer, Republican, Democrat, Independent, the rich, the poor, man, woman, and child. When He (God and not man) has blessed us with free will, the choice and inner ability to decide right from wrong, we can no longer hide behind association or a chain of command hierarchy in escaping

His Wrath. Now, later or for generations to come and throughout eternity, you are sealing your fate based on your actions!

God is the root of our existence as our Divine Creator (all of mankind, the entire human race), YASHUA (Jesus) is the vine who made the ultimate sacrifice for our *salvation,* and we (all of mankind, the entire human race) are the branches. Just as we are connected to the Creator, we are connected to each other through the Spirit of God regardless as to whether we believe it or not. Through that connection, God feels all of our pain, and He will avenge the innocent (and this world) in due time!

*And we know that in all things*
*God works for the good of those who love him,*
*who have been called according to his purpose.*

~ Romans 8:28 NIV

# WHAT IS YOUR DEFINITION OF ESSENTIAL?

June 25, 2020

Revised October 9, 2020

It's amazing to see how the meaning of "essential worker" changes out of convenience to include who it covers, depending upon the circumstances facing our nation or any given situation. It's similar to being labeled a "subject matter expert" who is not being compensated as such to fit the subjective title.

> Essential[63]:
> absolutely necessary, extremely important, crucial, vital

There are a number of folks on the frontline who have been pushing forward since the beginning of the COVID-19 quarantine who are not being compensated adequately or appreciated and valued. That includes leave (paid time off), healthcare

---

63  www.lexico.com/en/definition/essential

coverage, raises, and bonuses for their sacrifices! Prior to this pandemic, there was an unprecedented number of underpaid and devalued laborers trying to make a living to stay afloat. Hardworking people trying to make ends meet from the middle to stretch from one week to the next. Can you imagine single-parent households earning just enough to pay for a roof over their heads with nothing left over some months to put food in their stomachs? Or, what about the single mother or widow who has just enough left over to feed her children while she sacrifices herself and goes to bed hungry many nights? But the next morning, she is up bright and early, out of the house, and at work on time to start her day all over again!

Initially, there was a campaign in progress to round up immigrants and build a wall to keep them out of the United States. Have you noticed them out there in the trenches, along with many of their Black and Brown sisters and brothers (low-paid unskilled blue collar laborers as defined or classified by the Department of Labor) keeping businesses and offices afloat? Some are students attempting to do their part to help their families, fund their education, and pay back student loans! Where is the love and the appreciation? We all matter! Black lives matter! People matter! The human race matters. And according to our Abba Father, there is only "one race" as created and defined by Him! That race is the human race!

Why do we refuse to examine our hearts? Why do we allow hate and division to come between us and God to overlook and dismiss His word of truth? Why do we refuse to open our minds to truth? My heart aches for unity! My heart aches for a system of government that acknowledges God, His principles, and the concept of love in acceptance of all people fighting for the human race!

> *Make every effort to live in peace*
> *with everyone and to be holy;*
> *without holiness no one will see the Lord.*
>
> ~ Hebrews 12:14

# BONUS

# IN THE LINE OF FIRE

*For my thoughts are not your thoughts,*
*neither are your ways my ways, saith the LORD.*
*For as the heavens are higher than the earth,*
*so are my ways higher than your ways,*
*and my thoughts than your thoughts.*

~ **Isaiah 55:8-9 KJV**

March 24, 2016

As soon as I get comfortable in accepting a particular thing, situation, or the ways of people, change occurs and my world is turned slightly upside down. But if I believe there is no such thing as coincidences or accidents as it pertains to the *Will of God* for my life, then I must understand that everything—to include all change (good, bad, or indifferent)—occurs for His glory and my good to propel me closer toward my destiny in accordance to Romans 8:28, which states, *And we know that all things work together for good to them that love God, to them who are the called according to* his *purpose.* In addition, *for whom he did foreknow, he also did predestinate to be conformed to the image of his Son, that he might be the firstborn among many brethren. Moreover whom he did predestinate, them he also called: and whom he called, them he also justified: and whom he justified, them he also glorified* (Romans 8:29-30).

With that said, as long as I align myself with God, I must also always keep in mind that although the weapons of mass destruction may form against me, they will not prosper! Why? Because the more I attempt to align myself according to His word, His adversary—Lucifer along with those he is able to influence in carrying out his agenda—will attack me as a form of punishment or retaliation for making a choice to follow Christ in an attempt to dissuade me. Nonetheless, God gives me His word as spelled out in Isaiah 54:17, and it states, *No weapon that is formed against thee shall prosper; and every tongue that shall rise against thee in judgment thou shalt condemn. This is the heritage of the servants of the LORD, and their righteousness is of me, saith the LORD.*

I AM so grateful to know, God is like no other man on the face of this earth! He is a man of His word who honors every detail. He irrevocably does what He means and means exactly what He says! He is perfect in all His ways! He is not intimidated, easily persuaded, or influenced by associations to include stuff that has no real importance. He is guided by truth and encourages us to do the same in being led by His Spirit.

> *Therefore we also,*
> *since we are surrounded by so great*
> *a cloud of witnesses, let us lay aside every weight,*
> *and the sin which so easily ensnares us,*
> *and let us run with endurance the race that is set before us.*
>
> ~ Hebrews 12:1 NKJV

Quite frankly, the minute we allow ourselves to become too comfortable with our surroundings that operate outside of the *Will of God* as they threaten to trip us up, it is possible to blend in while putting our soul in jeopardy and stealing our joy. We must be careful not to become complacent and blind to the present darkness in being led to adapt and transform to the ways of the world even if others around us have lost their way. We must not allow the majority rule or the pressures of this world to heavily weigh us down to push us into doing what we know is not of God for our lives. No matter how great the temptation as the world attempts to seduce us, we must evade being tempted. We must be committed to doing the right thing no matter the sacrifice, which may bring us grave pain or disappointment in not achieving what we personally want. We must die to self daily and renew our mindsets as often as it takes to draw our strength from the Lord in waiting on Him, thus seeking truth along the way!

> *And ye shall know the truth,*
> *and the truth shall make you free.*
>
> ~ John 8:32

Over the years, I have come to learn that there are many people walking around in darkness—oblivious to the truth—who are not willing to let their minds be freed from the strongholds that bind them. Out of fear, temptation, and influence, they allow themselves to get pulled in to accomplish other people's agendas. And, in turn, they often oppress others by using intimidation and manipulation to reach the top of a hierarchically induced Babylonian-Roman empire that only proves to enslave their souls through the captivity of their minds as God is pushed far away from their thoughts into being nonexistent. What better way to attempt to exert full control over another human being than to succeed at stripping them of every ounce of hope and belief in Him who has given us all life. *But I will HOPE continually, and will yet praise thee more and more* (Psalm 71:14). *I'm glad in God, far happier than you would ever guess—happy that you're again showing such strong concern for me. Not that you ever quit praying and thinking about me. You just had no chance to show it. Actually, I don't have a sense of needing anything personally. I've learned by now to be quite content whatever my circumstances. I'm just as happy with little as with much, with much as with little. I've found the recipe for being happy whether full or hungry, hands full or hands empty. Whatever I have, wherever I am, I can make it through anything in the One who makes me who I am. I don't mean that your help didn't mean a lot to me—it did. It was a beautiful thing that you came alongside me in my troubles* (Philippians 4:10-14 MSG).

## MISSION CRITICAL

This title, *In the Line of Fire*, was dropped in my spirit by God during the first or second week of January. Struggling to get started and attempting to gather my thoughts, I also had difficulty determining which direction or approach God wanted me to take. I knew there was a lesson or revelation specifically directed at me as designed for this season in my life, but I was extremely perplexed and somewhat frustrated about the unsettling issues I was dealing with pertaining to the various aspects of my life, physically (in the natural) and spiritually (in the supernatural). I needed to grasp hold of the understanding, knowledge, and wisdom of what God was intending to teach me before I could move forward. Whenever He gives me something to write and share with others, it is always for me first and foremost. So, needless to say, it has, unfortunately, taken me until now to attempt to complete this message as instructed. However, after attending the 7:15 a.m. Reid Temple AME service on March 13, 2016, the message delivered by Reverend Hilda L. Hudson gave me much insight and revelation. What a word! She called it, "This Mission is Still Critical!" No matter how long it takes to include the difficulty of the road less traveled, my God-appointed mission or assignment is always critical. And, to top it off, on March 20, 2016, Reverend Dr. Lee P. Washington "enlightened me even further during his 9:30 a.m. message called, "All Shook Up." When the going gets tough, some of us have a tendency to want to run away and hide! But a true soldier or warrior on a mission runs toward the fight in a battle, meeting it head on!

> *Then I heard the voice of the Lord, saying,*
> *"Whom shall I send, and who will go for Us?"*
> *Then I said, "Here am I. Send me!"*

~ Isaiah 6:8

When things seem to take a turn, we must continue to believe and not lose faith! *But without faith it is impossible to please* him: *for he that cometh to God must believe that he is, and* that *he is a rewarder of them that diligently seek him* (Hebrews 11:5). We must be determined to muster up every ounce of courage to stay on course, hold on, or be still and wait on the Lord for further guidance or instructions! In fact, when a change of uncertainty takes place, why is it our first instinct to believe something is wrong? Did you ever stop to think that God was up to something and things were simply being shaken or stirred up, uprooted, and rearranged to fall into place as commanded by Him? Life is full of challenges and tribulations. No matter where God sends us, there will be opposition and conflict in an attempt to keep us from completing the mission at hand. Someone, in a rather roundabout, indirect or not-so-subtle way, recently alluded to me being bitter. Now, I will admit to being disappointed, frustrated, and angry about certain situations I have endured, to include how others have allowed themselves to be used or influenced in being a part of my misfortune, but being bitter only hinders me from moving forward as commanded by God in carrying out His mission. So, I must find a way to dismiss that which is irrelevant in being mindful of the bigger picture! Why? Because it is not about me or you! Therefore, not taking the comment to heart in being careful not to allow the statement or the individual to deter me, I took a step back to consult with God while hearing, "What Did I Say!" God forever cautions me not to consider the word of others over what He has already revealed to me and to be mindful not to take offense to anything, however difficult it can be at times to not fight with my flesh. Nonetheless, if He hasn't spoken a word to me to confirm what is spoken by others to me, then I must not receive that information to store it in my memory cortex. In other words, if what is said does not line up with what God has given you, you must not waste time dwelling on it and instead move forward with your mission, at all costs.

We all have our own agendas or ulterior motives for how we conduct ourselves as conditioned or influenced by our experiences. But, as part of a whole, there is something far greater than little old me, and I have been given an important role or part to play in God's army! *For just as the body is one and yet has many parts, and all the parts, though many, form [only] one body, so it is with Christ. For by one [Holy] Spirit we were all baptized into one body, [spiritually transformed—united together] whether Jews or Greeks (Gentiles), slaves or free, and we were all made to drink of one [Holy] Spirit [since the same Holy Spirit fills each life]. For the [human] body does not consist of one part, but of many [limbs and organs]* (1 Corinthians 12:12-14 AMP). Therefore, as referenced in Proverbs 3:5, we must *Trust in the LORD with all thine heart; and lean not unto thine own understanding.* That means putting our flesh under the subjection of the Lord to do things "completely" His way; not ours!

*Thou hast put all things in subjection under his feet.*
*For in that he put all in subjection under him,*
*he left nothing that is not put under him.*
*But now we see not yet all things put under him.*

~ Hebrews 2:8

It is the enemy's main objective to hit us from every angle—sometimes all at once—to distract us. We could quite possibly make the wrong choices to abort the mission by attempting to run scared in hopes of escaping conflict (trouble) or we can embrace our challenges (run the race) to learn and grow through the struggle in obtaining spiritual elevation. *My friends, consider yourselves fortunate when all kinds of trials come your way, for you know that when your faith succeeds in facing such trials, the result is the ability to endure. Make sure that your endurance carries you all the way without failing, so that you may be perfect and complete, lacking nothing. But if any of you lack wisdom, you should pray to God, who will give it to you; because God gives generously and graciously to all* (James 1:2-5 GNT). There are times when we are challenged by God as much as we are challenged by His adversary, the devil! But, to what end? Ironically, we could be challenged and tested by both at the same time to get different results, of course. One is with good intentions, and the other is intended to trip us up. However, God is forever in control, and it is He who allows the events in our lives to take place, which are beneficial for directing us to choose wisely whom we will serve. God never intends to harm us; His objective is always to prosper us toward an expected glorious and victorious end in realizing who we are and were created to be in carrying out our mission! So when change comes, whether good or bad, God can always use both ends of the spectrum to propel us toward our destiny as long as we are willing to stay in alignment with Him. Our objective, even in the midst of toxic environments, should be to develop a strong constitution for overcoming every challenge in accordance to the *Will of God*. Being forever flexible and ready to move into position for as long as it takes! *Therefore, my beloved brothers and sisters, be steadfast, immovable, always excelling in the work of the Lord [always doing your best and doing more than is needed], being* continually *aware that your labor [even to the point of exhaustion] in the Lord is not futile* nor *wasted [it is never without purpose]* (1 Corinthians 15:58 AMP).

## THE MAKING OF A SOLDIER

When we are born into this world, we have no immediate knowledge of who we are or who we were created to be by our Heavenly Father. In fact, we know nothing of our Creator to understand He created us for a *divine purpose* and strategically placed us in a particular environment designed to produce a desired outcome. Each detail is uniquely thought out to bring us to an expected end for the sole purpose of us becoming fully awakened to the elements and dynamics of this world with the hope of us making the right decisions in choosing a side. Unbeknownst to many, there are only two very distinctive opposing forces in this world: good versus evil! There is no middle ground or high road, although many people like to believe there is and seek to justify their actions according to that belief in an effort to avoid taking responsibility for anything. However, taking no responsibility is not an option; they just haven't figured that out yet to understand how the law of gravity works! What goes around comes around. What goes up must come down. And what you sow, you will most certainly reap in addition to this being the year of Jubilee! *And you shall consecrate the fiftieth year and proclaim freedom [for the slaves] throughout the land to all its inhabitants. It shall be a Jubilee (year of remission) for you, and each of you shall return to his own [ancestral] property [that was sold to another because of poverty], and each of you shall return to his family [from whom he was separated by bondage]. That fiftieth year shall be a Jubilee for you; you shall not sow [seed], nor reap what reseeds itself, nor gather the grapes of the uncultivated vines. For it is the Jubilee; it shall be holy to you; you shall eat its crops out of the field. 'In this Year of Jubilee each of you shall return to his own [ancestral] property* (Leviticus 25:10-13 AMP).

In this game of life on Earth, I view it synonymously to chess or checkers. Chess, however, is a much more strategic game than checkers; you have to be more skilled or cunning and greatly matched with your opponent if you intend to stay in the game long. That means you need to be able to scope out the entire board (your territory) while studying your opponent (all the players) to anticipate his or her (their) every move before it is made. You have to be ready to maneuver and think of successful countermeasures to survive (spiritual warfare). Your head and your heart must be in the game, which means you cannot allow any distractions (personal or otherwise) to emotionally hinder you! You must be clear and level headed, focused on the extreme mission! As a matter of fact, contrary to popular belief, the making of a soldier is more involved than getting through military basic training or boot camp. Literally, if you never learn to physically play chess, you would need to master the concept of the game to understand how to win at making wise moves. Winning can also be defined by your willingness to stay in the game specific to building endurance, i.e., staying power, standing firm and strong, and holding your position!

## SHARING MY TESTIMONY

Approximately one month after my arrival to the US Department of Energy (DOE), I started to notice a great deal of adversity and disorganization, along with a lack of integrity. I witnessed dishonest leadership, with an emphasis on unfairness and the unwillingness to take accountability for their actions. I started questioning God as to why He allowed such disarray in addition to me being assigned to work at such a place, especially considering what I had endured prior to coming here. Ironically, here I was, once again, witnessing practices not lining up with what God was expecting of me or His children as leaders. As time went on, I asked more questions to include my desire to flee from here, not wanting His permissive will but needing His perfect will. I asked, "How much longer would I simply need to endure my surroundings before You would grant me the opportunity to leave?" Directing me to a book addressing David's Adullam, He finally gave me my answer. Needless to say, with mixed emotions, I cried in disbelief of what I was hearing, but I desperately want to complete my God-given assignment with the intent of learning all of what God has intended for me. Laying it all out, He ministered to me about David's plight and the necessary lesson he needed to learn about enduring before he could move forward.

God reminded me that I desperately wanted to leave my previous employer, where I was sent on assignment. And, it was my desire to return to the employment of federal government after a twenty-three- to twenty-four-year intermission. I actually left the federal government three to four times, and I had simply forgotten about the endearing politics, which was no different upon my return in 2008. I truly do not know why I thought things had changed for the better toward fair and righteous advancement. Because I asked, God honored my request to leave an unpleasant working environment, but not from my assignment or the need for learning a much-needed lesson. He was no longer granting me the opportunity to flee from each and every situation just because I was experiencing conflict. He was forcing me to work through the process for reaching my God-appointed destiny! So while I am here, God is using this situation to fortify me, equip me, and continually develop me for His Kingdom. He is teaching me about spiritual warfare and the need to stand, so He has deliberately put me in the midst of chaos to help strengthen me.

The DOE headquarters symbolize a dark and dingy cave, dungeon, or black hole. God sent me (to include others) to be the light in the midst of darkness. We are encouraged not to become weary in well doing. In addition, He is teaching me to conquer my fears by intercepting my option to take flight or freeze (remaining docile) by forcing me to fight the good fight of faith. Literally, He is teaching me how not to leave a mission prematurely to include not giving up or giving in to my circumstances. And if at any time I should fall while in battle, I was permitted to lie down, however, not to rollover! Meaning, my rest was only necessary to retreat and regroup to stand back up and continue the mission. If I truly want to leave this place, I was told I would have to stay for *at least* seven years to accomplish the task in completing my assignment with joy—and not dread—before being able to move forward and onward. David was elevated every seven years.

SAMPLE: Spiritual Meaning of Numbers - Seasons

| | |
|---|---|
| January 22, 2008 | Beginning date of employment at DOE |
| | 8 = New Beginnings / 2 + 8 = 10 = 1 = Unity |
| 2014 | 7 = Completion = Elevation |
| January 22, 2015 | 2 + 1 + 5 = 8 = New Beginnings |
| | 1 = Unity |
| | 2 = Duality and/or opposition (symbolism), balance, truth |
| | 5 = Grace |
| January 2016 | 2 +1 + 6 = 9 = Birth |
| The HEBREW YEAR | 5776 = 2016 = The year of "jubilee" RESTORATION, Order restored, God's favor |

## SERVING THE LORD

Accepting my calling, I pledge my soul (mind, will, and emotions), body (joints and marrow), and spirit (meaning and purpose) to fulfilling God's purpose in connection to my God-appointed assignments. Like that of others before me, I will gladly go where I AM sent to scope out the land and report what I see. If need be, I will be the gatekeeper who sits on the wall to keep watch. As a willing vessel, I will be the conduit in the earth to pray for and with others. I will devote all of me in denouncing and sacrificing self. I must embrace each and every lesson as allowed and orchestrated by God to reach my full potential in Him. No matter how hard or difficult I think the "perceived" defeating environment (situation or circumstances) may be, I must be mindful of the importance of exercising control over the very essence of who I AM and who I was called to be. We do not have to defeat the devil or his minions; we just have to remind the adversary that he is a defeated foe. Therefore, it does not matter what it looks like or feels like to others including myself, because, if the truth be told, it's really not about me! And why is that? *For many are called, but few are chosen* (Matthew 22:14). Because *ye are a chosen generation, a royal priesthood, an holy nation, a peculiar people; that ye should shew forth the praises of him who hath called you out of darkness into his marvellous light* (1 Peter 2:9), and as the children of God, we have been granted His mercy (1 Peter 2:10), grace, glory, and strength to accomplish the impossible. We can do all things through Christ who strengthens us!

Seeking and receiving clarity from the Father is a very wonderful thing! Not everyone understands or knows what it looks like to have the passion and desire to serve the Lord completely! When God loves you enough to not only show you the very best of Himself, but the very best and worst of who you are in comparison to who you were created to be through His eyes, your love and passion grow for wanting to please Him at all cost to push past your fears to live and die for Him while striving to be your best—far beyond the understanding of others. It's more than just simply going through the motions! Through the depth of my experience at DOE, I have come to learn, understand, and accept that our God-appointed assignments encourage an awakening or awareness to our divine purpose and identity. Initially, it may not be feasible for us to know everything to include hiding who we are from those within the environment in which He sends us. When He sends us out as His mouthpiece, He cloaks us while we are given time to see what we need to see. Meaning as watchers, we are sent to observe the situation or the environment before He gives us permission to speak. God also uses that time to teach us who we were created to be as we develop into our perspective positions for His Kingdom. Sometimes, He may send us out on assignment for a temporary or extended period of time. Some He sends in and out immediately to give a word and leave. Because timing is everything— you must be obedient and disciplined to hearing the voice of the Lord and following through with your assignment as dictated. You should never leave an assignment before you have been released by God and you should never stay past your appointed time after being released. Until my time comes, I will continue to ride the waves while standing tall with my feet firmly planted!

> *For I know the thoughts that I think toward you, saith the LORD, thoughts of peace, and not of evil, to give you an expected end. Then shall ye call upon me, and ye shall go and pray unto me, and I will hearken unto you. And ye shall seek me, and find me, when ye shall search for me with all your heart. And I will be found of you, saith the LORD: and I will turn away your captivity, and I will gather you from all the nations, and from all the places whither I have driven you, saith the LORD; and I will bring you again into the place whence I caused you to be carried away captive. Because ye have said, The LORD hath raised us up prophets in Babylon; Know that thus saith the LORD of the king that sitteth upon the throne of David, and of all the people that dwelleth in this city, [and] of your brethren that are not gone forth with you into captivity; Thus saith the LORD of hosts; Behold, I will send upon them the sword, the famine, and the pestilence, and will make them like vile figs, that cannot be eaten, they are so evil.*
>
> ~ Jeremiah 29:11-17

# DEBORAH THE BEE:
## JUDGE, PROPHET, DELIVERER, MOTHER, WIFE, WARRIOR—AND MORE

*Because he [Sisera] had nine hundred chariots fitted with iron and had cruelly oppressed the Israelites for twenty years, they cried to the LORD for help. Now Deborah, a prophet, the wife of Lappidoth, was leading Israel at that time. Villagers in Israel would not fight; they held back until I, Deborah, arose, until I arose, a mother in Israel.*

~ **Judges 4:3-4 and 5:7 NIV**

February 18, 2019

Revised/Finalized February 28, 2019

**Do you know who you are and what you are capable of achieving?** Women have been undervalued and told to stay in their place, which was defined by men who lack the ability to appreciate the true beauty, strength, and wisdom of a woman. God created men and women to coexist in bringing balance to the world. He positioned women just as He positioned men with purpose for a purpose.

The Bible references many who were chosen to carry out a role designated (or tailor made) just for them. As assignments are streamlined and missions are directed with the right person in mind (male or female), individuals are uniquely chosen based on who they were created to be! From their upbringing to various experiences through trials and tribulations dedicated to shaping character, men and women courageously defended their territories with no hesitation. Today, I would like to put the spotlight on Deborah as referenced in the Book of Judges.

*Then the Israelites did evil in the sight of the Lord and worshiped and served the Baals, and they abandoned the Lord, the God of their fathers, who brought them out of the land of Egypt. They followed other gods from the gods of the peoples who were around them, and they bowed down to them, and offended and provoked the Lord to anger. So they abandoned the Lord and served Baal [the pagan god of the Canaanites] and the Ashtaroth. So the anger of the Lord burned against Israel, and He gave them into the hands (power) of plunderers who robbed them; and He sold them into the hands of their surrounding enemies, so that they could no longer stand [in opposition] before their enemies. Wherever they went, the hand of the Lord was against them for evil (misfortune), as the Lord had spoken, and as the Lord had sworn to them, so that they were severely distressed. Then the Lord raised up judges who rescued them from the hands of those who robbed them.*

*~ Judges 2:11-16 AMP*

The children of Israel were brought out of Egypt into the Promised Land of Canaan, and they were specifically told by God to be obedient to His demands as outlined in the covenant agreement—the same covenant treaty initially entered into with their forefathers (Abraham, Isaac, and Jacob) prior to the death of Joshua. We are told that although we are in the world, we are not to allow ourselves to be consumed by the world in conforming to the ways of the world. The children of Israel were to enjoy the fruits of the land, but they were to remain separate and apart from the natives of the land of Canaan while being mindful to honor the ways of the Lord. **In disobedience, many members of the Tribes of Israel mingled and comingled with the Canaanites and adapted to their ways by fornicating and worshipping other gods like Baal.** So God stepped aside and allowed them to be defeated by their own devices. In other words, He turned them over to a reprobate mind! They refused to do that which was right and honorable. The death of Joshua, who was righteous, left a vacant position for an influential obedient and loyal leader who was not afraid to go into battle on behalf of the Lord. But I'm sure they were not expecting it to be a woman.

As the need arises for warriors to be born, step up, and take their rightful place, God calls them to order to reign one by one. *In that day the LORD will whistle for the army of southern Egypt and for the army of Assyria. They will swarm around you like flies and bees. They will come vast hordes and settle in the fertile areas and also in the desolate valleys, caves, and thorny places* (Isaiah 7:18-19). Man believes in titles with one manner of importance on the basis of visibility with no action of follow-up or follow-through. God not only grows us up and grooms us to be in position with titles, He equips us to fully operate in every role He titles us to perform with honors. Each and every name or title has definitive meaning in accordance to our God-appointed destiny! Sometimes, the Lord would raise up a Judge for the people and the people would turn to the Lord and serve Him throughout the lifetime of that Judge's position in office (see Judge 2:18).

There is *true* meaning in a name! If we were to take a little time to consider the origin or derivative of a word to study it through a system or process called etymology, you would be surprised at what you are able to uncover. Everything about who we are is significantly planned out in accordance to the will of God, down to the date and time of birth! The New International Version of Jeremiah 29:11 makes that very clear: *For I know the plans I have for you," declares the Lord, "plans to prosper you and not to harm you, plans to give you hope and a future.* If more confirmation is needed, here is a paraphrased version of Jeremiah 1:5: Before God formed us in our mother's womb, He knew us, before we were born into the world, He set us apart! We were anointed and appointed to be a Prophet to the nations.

The game of life, which is more symbolic to a journey than many would like to admit, offers peaks and valleys. Some of us have been fortunate enough to keep the momentum going by staying on track, and some have taken detours only to find their way back to fulfilling the destiny or calling upon their life while others have simply gone astray in taking a different path altogether. But, in my review of Deborah, I get the impression that she was **as steady as a rock** and stayed on course!

## ETYMOLOGY

Before we go any further, I want to talk about etymology (the study of words) to give you a greater understanding of how to dig down deep into the meaning of your name (or any word) by using the Hebrew language (and possibly a combination of Greek and Latin as things unfold). Through my research, I understand that the Hebrew language is one of the oldest languages in the history of the world. It is written and read from right to left, while the English language is written and read from left to right. For every English word, there is a root derivative and meaning drawn from the Hebrew, Greek, or Latin origin. Unfortunately, the meanings of many English words have been changed and deviate from their true intended meaning. But the Hebrew language has always remained true to its origin to include being more gender specific for nouns.

Although there is a variation of different spellings for Deborah—such as Devorah, Devora, Dvora, and Dvorah—Deborah means "bee," and it speaks to her personality and purpose. You can tell a lot about a person based on their birth name to include what it may be changed to later. Let's take a closer look. The root word or Hebrew derivative of Deborah is *debar*, which means to speak, communicate openly, or to pronounce. Considering her role as a *prophet* and a *judge*, Deborah cannot have a fear of speaking up or out about various topics or situations to promote change or justice on behalf of the people God has assigned her to represent. Using divine wisdom, she must be an open-minded listener who is able to extend unbiased compassion to all in reaching a fair (justifiable) judgment. Too often, we are given a charge or a voice to speak with authority and integrity, but we sit silently on the sidelines while allowing injustices to take center stage. By saying nothing or doing nothing, we become like everyone else around us.

As mentioned above, Deborah means "bee"! There are various species or types of bees, such as the honeybee, bumblebee, hornet, and wasp. Each is significantly created and purposed to carry out a role, but in general, bees are noted for their work ethic. According to my research, all of the worker bees are female. They symbolize family unity and a sense of community. They are very loyal to each other, strategic, methodical, and organized. Their sting can be deadly! The queen bee is very maternal and nurturing. She takes her role as a leader of her colony very seriously in directing and leading them for survival, similar to Deborah in the manner in which she took control of the situation for the survival of those within her community and under her command.

*She used to sit [to hear and decide disputes] under the palm tree of Deborah between Ramah and Bethel in the hill country of Ephraim; and the Israelites came up to her for judgment.*

~ Judges 4:5 AMP

Equipped with endless potential, Deborah was **chosen** to reign with victory and significantly positioned in place between Ramah and Bethel. Ramah means "a place of idolatry or idol worship," and Bethel means "the house of God." She was a very wise and God-fearing woman with extreme loyalty! You know she had to be bad if she had her own palm tree named in her honor. After researching "palm tree," I learned it symbolizes strength and victory. It all fits! Everything works together for the good of those who love God and are called according to His Purpose!

Can you imagine being able to flourish in extremely hot temperatures with little to no water for days? Have you ever seen a palm tree up close and personal? It stands tall and firm with such a commanding presence. They are not very large in circumference, but their trunks look sturdy, robust, and powerfully structured to withstand strong winds. The top branches out and exposes many leaves, which provide protection and shelter from the sun. I guess you could say, it bears much fruit! That is what we are expected to do as children of God. Bear much fruit. Stand without wavering under the pressure and weight of the elements around us. Be rooted and grounded in perfect alignment with the Father in carrying out our assignments, embracing each role, no matter the title!

**Deborah's Roles** (not limited to the below attributes)

- Wife: Ishah or ishshâh in Hebrew, meaning "woman." Ezer Kenegdo – not just a helpmate or helpmeet, but an equal (suitable) counterpart (partner in marriage).

- Mother: Hebrew meaning (strong #517) – strong water which symbolizes the glue that holds the family together, binding.

- Nurturer: Maternal tenderness or affection.

- Warrior: A woman of valor (hayil). A double meaning: Ezer kenegdo also means warrior; strong help; man's perfect match.

- Prophet: Hebrew (strong #5030) is navi or nabi (pronounced naw-bee'), God's spokesman to the people.[64]
- Judge: Hebrew is shofet, also spelled shophet, meaning chief, admiral, general, leader. Discern, examine, investigate, question, and separate throughout.
- Chief: Reviewed as being the highest rank or office of greatest importance, significance, or influence. One who is yoked to another to lead and teach!
- Deliverer
- Intercessor

She was a wife, mother, Prophet, Judge, and Deliverer, but was still not limited in range and capacity! In each capacity, one role was as important as the next, individually or collectively, like being able to operate in performing with ease in each of the roles of the fivefold ministries. Deborah was the only female judge mentioned in the Bible, and her success in this role should be credited for opening the door to other women to reside in this role without question! She was a woman of great stature and authority who spoke on behalf of the Lord and acted as a respected mediator between the people and God. She delivered her people out of the hands of their oppressors and liberated them to freedom and safety. She rescued them and gave them a reason to fight because she was a warrior with a warrior spirit who interceded for those in her care.

---

64  https://biblehub.com/hebrew/5030.htm

*Now she sent word and summoned Barak the son of Abinoam from Kedesh-naphtali, and said to him, "Behold, the LORD, the God of Israel, has commanded, 'Go and march to Mount Tabor, and take with you ten thousand men [of war] from the tribes of Naphtali and Zebulun. I will draw out Sisera, the commander of Jabin's army, with his chariots and his infantry to meet you at the river Kishon, and I will hand him over to you.'" Then Barak said to her, "If you will go with me, then I will go; but if you will not go with me, I will not go." She said, "I will certainly go with you; nevertheless, the journey that you are about to take will not be for your honor and glory, because the Lord will sell Sisera into the hand of a woman." Then Deborah got up and went with Barak to Kedesh. And Barak summoned [the fighting men of the tribes of] Zebulun and Naphtali to Kedesh, and ten thousand men went up under his command; Deborah also went up with him.*

~ Judges 4:6-10 AMP

Barak recognized Deborah's courage and refused to go to war as commanded by God unless she went with him, but he also did not realize that his decision to hesitate would come with a price. However, his decision to request Deborah to accompany him to battle and her acceptance spoke volumes about her drive and warrior spirit. She was a woman, and Barak was a man, but it was her who inspired him to take a stand and fight for their territory, their rightful inheritance! Deborah was a natural born leader who didn't run from a fight. She was a seeker of JUSTICE with a vision, and God encourages us to write the vision and make it plain (Habakkuk 2:2). Where there is no vision, the people perish (Proverbs 29:18)!

The Hebrew word for judge is *shofet*, also spelled *shophet*. In various contexts, it represents general, ruler, or leader of the military. In Latin, it is *shophetim*. Being a judge is about standing out and separate, set apart in observation of your surroundings with clarity of thought and fairness. The decision of a judge should not be tainted by outside influences and self-interest. Taking a stand for righteousness and holding your ground is an important attribute for a judge. *The righteous will flourish like a palm tree, they will grow like a cedar of Lebanon; planted in the house of the LORD, they will flourish in the courts of our God. They will still bear fruit in old age, they will stay fresh and green, proclaiming, "The LORD is upright; he is my Rock, and there is no wickedness in him"* (Psalm 92-12-15).

In this season, God is raising up an army of Deborahs! Women who are not afraid to talk openly about their love for and connection to God! They are not afraid to be obedient to the Lord and the calling on their lives. It is important for women to get out the shadows and take their rightful places to claim their inheritance in being warriors. They must be willing to open their mouths and lead by example to teach girls and other women that they too can be courageous, stern, and gentle at the same time in demanding justice for themselves and others. You cannot be afraid of doing the right thing on behalf of the Lord and the Kingdom of God even if persecution comes. Make no mistake, God is the Judge of judges!

# AMAZING GRACE

*[Growing in grace]*
*they will still thrive and bear fruit and prosper in old age;*
*They will flourish and be vital and fresh [rich in trust and love and contentment]; [They are living memorials] to declare that the Lord is upright and faithful [to His promises]; He is my rock, and there is no unrighteousness in Him.*

**~ Psalm 92:14-15 AMP**

September 23, 2020

It's my birthday, and I give God all the glory! I generally don't celebrate or alert others concerning my big day; however, for some reason, this year feels extremely special, and I am overjoyed about reaching this milestone! God does everything with divine purpose, and none of us were accidents. There is no such thing as an accidental birth to God! Our existence is planned by design in accordance to God's specific timing. Right down to the exact month, day, year, and hour. How the stars and the planets aligned on the day and time of your birth has significance. Consider the energy in the atmosphere that played an important part in the development of your spiritual attributes.

I am *60 years young*, and although I have had more than my share of health scares to include aches and pains over the years, this season is to be greatly celebrated and appreciated. Actually, I feel we all should celebrate this year, particularly, as being a glorious milestone in claiming victory over the coronavirus to see the manifestation of the presence of God! Embrace the opportunity for rest, growth, and shifting! See God working in the undercurrent!

September has been referenced to be the month of *divine visitation*. September was originally the seventh month, and the Latin meaning or root word septem means seven. Whether in its seventh or ninth place, September is a very special month with a very specific meaning. It marks the beginning and end of a cycle or season in representing a change from summer to winter with fall in between. After seven comes eight, which symbolizes new beginnings. Did you feel a shift in the *energy* on September 21, 2020? I did! There is a physical and *supernatural shift* taking place!

Today is the twenty-third day of September, and if you take this number down from a two-digit to one by adding 2 + 3, you get 5; and 5 represents **GRACE**. My first name is Ann, which means or symbolizes grace. And specific to me as learned through revelation from the Lord as associated with my personality—*much grace!* My middle name, Gwen, symbolizes or means bless, pure and holy!

Lord God, thank YOU for blessing me to be a blessing to others! Thank YOU for that initial thought to create me into existence and breathing life in me. Thank YOU for each individual YOU have allowed to have access as we connect through YOU to celebrate life (ours and YOURS)!

# GOD, ALL I WANT FOR MY BIRTHDAY IS MORE OF YOU!

September 23, 2011

Dear God,

How are you today? Fine, I hope. Today, I am one year older, but my greatest desire is to receive more of you. As I reflect on many birthdays passed, I must give you the thanks, the glory, and the honor for saving me and allowing me to see another year. Not just any year but a year of great expectation of what is to come. A period of restoration to experience miracles, signs, and wonders from days of old!

Though you have cautioned me through your word not to be anxious for nothing, I am, in deed, anxious to be in your presence and to have you stretch out your hands to me. I long to have you hold me and to enlighten me with me your wisdom.

I want to have a greater understanding of your wisdom, knowledge, and understanding as I explore your peace. You said, *Peace I leave with you; my peace I give to you; I do not give it to you as the world does. Do not let your hearts be distressed or lacking in courage.* (John 14:26 NET).

Father, I want your peace that surpasses all my understanding. I want to be a vessel, a willing participant of discipleship in doing that which you have created me to do and be. I want to please you and walk upright without fear or lacking in courage. Please continue to take me under your wing and teach me forever more on how to be. Holy and true!

Operate on my heart and remove any damaged parts. Work on me, Lord, and use me as only you can use me. For I dedicate this day, the day of my birth and every day of my life to you in saying out loud with zest and passion, "I CHOOSE YOU, LORD!" I say yes to your will and ask that you repair me. Repair me to the fullness and newness of you. Before I was bruised and spoiled (damaged) by hurt and pain.

Though my suffering was for naught, I have learned to appreciate everything that has taken place in my life, which is for the betterment of me for You! I changed in ways I did not know were possible, seeing and believing what I thought was the impossible. Loving you for the renewing of my mind. Loving you with great joy in my heart. Thanking you for not leaving me nor forsaking me. Thanking you for the encouragement to go on and forcing me to push beyond my fears. Thanking you for the divine connections.

This was truly the best birthday ever. Why? Because it was celebrated more differently than ever before with an exciting knowledge and acceptance of You in my life! This birthday was all about You, and it actually started on Thursday with Bible Study Night under the leadership of Karyn Collins. And it ended Sunday, September 25, 2011, upon attending and partaking in communion with the First Baptist Church of Glenarden along with my neighbor in support of Tonya Cooper's acceptance of covenant partnership or her First Hand of Fellowship as an official member.

Oh God! I cannot express how grateful I am for those divine connections, allowing me to unite with spiritual brothers and sisters whose only agenda is to love me as they love themselves in honoring your greatest commandment. Non-believers in the concept or theory of "doing as I say and not as I do!" For you have called your children to be hearers and doers of the word. Lord, they flow in the Spirit. Walk in the Spirit. Live by the Spirit.

God, thank you for hearing me, loving me, accepting me, and choosing me!

Sincerely,
Your daughter, Ann

# APPENDIX

# THE NAMES OF GOD

Each of the many names of God[65] describes a different aspect of His many-faceted character. Here are some of the better-known names of God in the Bible:

**EL, ELOAH:** God "mighty, strong, prominent" (Genesis 7:1; Isaiah 9:6) – etymologically, *El* appears to mean "power," as in "I have the power to harm you" (Genesis 31:29). *El* is associated with other qualities, such as integrity (Numbers 23:19), jealousy (Deuteronomy 5:9), and compassion (Nehemiah 9:31), but the root idea of might remains.

**ELOHIM:** God "Creator, Mighty, and Strong" (Genesis 17:7; Jeremiah 31:33) – the plural form of *Eloah*, which accommodates the doctrine of the Trinity. From the Bible's first sentence, the superlative nature of God's power is evident as God (Elohim) speaks the world into existence (Genesis 1:1).

**EL SHADDAI:** "God Almighty," "The Mighty One of Jacob" (Genesis 49:24; Psalm 132:2,5) – speaks to God's ultimate power over all.

---

65  Booklet - Names of God (biblespeaks.org)

**ADONAI:** "Lord" (Genesis 15:2; Judges 6:15) – used in place of YHWH, which was thought by the Jews to be too sacred to be uttered by sinful men. In the Old Testament, YHWH is more often used in God's dealings with His people, while *Adonai* is used more when He deals with the Gentiles.

**YHWH / YAHWEH / JEHOVAH:** "LORD" (Deuteronomy 6:4; Daniel 9:14) – strictly speaking, the only proper name for God. Translated in English Bibles "LORD" (all capitals) to distinguish it from *Adonai*, "Lord." The revelation of the name is first given to Moses "I Am who I Am" (Exodus 3:14). This name specifies an immediacy, a presence. Yahweh is present, accessible, near to those who call on Him for deliverance (Psalm 107:13), forgiveness (Psalm 25:11), and guidance (Psalm 31:3).

**YAHWEH-JIREH:** "The Lord Will Provide" (Genesis 22:14) – the name memorialized by Abraham when God provided the ram to be sacrificed in place of Isaac.

**YAHWEH-RAPHA:** "The Lord Who Heals" (Exodus 15:26) – "I am Jehovah who heals you" both in body and soul. In body, by preserving from and curing diseases, and in soul, by pardoning iniquities.

**YAHWEH-NISSI:** "The Lord Our Banner" (Exodus 17:15), where *banner* is understood to be a rallying place. This name commemorates the desert victory over the Amalekites in Exodus 17.

**YAHWEH-M'KADDESH:** "The Lord Who Sanctifies, Makes Holy" (Leviticus 20:8; Ezekiel 37:28) – God makes it clear that He alone, not the law, can cleanse His people and make them holy.

**YAHWEH-SHALOM:** "The Lord Our Peace" (Judges 6:24) – the name given by Gideon to the altar he built after the Angel of the Lord assured him he would not die as he thought he would after seeing Him.

**YAHWEH-ELOHIM:** "LORD God" (Genesis 2:4; Psalm 59:5) – a combination of God's unique name YHWH and the generic "Lord," signifying that He is the Lord of Lords.

**YAHWEH-TSIDKENU:** "The Lord Our Righteousness" (Jeremiah 33:16) – As with YHWH-M'Kaddesh, it is God alone who provides righteousness to man, ultimately in the person of His Son, Jesus Christ, who became sin for us "that we might become the Righteousness of God in Him" (2 Corinthians 5:21).

**YAHWEH-ROHI:** "The Lord Our Shepherd" (Psalm 23:1) – After David pondered his relationship as a shepherd to his sheep, he realized that was exactly the relationship God had with him, and so he declares, "Yahweh-Rohi is my Shepherd. I shall not want" (Psalm 23:1).

**YAHWEH-SHAMMAH:** "The Lord Is There" (Ezekiel 48:35) – the name ascribed to Jerusalem and the Temple there, indicating that the once-departed glory of the Lord (Ezekiel 8—11) had returned (Ezekiel 44:1-4).

**YAHWEH-SABAOTH:** "The Lord of Hosts" (Isaiah 1:24; Psalm 46:7) – *Hosts* means "hordes," both of angels and of men. He is Lord of the host of heaven and of the inhabitants of the earth, of Jews and Gentiles, of rich and poor, master and slave. The name is expressive of the majesty, power, and authority of God and shows that He is able to accomplish what He determines to do.

**EL ELYON:** "Most High" (Deuteronomy 26:19) – derived from the Hebrew root for "go up" or "ascend," so the implication is of that which is the very highest. *El Elyon* denotes exaltation and speaks of absolute right to lordship.

**EL ROI:** "God of Seeing" (Genesis 16:13) – the name ascribed to God by Hagar, alone and desperate in the wilderness after being driven out by Sarah (Genesis 16:1-14). When Hagar met the Angel of the Lord, she realized she had seen God Himself in a theophany. She also realized that *El Roi* saw her in her distress and testified that He is a God who lives and sees all.

**EL-OLAM:** "Everlasting God" (Psalm 90:1-3) – God's nature is without beginning or end, free from all constraints of time, and He contains within Himself the very cause of time itself. "From everlasting to everlasting, You are God."

**EL-GIBHOR:** "Mighty God" (Isaiah 9:6) – the name describing the Messiah, Christ Jesus, in this prophetic portion of Isaiah. As a powerful and mighty warrior, the Messiah, the Mighty God, will accomplish the destruction of God's enemies and rule with a rod of iron (Revelation 19:15).

# REFERENCES

Go Show Them What He Told You

- www.gotquestions.org/emotional-abuse.html

Stop Denying the Holy Spirit

- Scriptures: Genesis 11:7; Joshua 1:8; Ephesians 4:18, 6:12; Jeremiah 17:5; 1 John 5:7; 1 Corinthians 14:33; Acts 2:1-4

Bearing Witness to the Pain and the Glory: A Moment of Truth!

- Destruction is damage so bad, things must be replaced, not fixed. Other words or similar meanings and types of destruction: annihilation, assassinate, decay, demolition, devastation, eliminate, eradicate, harm, havoc, invalidate, massacre, ruin, sabotage, subjugate.

    > The Latin word destructionem, "a pulling down," is the root of destruction.

    > Greek, strong's concordance #684; apóleia: causing someone (something) to be completely

severed; cut off (entirely) from what could or should have been.

> Hebrew: 'abhaddon (from verb 'abhadh meaning "to be lost," "to perish"); Hebrew: cherem (from verb charam) and closer in meaning is to "exterminate, ostracize or excommunicate."

Ministering in the Earth, the Church, the Marketplace, and on the Job

- Scriptures: Genesis 1, John 1, Romans 1
- Apostle – (1) messenger, (2) one who is sent.
    > www.jewishvirtuallibrary.org/apostle
- Apostolic Authority Established by Dr. Kluane Spake
- Apostolic Doctrine – the message of Jesus, His redemptive work, and His call to selfless discipleship that is found in the twenty-seven books of the New Testament.
    > www.eastsideapostolic.com/apostolic.php
    > http://biblehub.com/sermons/auth/thomson/the_apostolic_doctrine.htm
- Order – (1) the arrangement or disposition of people or things in relation to each other according to a particular sequence pattern or method; (2) an authoritative command, direction, guidance, or instruction.

- Position – (1) a relative place, situation, or standing; (2) an arranged order of advantage or preference; (3) a social, official/unofficial rank or status.

- Sunset or sundown – the time in the evening when the sun disappears or daylight fades

- Zmanim – Hebrew word for times; specific periods of time or times of the day significant to Jewish law.

  > www.chabad.org/calendar/zmanim_cdo/jewish/Halachic-Times.htm

What Is the Nature of a SCRIBE? – Part 2

- Religion

  > The belief in and reverence for a supernatural power or powers, regarded as creating and governing the universe: respect for religion.

  > A particular variety of such belief, especially when organized into a system of doctrine and practice: the world's many religions.

  > A set of beliefs, values, and practices based on the teachings of a spiritual leader.

Witnessing

- Yashua/Yeshua HaMashiach – Jesus Christ; the Anointed One, the Messiah; the Son of God the Father.

- Scriptures

  - Revelation 20:12 & 15 ~ [12]And I saw the dead, small and great, stand before God; and the books were opened: and another book was opened, which is the book of life: and the dead were judged out of those things which were written in the books, according to their works. [15]And whosoever was not found written in the book of life was cast into the lake of fire."

  - Exodus 32:33 ~ "And the LORD said unto Moses, Whosoever hath sinned against me, him will I blot out of my book."

  - Psalm 139:13-16, MSG ~ "Oh yes, you shaped me first inside, then out; you formed me in my mother's womb. I thank you, High God—you're breathtaking! Body and soul, I am marvelously made! I worship in adoration—what a creation! You know me inside and out, you know every bone in my body; You know exactly how I was made, bit by bit, how I was sculpted from nothing into something. Like an open book, you watched me grow from conception to birth; all the stages of my life were spread out before you, The days of my life all prepared before I'd even lived one day."

- Links

  - www.studylight.org/dictionaries/hbd/w/witness-martyr.html

> https://biblehub.com/topical/w/witness.htm

> www.bibletools.org/index.cfm/fuseaction/ Library.sr/CT/ARTB/k/310/You-Are-My-Witnesses.htm

Time

- Suggested reading:

    > *Eternity Invading Time*

    Author: Renny McLean

    ISBN: 1-59755-038-8

    > *Dispensations in Time*

    Author: Patience Dean

    ISBN-10: 0692458026

    ISBN-13: 978-0692458020

- Inspiration

    > www.blacknews.com/news/reginald-dwayne-betts-ex-felon-graduated-yale-lawyer/

The Highest Honor

- Numbers 26:33-34 ~ Zelophehad the son of Hepher had no sons, but only daughters, and the names of Zelophehad's daughters were Mahlah, Noah, Hoglah, Milcah, and Tirzah. These are the families (clans) of

Manasseh, and those who were numbered of them were 52,700.

- Numbers 26:52-56, AMP ~ And the Lord spoke to Moses, saying, "Among these the land shall be divided as an inheritance according to the number of names. To the larger *tribe* you shall give the larger inheritance, and to the smaller *tribe* the smaller inheritance; each *tribe* shall be given its inheritance according to its numbers. But the land shall be divided by lot. They shall receive their inheritance according to the names of the tribes of their fathers (tribal ancestors). According to the [location selected by] lot, their inheritance shall be divided between the larger and the smaller [groups]."

- A Law of Inheritance: Numbers 27:1-10, AMP ~ Then the [five] daughters of Zelophehad[66] the son of Hepher, the son of Gilead, the son of Machir, the son of Manasseh, from the tribes of Manasseh [who was] the son of Joseph, approached [with a request]. These are the names of his daughters: Mahlah, Noah, Hoglah, Milcah, and Tirzah. They stood before Moses, Eleazar the priest, the leaders, and all the congregation at the doorway of the Tent of Meeting (tabernacle), saying, "Our father died in the wilderness. He was not among those who assembled together against the Lord in the company of Korah, but he died for his own sin [as did all those who rebelled at Kadesh], and he had no sons. Why should the name of our father be removed from

---

66    https://jwa.org/encyclopedia/article/daughters-of-zelophehad-bible

his family because he had no son? Give to us a possession (land) among our father's brothers." So Moses brought their case before the Lord. Then the Lord said to Moses, "The request of the daughters of Zelophehad is justified. You shall certainly give them a possession as an inheritance among their father's brothers, and you shall transfer their father's inheritance to them. Further, you shall say to the Israelites, 'If a man dies and has no son, you shall transfer his inheritance to his daughter. If a man has no daughter, then you shall give his inheritance to his brothers. If a man has no brothers, then you shall give his inheritance to his father's brothers. If his father has no brothers, then you shall give his inheritance to his nearest relative in his own family, and he shall take possession of it. It shall be a statute and ordinance to the Israelites, just as the Lord has commanded Moses.'"

- Five daughters of Zelophehad

    > Five = GRACE

    > Ironically, one of the ways in which God chooses to communicate with me is through numbers. I have learned to uncover the significance of specific events in connection to numbers to receive confirmation from God of His approval and blessing in my life.

- Dignity, Glory, and Honor; the Hebrew word(s) for honor is kâbad (H3513), kaw-bad' or kâbâd and, literally means: to be heavy, be weighty, be grievous, be hard, be rich, be honorable, be glorious, be burdensome, be honored[67].

> Exodus 20:12 ~ *Honour thy father and thy mother: that thy days may be long upon the land which the Lord thy God giveth thee.*

> Proverbs 25:2 ~ *It is the glory of God to conceal a matter, but the glory of kings is to search out a matter.*

▷ Liberty[68]; the Hebrew word is derowr [pronounced der-ore or darar, H1865] which means to flow freely or move rapidly, to fly away or freedom, pure.

> Isaiah 61:1-2 ~ "The Spirit of the Lord God is upon me; because the Lord hath anointed me to preach good tidings unto the meek; he hath sent me to bind up the brokenhearted, to proclaim liberty to the captives, and the opening of the prison to them that are bound; To proclaim the acceptable year of the Lord, and the day of vengeance of our God; to comfort all that mourn; To appoint unto them that mourn in Zion, to give unto them beauty for ashes, the oil of joy for mourning, the garment of praise for the spirit

---

67  www.blueletterbible.org/lang/lexicon/lexicon.cfm?Strongs=H3513&t=KJV

68  www.blueletterbible.org/lang/lexicon/lexicon.cfm?t=KJV&strongs=H1865

of heaviness; that they might be called trees of righteousness, the planting of the Lord, that he might be glorified."

## What Is Perception?

- Stereotypes – rigid and generally negative beliefs that people use to categorize members of group (race) who share general characteristics. (Biases and bigotry are based on uniformed stereotypes.)

## Covering

- Some use the term Holy Ghost or Holy Spirit; both mean the same.
- Cover (or covering): to shelter; to protect; to defend.
- http://bibleresources.org/head-coverings/
- www.eskimo.com/~scoleman/cover.html
- www.bible.ca/interactive/worship-10-weekly-attendance.htm
- Hebrews 10:25-27 AMPC ~ "Not forsaking or neglecting to assemble together [as believers], as is the habit of some people, but admonishing (warning, urging, and encouraging) one another, and all the more faithfully as you see the day approaching. For if we go on deliberately and willingly sinning after once acquiring the knowledge of the Truth, there is no longer any sacrifice left to atone for [our] sins [no further offering to which

to look forward]. [There is nothing left for us then] but a kind of awful and fearful prospect and expectation of divine judgment and the fury of burning wrath and indignation which will consume those who put themselves in opposition [to God]."

## Spiritual Maturity

- Scriptures:
    - Romans 7:14 ~ "For we know that the law is spiritual: but I am carnal, sold under sin."
    - Romans 8:6 ~ "For to be carnally minded is death; but to be spiritually minded is life and peace."
    - Romans 8:7 ~ "Because the carnal mind is enmity against God: for it is not subject to the law of God, neither indeed can be."
    - 1 Corinthians 3:3 ~ "For ye are yet carnal: for whereas there is among you envying, and strife, and divisions, are ye not carnal, and walk as men?"
    - 1 Corinthians 3:4 ~ "For while one saith, I am of Paul; and another, I am of Apollos; are ye not carnal?"
    - 1 Corinthians 9:11 ~ "If we have sown unto you spiritual things, is it a great thing if we shall reap your carnal things?"

- > 2 Corinthians 10:4 ~ "(For the weapons of our warfare are not **carnal**, but mighty through God to the pulling down of strong holds;)"

- > Hebrews 9:10 ~ "Which stood only in meats and drinks, and divers washings, and carnal ordinances, imposed on them until the time of reformation."

- www.allaboutfollowingjesus.org/spiritual-maturity.htm
- www.youtube.com/watch?v=v3K1KL5JPDE
- www.gotquestions.org/names-of-God.html

In the World, but Not of the World

- *The Discerning of Spirits*

    Author: Frank Hammond

    ISBN 10: 0-89228-368-8

    ISBN 13: 978-089228-368-2

Supernatural Manifestation Defeating Flesh

Bishop C. Anthony Muse (Senator)

- www.arkofsafetychristianchurch.com/
- http://msa.maryland.gov/msa/mdmanual/05sen/html/msa12282.html

Bishop Norman Hutchins (Pastor and Musician)

- http://normanhutchins.com/
- www.youtube.com/watch?v=l-6HpdmIiZM
- http://pathmegazine.com/news/gospel/norman-hutchins-wife-gives-gospel-legend-kidney-pastor-hutchins-later-flatlines-on-hospital-bed/

Heaven's Best Healing and Deliverance Church

- http://angeloojones.com/heaven-s-best-history.html
- www.facebook.com/ClintonMDcampmeeting/
- www.youtube.com/watch?v=9ZsjATfnnkE

The Souls of My Ancestors

- Scriptures:
  > 2 Corinthians 1:3-11 MSG ~ "All praise to the God and Father of our Master, Jesus the Messiah! Father of all mercy! God of all healing counsel! He comes alongside us when we go through hard times, and before you know it, he brings us alongside someone else who is going through hard times so that we can be there for that person just as God was there for us. We have plenty of hard times that come from following the Messiah, but no more so than the good times of his healing comfort—we get a full measure of that, too. When we suffer for Jesus, it works out

for your healing and salvation. If we are treated well, given a helping hand and encouraging word, that also works to your benefit, spurring you on, face forward, unflinching. Your hard times are also our hard times. When we see that you're just as willing to endure the hard times as to enjoy the good times, we know you're going to make it, no doubt about it. We don't want you in the dark, friends, about how hard it was when all this came down on us in Asia province. It was so bad we didn't think we were going to make it. We felt like we'd been sent to death row, that it was all over for us. As it turned out, it was the best thing that could have happened. Instead of trusting in our own strength or wits to get out of it, we were forced to trust God totally—not a bad idea since he's the God who raises the dead! And he did it, rescued us from certain doom. And he'll do it again, rescuing us as many times as we need rescuing. You and your prayers are part of the rescue operation—I don't want you in the dark about that either. I can see your faces even now, lifted in praise for God's deliverance of us, a rescue in which your prayers played such a crucial part."

> 1 Corinthians 14:40 ~ "Let all things be done decently and in order."

- Racism – a belief system hinging on racial/cultural prejudice and discrimination supported by institutional power and authority; designed to overtly or covertly limit advancement opportunities by keeping certain individuals at a particular level regardless of their training or education and qualifications to successfully perform at a higher level that may afford them higher wages.

    > Discrimination[69] – the process of responding to a person differently by imposing unfair treatment upon him/her, or denying a person or group equal opportunities stemming from biases or prejudices or stereotypes based on that individual's or group's gender, race, age, religion (beliefs), sexual orientation, social class, or national origin. Specific types of discrimination[70]: age, culture (National Origin) and ethnicity, disability, equal pay/compensation, genetic information, harassment, pregnancy, race/color, religion, retaliation, sexual orientation, sexual harassment.

    > Prejudice:

    negative attitudes and feelings toward individuals based solely on their membership in a particular group.

---

69   www.eeoc.gov/youth/what-employment-discrimination
70   www.eeoc.gov/discrimination-type

an assumption (stereotype) or prejudgment in favor of or against a person (gender and/or appearance), a group, an event, an idea (beliefs) or a particular thing.

an assumption (stereotype) or prejudgment in favor of or against a person (gender and/or appearance), a group, an event, an idea (beliefs) or a particular thing.

- Suggested sources for review:
    - > Robert and Regina Rudolph Ministries; www.alfc-pa.org/product/supernatural-warfare-bundle/
    - > Patience Dean; Spiritual Anatomy: Understanding the compartments of a human being; www.youtube.com/watch?v=oupOVxgAtD4

Frequency

- 528 hz – The natural frequency of the earth. Repairs DNA to bring about transformation and miracles in your life.
- 639 hz – Enhances communication, tolerance, and love to strengthen relationships.
- 741 hz – Encourages self-expression. Cleanses cells of toxins.

- 852 hz – Awaken intuition and realigns spiritual order.
- 963 hz – Restores the SPIRIT to its original setting by directly connecting it or putting it in direct alignment with God.
- www.youtube.com/watch?v=_aeeNMk04l0

Until Now

- www.appliedfaithministries.org/about-us
- https://my.clevelandclinic.org/health/treatments/10142-hysteroscopy

Integrity

- Isaiah 45:23 ~ "I have sworn by myself, the word is gone out of my mouth in righteousness, and shall not return, That unto me every knee shall bow, every tongue shall swear."
- Philippians 2:10-11 ~ "That at the name of Jesus every knee should bow, of things in heaven, and things in earth, and things under the earth; And that every tongue should confess that Jesus Christ is Lord, to the glory of God the Father."
- www.united2restore.com/2016/05/05/heresy/
- www.united2restore.com/2016/04/05/the-hebrew-roots-dichotomy/

- www.federaldisability.com/blog/2016/06/federal-agency-may-prove-employees-lack-candor/
- www.quora.com/What-is-meant-by-lack-of-candor
- https://mspbattorneys.com/blawg/subjective-disciplining-candor/

Culture

- Culture – predominating attitudes and behaviors that characterize how a group functions or behaves.

- Double Standard(s) – a set of principles that applies differently and usually more rigorously to one group of people or individual than another in the same situation under the same circumstances.

- Oppression – an act to rule in a nondiplomatic, dehumanizing way oftentimes coupled with unjust harshness whereby those being oppressed become high-risk candidates for emotional or physical collapse.

- Retaliation[71] – a counter attack, tit for tat, revenge. Widely common in the workplace: employer vs. employee. Retaliation has been the most frequently alleged basis of discrimination in the federal sector since fiscal year 2008.[72]

---

71  www.eeoc.gov/retaliation
72  www.eeoc.gov/retaliation-making-it-personal

Struggling to Understand

- www.cdc.gov/alcohol/fact-sheets/minimum-legal-drinking-age.htm
- www.nytimes.com/interactive/2019/09/10/us/men-military-sexual-assault.html
- www.stripes.com/news/us/pentagon-reports-of-sexual-assault-harassment-in-the-military-have-increased-1.627966
- www.militarytimes.com/news/your-military/2020/04/30/a-culture-that-fosters-sexual-assaults-and-sexual-harassment-persists-despite-prevention-efforts-a-new-pentagon-study-shows/
- https://youtu.be/M4pBfWYbJYY
- www.thoughtco.com/bible-verses-about-lust-712095

The Government Shutdown

- www.dol.gov/oasam/programs/history/flsa1938.htm
- www.dol.gov/general/aboutdol/history/dolhistoxford
- www.npr.org/sections/ed/2018/06/21/622189097/white-house-proposes-merging-education-and-labor-departments
- https://abcnews.go.com/beta-story-container/GMA/Living/syrian-refugee-falafel-shop-named-nicest-place-america/story?id=60417144

Justice or Just Us!

- 1 Corinthians 6

Chain of Command: New Level, New Devil

- **A true pyramid** – three equal and identical points of measurement. No matter which side you turn it on, it is the same measurement in height and value! Trinity: three equal parts of value. One in the same with three distinct functions as part of a whole. You simply can't acknowledge one without acknowledging the other (the Father, the Son, the Holy Spirit), although many do, which is unacceptable!

- **New level** – When I speak of a new level, I am speaking of a different plateau in one's learning and growth. To be promoted rather than demoted is truly a great reward in itself, but you must also be willing to take into account the wisdom, knowledge, and understanding you gain from transitioning from one position to another even if it is just a lateral move.

- **New devil** – Many people do not put themselves in a position to think, learn, and grow on their own. They have the tendency to rely more on technology as well as the knowledge of others pertaining to what they are willing to believe or accept as being the truth. You have to be willing to look at everything with an open mind and objective view. Research and study for yourself to grasp the meaning and depth of what you should know.

> Just as there are many degrees or levels in positioning, there are many influences in the world with varied levels of power. Figuratively speaking, a new devil is a spirit of influence at a higher level than the one before it. Just like the military structure of hierarchical ranking comes with more power of influence and control, there is that same hierarchical ranking amongst those within the spirit world or realm: angels on the side of God and those on the side of Lucifer, the devil. Once you pass your spiritual test in succeeding or transitioning to a higher level, do you honestly think that Lucifer will reassign one of his minions that you already defeated in spiritual warfare?

Deborah the Bee: Judge, Prophet, Deliverer, Mother, Wife, Warrior—and More

- Websites:
  - www.linguajunkie.com/hebrew/introduction-hebrew-basics
  - www.britannica.com/topic/shofet
  - www.biblestudytools.com/dictionary/judge/
  - biblehub.com/sermons/auth/clarkson/the_significance_of_the_palm_trees.htm
  - www.tblfaithnews.com/faith-religion/palm-trees-do-you-have-the-character-that-they-do
  - www.faithgateway.com/ezer-unleashed/

- Suggested reading:
  - *Gender Across Languages: The linguistic representation of women and men, Volume I,* John Benjamins B.V., John Benjamins Publishing Company, Amsterdam/Philadelphia, © 2001, page 177; Hebrew: Gender switch in Modern by Yishai Tobin.

Amazing Grace

- Seven - www.biblestudy.org/bibleref/meaning-of-numbers-in-bible/7.html
- Nine - www.biblestudy.org/bibleref/meaning-of-numbers-in-bible/9.html
- September
  - www.sunsigns.org/september-meaning-symbolism/!
  - https://touchedbyanangelhealings.blogspot.com/2018/09/new-month-september-meaning-symbolism.html
  - www.ducksters.com/history/septemberinhistory.php

# BIBLICAL REFERENCES

Unless otherwise indicated, scripture quotations are from the Holy Bible, King James Version. All rights reserved.

Scriptures marked AMP are taken from Amplified Version. Copyright © 2015 by The Lockman Foundation. All rights reserved.

Scriptures marked AMPC are taken from the Amplified Version®, Classic Edition. The "Amplified" trademark is registered in the United States Patent and Trademark Office by The Lockman Foundation. Use of this trademark requires the permission of The Lockman Foundation.

Scriptures marked BSB are taken from The Holy Bible, Berean Study Bible, BSB Copyright ©2016 by Bible Hub. Used by Permission. All Rights Reserved Worldwide.

Scriptures marked CEV are taken from the Contemporary English Version®. Copyright © 1995 by American Bible Society. All rights reserved.

Scriptures marked CJB are taken from the Complete Jewish Bible. Copyright © 1998 by David H. Stern. All rights reserved. No portion of this book may be reproduced, stored in a retrieval system, or transmitted in any form or by any means without prior written permission of the publisher.

Scriptures marked ESV are taken from English Standard Version. Copyright © 2001 by Crossway, a publishing ministry of Good News Publishers. All rights reserved.

Scriptures marked GNT are taken from the Good News Translation® — Second Edition. Copyright © 1992 by American Bible Society. All rights reserved.

Scriptures marked GW are taken from God's Word Translation. Copyright © 1995, 2003, 2013, 2014, 2019, 2020 by God's Word to the Nations Mission Society. All rights reserved.

Scriptures marked ISV are taken from *The Holy Bible: International Standard Version.* Release 2.0, Build 2015.02.09. Copyright © 1995-2014 by ISV Foundation. ALL RIGHTS RESERVED INTERNATIONALLY. Used by permission of Davidson Press, LLC.

Scriptures marked MSG are taken from The Message. Copyright © 1993, 1994, 1995, 1996, 2000, 2001, 2002. Used by permission of NavPress Publishing Group.

Scriptures marked NASB are taken from the New American Standard Bible. Copyright © 1960, 1962, 1963, 1968, 1971, 1972, 1973, 1975, 1977, 1995 by The Lockman Foundation. Used by permission.

Scriptures marked NIV are taken from the New International Version. Copyright © 1973, 1978, 1984, 2011 by Biblica, Inc, TM. All rights reserved.

Scriptures marked NKJV are taken from the New King James Version. Copyright © 1982 by Thomas Nelson. All rights reserved.

Scriptures marked NLT are taken from the New Living Translation*. Copyright © 1996, 2004, 2007, 2013 by Tyndale House Foundation. All rights reserved.

Scriptures marked NET are taken from the NET Bible* copyright © 1996-2006 by Biblical Studies Press, L.L.C. http://netbible.com. All rights reserved.

Scriptures marked TLB are taken from The Living Bible copyright © 1971 by Tyndale House Foundation. Used by permission of Tyndale House Publishers Inc., Carol Stream, Illinois 60188. All rights reserved. The Living Bible, TLB, and The Living Bible logo are registered trademarks of Tyndale House Publishers.

Scriptures marked TCW are taken from The Clear Word Bible copyright © 1994 by James Blanco, Review and Harald Publishing. All rights reserved.

Scriptures marked VOICE are taken from The Voice Bible Copyright © 2012 Thomas Nelson, Inc. The Voice™ translation © 2012 Ecclesia Bible Society All rights reserved.

# ABOUT THE AUTHOR

Ann Gwen Mack, a native Washingtonian, was born on September 23, 1960, to Ruby H. and James S. Mack. Through life's lessons and challenges, she was determined to push beyond the boundaries and limitations she encountered to prove to herself that she could indeed accomplish what others believed and always told her she could not do. After finding herself unemployed for the third time, she made a conscious commitment to go back to school to pursue a degree in business management with an emphasis on human resources, business, and employment law!

Spending most of her life church hopping, Ann spent a great deal of time in church attempting to get closer to God because she believed there was much more to life than the pain, the ups and downs, the world had presented. God's persistence to bring her through every trial and tribulation has given her the push she's needed to endure with divine determination.

In August of 2010, Ann yielded to the call on her life to minister the Gospel, which led to the beginning of her first God-ordained writing assignment, the first edition of What Do I Do With My Pain? She went on to write her second book, entitled From What Tribe Were You Birthed?: Understanding the Significance of the Breastplate of Aaron.

To contact Ann, email her at author_ann@anngwenmack.com

## CREATING DISTINCTIVE BOOKS WITH INTENTIONAL RESULTS

We're a collaborative group of creative masterminds with a mission to produce high-quality books to position you for monumental success in the marketplace.

Our professional team of writers, editors, designers, and marketing strategists work closely together to ensure that every detail of your book is a clear representation of the message in your writing.

### Want to know more?
Write to us at info@publishyourgift.com
or call (888) 949-6228

Discover great books, exclusive offers, and more at
**www.PublishYourGift.com**

Connect with us on social media

@publishyourgift